THE LADY OF KABUL

Florentia Sale and the Disastrous Retreat of 1842

MICHAEL SCOTT

© Michael Scott 2019

Michael Scott has asserted his rights under the Copyright, Design and Patents Act, 1988, to be identified as the author of this work.

First published in 2019 by Endeavour Media Ltd.
Second Edition 2020

*Previous books
by author*

In Love and War
The Lives of General Sir Harry & Lady Smith
(*with David Rooney*)
2008

Surrender at New Orleans
General Sir Harry Smith in the Peninsula and America
(*paperback edition of In Love and War*)
2012

Scapegoats
Thirteen Victims of Military Injustice
2013

Royal Betrayal
The Great Baccarat Scandal of 1890
2017

DEDICATION

The book is dedicated to the Officers, Warrant and Non-Commissioned Officers,
and Guardsmen of the 1st Battalion Scots Guards who fought in Afghanistan in 2010.
In particular, those who were killed in action;

Colour Sergeant Alan Cameron

Sergeant David Walker

Lance Sergeant Dale McCallum

Lance Corporal Stephen Monkhouse

Nemo Me Impune Lacessit

TABLE OF CONTENTS

Chapters

PREFACE	15
1 The Great Game	23
2 Memsahib	35
3 March to Kabul	42
4 Kabul	53
5 Insurrection	65
6 Defeat	78
7 Surrender	89
8 Retreat	123
9 Kidnapped	139
10 Destruction of an Army	145
11 In the Hands of the Sirdar	164
12 Death of the General	189
13 The Final Months	221
14 Rescue	254
15 Aftermath	266

Annexes

A Civil and Military officers killed at or near Kabul and during the retreat

B Surviving Officers of the Kabul Force

C Prisoners released on General Pollocks arrival at Kabul

D Simplified family tree

Cover

Entrance to Bolan Pass from Dadur James Atkinson. "Sketches in Afghanistan"

Maps

A   Afghanistan
B   Kabul City and Cantonments
C   Retreat from Kabul

Note on Money

Florentia reckoned a Rupee was worth 2 shillings. Today it is £8.87.

A Lakh is 100,000.

Florentia reckoned a Lakh of rupees to be £10,000. Today it is £886,900.

I have merely multiplied Florentia's estimate by the percentage increase in the Retail Price Index.

AFGHANISTAN

TURKESTAN

CHARIKAR
BAMIYAN
KABUL
JALALABAD
Khyber Pass
HERAT
PESHAWAR
AFGHANISTAN
GHAZNI

PUNJAB

KANDAHAR

Khojak Pass

PERSIA

QUETTA
Bolan Pass
BALUCHISTAN

SCALE
0   100
Miles

Kabul

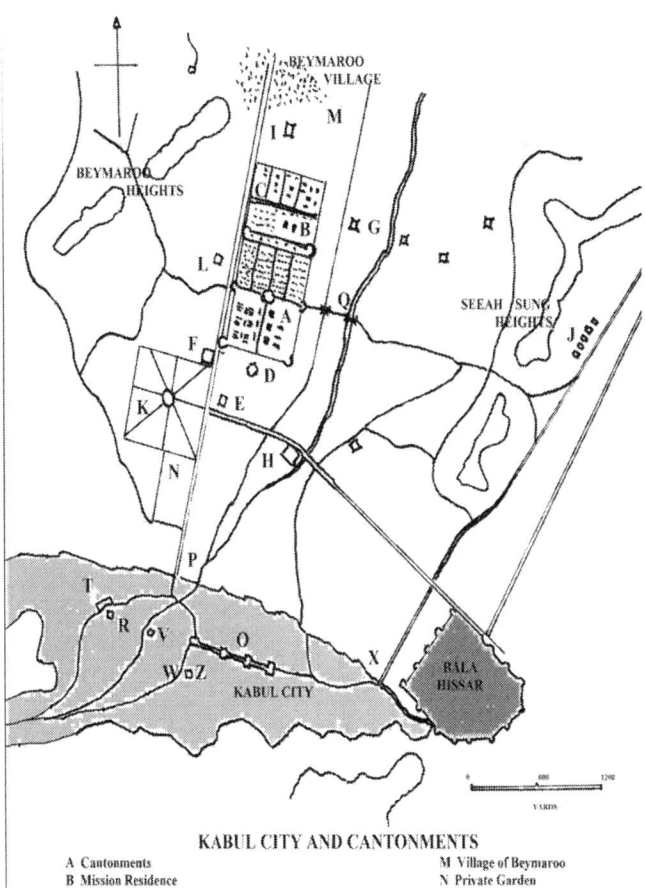

KABUL CITY AND CANTONMENTS

A Cantonments
B Mission Residence
C Mission Offices
D Magazine Fort (unfinished)
E Commissariat Fort
F Mohammad Shereef's Fort
G Rikabashee Fort
H Mahmood Khan's Fort
I Zoolficar's Fort
J Camp at Seeah Sung
K King's Garden
L Musjeed
M Village of Beymaroo
N Private Garden
O Bazaar
P Kohistan Gate
Q Empty Fort near Bridge
R Brig Anquetil's Fort
T Yahoo khaneh
V Capt Trevor's Tower
W Sir Alexander Burnes's house
X Lahore Gate
Z Capt Johnson's Treasury

After Eyre Sketch

RETREAT FROM KABUL

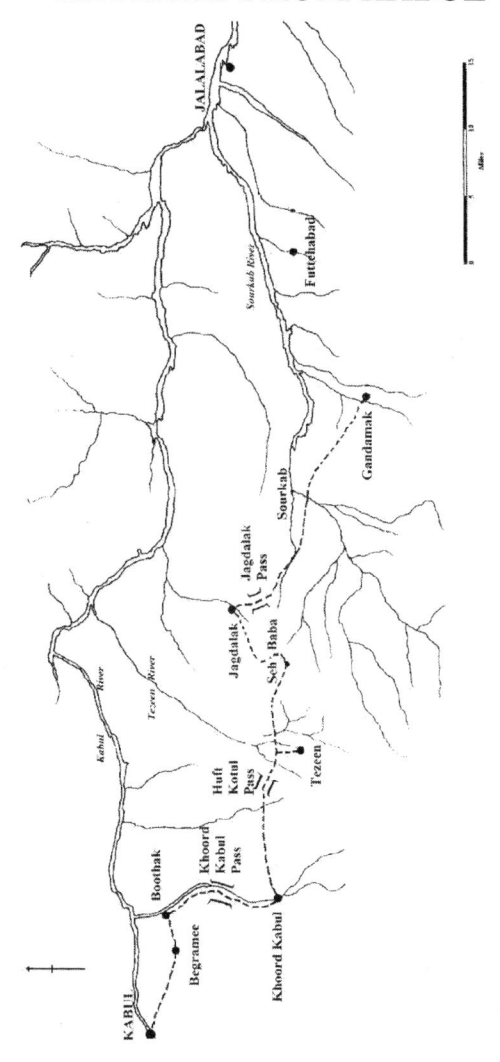

After A.Karl/ J.Kemp

PREFACE

'I had fortunately only one ball in my arm; three others passed through my *poshteen* (sheepskin coat) near the shoulder without doing me injury.' So wrote the indomitable Lady Florentia Sale of her wound on the retreat from Kabul in 1842.

This is the tale of an archetypal Victorian *memsahib* who could endure, arguably, the biggest military disaster of the 19th century and cope with nine month's captivity at the hands of the Afghans, with courage and superb confidence. Her captors must have regretted every day they had her in their power.

For the historian, nothing can be more exciting than the evidence of a witness who was on the spot. However, eyewitnesses can be unreliable, particularly if a long period of time has elapsed since the event. Memories can fade and facts – times, dates, places and names can become muddled. Soldiers present at the battle of Waterloo, for instance, and therefore with much store set by historians, often related their experiences, probably in a pub, many years later with consequent inaccuracies.

A witness can only see, hear or be aware of an event which is close at hand. A participant, at the centre of the action, may be seriously blinkered with a narrow vision of what is happening. Records of actions taking place at night, for instance, have obvious room for error. Letters, diaries and memoirs can be written with personal motives, glossing over the less attractive parts of the story.

However, the joy of Florentia Sale's account is that it was written during her time amongst the Afghans. 'I have not only daily noted down events as they occurred, but often have done so hourly,' she wrote. Her diary started in September 1841 in Kabul and ended a year later with her rescue from captivity. The diaries were published by John Murray in 1843 (*A Journal of the Disasters in Affghanistan, 1841-2*). Manuscript editions of many of her letters survive, particularly of those between her and her husband while she was a captive. Of course, some of the entries were coloured with her own, often stringent, views and, inevitably, she gets muddled with some names and facts. I have taken the liberty of correcting these and rationalising the spelling where I can, although, even amongst inhabitants themselves, places were differently spelt e.g. Cabul, Cabool, Kabool or Kabul.

Born in India into an old East India Company family, Florentia Wynch married Robert Sale in 1808. Sale was a brave, bluff, no-nonsense soldier, whose solution to military problems was to get in front and lead his men into action. In the early part of their marriage, they travelled widely, bearing twelve children, of whom four died in infancy and one aged ten.

In 1840, Sale was appointed second-in-command of the Army of the Indus which was despatched from India to Afghanistan to take Kabul and replace the existing ruler, Dost Mohammad with Shah Shuja. After a relatively peaceful year, in which officers were joined by their families, Sale's brigade, as part of a force reduction, was ordered back to India via Jalalabad, temporarily leaving Florentia, a daughter and son-in-law in Kabul.

This gave the Afghan insurgents the opportunity to attack the British cantonments and parts of the city. The British, badly led by indecisive senior officers, with winter closing in and little fuel, decided to withdraw to India via Jalalabad and Sale's protection. A hollow promise was made by the Afghans to allow safe conduct. Thus some 4,500 soldiers and 12,000 camp followers set out in January 1842.

The column was constantly harassed by the enemy, discipline collapsed and any military reaction hampered by camp followers. Every day hundreds died from hunger and cold, or sniper fire from the insurgents. At one point, Florentia, her daughter and a number of others, including some senior, and wounded, officers were taken hostage by an Afghan chieftain. Constantly being moved to avoid any British rescue attempt and interned as bargaining counters for safe conduct, life was miserable but Florentia, amazingly, was able to write a journal, which she managed to conceal from her captors, with whom she established a working relationship. (The musket ball in her arm was cut out, without anaesthetic, during her imprisonment). She was unfazed by the perils in which she found herself. Lice, earthquakes, rain, snow, lack of hygiene, glutinous mutton stew and little bedding were taken in her stride.

One of Florentia's fellow captives was the wounded Lieutenant Vincent Eyre of the Bengal Artillery. He also wrote an account of the disaster, which was published simultaneously with Florentia's (*The Military Operations in Cabul, which ended in the Retreat and Destruction of the British Army, January 1842. With a Journal of Imprisonment in Affghanistan*). Vincent was an accomplished artist and I have used some of his excellent sketches, particularly his map of Kabul which, curiously for a professional soldier, was upside down. Additionally, the most famous survivor, with the Lady Butler's iconic painting of his arrival at Jalalabad, was Dr Brydon. He wrote a report for General Sale, six days after his arrival in Jalalabad.[1] This completes the story of the retreat after Florentia was kidnapped. So I have tried to balance the three manuscripts, and recount Florentia's story of tragedy, appalling leadership, and her heroism and courage in the face of physical and mental hardship. I have made direct extracts from these accounts, without quotation marks, to ease the flow of the narrative. I was very grateful to Brigadier Alastair Fyfe, formerly of Robert Sale's Regiment, the Somerset Light Infantry, for his papers, particularly extracts from *The Light Bob Gazette*. Florentia's direct descendants, Camilla Rushbrooke and Susan Clark were interested and supportive from distant shores. I am indebted to Professor Jane Ridley for her encouragement and enthusiasm for this story and cannot wait for her book on George V. Where necessary, I have used as near as possible contemporary accounts but only as

---

[1] In 1874 Sir George Lawrence published as an appendix to his Reminiscences of Forty-Three Years in India a "Copy of William Brydon's Account from memory, and Memoranda made on Arrival at Jalalabad, of the Retreat from Cabool in 1842." In 1967 Louis and Nancy Hatch Dupree published a transcript, together with two indistinct facsimile pages, of the report as given by Assistant Surgeon William Brydon to General Robert Sale at Jalalabad. There is some discussion about the absolute accuracy of the transcript as it was copied by others, at the time, and therefore subject to minor mistakes. Nevertheless, it provides a sound account of Brydon's epic escape from the Afghans.

background colour, for instance Archibald Forbes's *The Afghan Wars 1839-42* and *Sale's Brigade in Afghanistan* by the Rev G R Gleig, Principal Chaplain to the Forces. There are many books about the 1st Afghan War, some very good (Patrick Macrory's[2] and William Dalrymple's[3] in particular) but in all of them Florentia only has a walk-on part. Now is the time for a book to herself.

I have delved into the papers in the National Archives containing memoranda and letters from the Governor General's office in India to General Pollock and to Major Pottinger (PRO 30/12/33/2 & 6) also Queen Victoria's Journals, now obtainable on-line. There are a number of good sources in the National Army Museum including the Testimonial signed by the British prisoners at Kabul in March 1842 and presented to their gaoler, Meerza Bawudeen Khan, *Narrative of the Disastrous Retreat from Kabul 1st Afghan War 1842* by Sergeant-Major Lissant, 37th Bengal Native Infantry, the papers of Lt Gen Sir Jasper Nicolls, Commander-in-Chief in India 1839-1843 and, of course, Captain Souter's letter to his wife.

Two threads ran through my mind while writing this story. The first was what an outstanding woman Florentia was. Steadfastly loyal to her soldier husband, courageous in the face of devastating hardship, physical danger and privation, she was a charismatic leader amongst demoralised and fearful captives. I have tried to penetrate the mind of a lady, in India, in the first half of the 19th Century. In Calcutta, she'd be waited on hand and foot,

---

[2] *Signal Catastrophe*, London, Hodder & Stoughton 1966.

[3] *Return of a King*, London, Bloomsbury 2013.

cooked for, her laundry instantaneously washed and ironed, her garden manicured; changing her clothes, perhaps, three times a day, and her horse brought round to the front door, beautifully groomed and harness sparkling. On the retreat from Kabul, she did not take her clothes off for ten days.[4] Her underwear was filthy, her blouse stiff with grime and sweat and her woollen outer layer stinking. Lice and fleas infested her whole body. What about the 'washing' arrangements? Was there loo paper? Did she ask for a pause on their endless trekking in order to 'go behind a bush?' She was at the mercy of a man who had personally shot the Government Envoy in cold blood. Her captors were quite prepared to kill Florentia and her companions if it suited them. They kept them alive either for ransom, sell them into slavery or retain as bargaining chips with the British Government. She had seen frozen, disembowelled bodies with suppurating entrails, decapitated children and men with their genitals cut off and heads spiked for display on a fort's ramparts. She knew the penalties.

This was also a world where women belonged to their husbands, could not own land properly themselves until the 1882 Married Women's Property Act, nor have the vote. She could show modern women a thing or two. Today, she would be a Cabinet Minister or CEO of a FTSE 100 company.

Secondly, Afghanistan. It is a well-worn cliché that we never learn our mistakes from history. Certainly we have learnt none from the 1st Afghan War. 'They had learned

---

[4] I did not take mine off for 14 days in the Falklands War, so I know the feeling.

nothing and forgotten nothing.'[5] Every time Auckland, Macnaghten or Elphinstone made yet another crass decision, I thought, 'Oh dear, this is going to come round again.' Here we are, *still* embroiled in a war that we should have got out of once Al Qaeda was finished in 2002.

But, for all that Florentia was the true Lady of Kabul. This is her story.

---

[5] Attributed to Talleyrand referring to the restored Bourbon dynasty after the abdication of Napoleon.

CHAPTER 1

The Great Game

Anyone who has served in Afghanistan, and many have in recent years, will tell you that it is a land of indescribable beauty, ranging from snowy peaks of the Hindu Kush to ochre deserts, vast sand dunes, and green valleys, with rushing brooks and lush pastures. The mountains, rivers and deserts divide the country into valleys, isolating their inhabitants into warring factions. Its history is one of hatred, bloodshed, treachery, and torture erupting from tribal rivalries, religious fanaticism and terrorism. Great Powers and their armies have involved themselves to inevitable rejection and disengagement. In the 19th century, eyeing the country from their borders, the Persians and the Sikhs were ready for any opportunity to cause mischief.

There were two main tribes in Afghanistan, the Duranis and the Ghilzais. The former, the most powerful, were divided into a number of clans, the most outstanding of which were the Barakzais from the Kandahar region, the Sadozais from north of Kandahar up to Kabul, and the Mohmands from the Khyber Pass. Dost Mohammad was Barakzai and Shah Shujah, a Sadozai. The Ghilzais were, essentially, nomads roaming from Kandahar in the south, along the Helmand River valley into Kabul province and Bamiyan. The Eastern Ghilzais inhabited the mountain region between Kabul and Jalalabad. There were others, some of whom were Persian or Arab extraction like the

Tajiks and the Hazaras.[6] Loyalty was skin deep; an individual would just about owe allegiance to his local chieftain, certainly not some Shah in far-off Kabul. Victories over rivals were usually the result of negotiation and one side betraying its leaders rather than out and out battles. Real central control over the country was non-existent; it depended wholly on tribal and family cohesion. Taxing the population was out of the question. In fact the opposite was true; opponents had to be bought off with bribes and subsidies.

By 1809, Shah Shuja of the Sadozais was in the seventh year of his difficult and unstable reign over a steadily disintegrating country. His power and influence only really extended to the distance his soldiers could travel from whatever base they were currently occupying. Therefore to his pleasant surprise, he learnt of emissaries of the East India Company approaching his capital with diplomatic overtures. Like all independently-minded rulers he regarded the Company with suspicion at best and downright hostility at worst. However, an alliance with the Company could provide him with the financial and armed support and stability he so desperately needed.

The East India Company had devolved from a small enterprise run by a group of City of London merchants in the early 17th century into a company with military supremacy over rival European trading companies and local rulers, culminating in 1757 in the seizure and control of the province of Bengal. Further territorial acquisitions in India

---

[6] A few years ago, the author's local 'convenience' store was run by Afghans. The shopkeeper was a Tajik and his sidekick was a Hazara. It was quite clear which one did the running around.

during the late eighteenth and early nineteenth centuries cemented the change in the Company's role from mere trader to a significant independent power at a very long arm's length from its Directors in London.

The Company's strength lay with its army. The first Indian troops recruited by the British were watchmen employed to protect their trading stations. From the mid-eighteenth century, the Company began to maintain forces at each of its three main stations; Calcutta, Madras and Bombay. These armies were quite distinct, each with their own Regiments and commanded by European officers. All three contained European, effectively mercenary, regiments in which both the officers and men were Europeans, as well as a larger number of 'Native' regiments, in which the officers were Europeans and the other ranks were Indians. They included artillery, cavalry and infantry regiments, often designated the Bengal/Madras/Bombay Artillery/Cavalry/Infantry (the latter often termed 'Native Infantry' or 'N.I.'). From the mid-eighteenth century onwards, the Crown began to dispatch regiments of the regular British Army to reinforce the Company's armies. These troops were often referred to as 'H.M.'s Regiments' or 'Royal Regiments'.

By 1824, the size of the combined armies of Bengal, Madras, and Bombay was about 200,000 and had at least 170 *sepoy* (an Indian infantry private; a cavalry trooper was called a *sowar*) and 16 European regiments. A force, in the right hands, to be reckoned with.

However, the diplomats approaching Kabul hardly had the Shah's well-being in mind.

To discover the real reason for this powerful overture to a rapidly weakening prince, we must go back to Napoleon.

On 7 July 1807, Napoleon and the Russian Emperor, Alexander II, negotiated the Treaty of Tilsit. The Treaty, on the surface, merely concerned itself with post-war arrangements in Europe. However, the secret clauses, which like all secrets, soon became known to the intelligence agents of the non-signatories, including Britain. These clauses amounted to an agreement between the two nations for a joint attack on Britain's richest resource, India. This had always been Napoleon's dearest wish since his abortive foray into Egypt a few years earlier and now the opportunity arose again. He saw himself as the latter day Alexander the Great, heading his army through Persia, across Afghanistan, to the Indus. The Russians, likewise, saw opportunities in allying themselves to the French for the invasion, then conveniently reneging on the deal once established on the Afghan border to threaten India.

Lord Minto, Governor General of India, was soon briefed and given instructions to warn countries in the path of the invaders and conclude alliances with them. Troops in England would be stood by to reinforce Indian forces should the need arise. Minto wasted no time and negotiated agreements, backed by lavish presents to the rulers of Persia; Ranjit Singh of the Sikhs in the Punjab and the Amir of Sindh. He then dispatched Mountstuart Elphinstone of the East India Company to woo Shah Shuja in Kabul. Elphinstone was no slouch, having fought under Arthur Wellesley, the future Duke of Wellington, in the Maratha Wars. He determined to show the Afghans what a proper Embassy should look like. The Ambassador was accompanied by 200 cavalry, 4,000 infantry, 12 elephants and 600 camels. It became apparent, even to the doziest member of Shah Shuja's court, that this panoply of power was not just for them but to demonstrate, with crystal clarity, that this was to persuade any invader that Britain would not tolerate a usurpation of her power in India by imperial rivals. The Great Game had begun.

Six months after leaving Delhi, Elphinstone met Shah Shuja at Peshawar soon to find all was not well. The Barakzai rebels had taken Kandahar and, in April 1809, captured Kabul itself. The remnants of the Shah's army in Kashmir straggled back, defeated. Now in serious danger, Elphinstone and his men sensibly headed back to Delhi. Shah Shuja's remaining followers were massacred outside Jalalabad and his retinue deserted him. He left, alone, for exile. Years of betrayal, humiliation and despair were to follow.

By 1812, the Napoleonic threat had evaporated to be replaced, more strongly, by the Russian. While Russia was really more concerned with Central Asia and taking on the Turks and the Persians, the *perception*, from the British point of view at least, was that Russia had its eye firmly on India. As often in politics and diplomacy, it was *perception* that mattered rather more than reality. The 'Great Game' took on a new dimension with the advent of the intelligence agents; intrepid men like Conolly, Pottinger, Rawlinson and Burnes. They were accomplished linguists and less scrupulous than their uniformed brethren. In disguise they penetrated the souks and tribal lands, bringing back, sometimes exaggerated, information. They were also adept intriguers with the skill to deal with men like Ranjit Singh, the formidable Sikh chieftain of the Punjab, on their own terms. By the 1830s, the Barakzais were loosely in control in Afghanistan, with Dost Mohammad Khan exerting power from Kabul. The latter was thought by Burnes to be very impressive against the now elderly and disenfranchised Shah Shuja. This was not, however, the view of mainstream British policy; Shah Shuja was seen as the most pliable ally they could have in Kabul. Nevertheless, the British were being two-faced; on the one hand Burnes and the Governor General, Lord Bentinck, were buttering up Dost Mohammad, on the other, Wade and Bentinck's chief adviser, William Macnaghten, were discreetly funding Shah Shuja. However, after an abortive effort to take Kandahar, Shah Shuja was, yet again, beaten back by Dost Mohammad's men. The British had backed a loser, unless...

If the Russians were to make a move into Afghanistan, with Dost Mohammad's backing, then, just maybe, the British could seize the excuse to put *their* man on the throne?

By 1837, it became apparent to British intelligence that Russia was becoming very close to the Shah of Persia, even to guarantee a proposed treaty between the Shah and the Barakzai gang in Kandahar. This bad news was relayed to Lord Palmerston in London and the new Governor General in India, Lord Auckland. Dost Mohammad made it clear to the Russians that the British were about to conquer all India and only he, armed and financed, by the Russians could hold them back from Afghanistan. Russian agents were then given clandestine orders to establish a mission to Dost Mohammad, urging him to unite with his Barakzai brethren in Kandahar. British spies remained unaware at this stage but, known to the Russians, Burnes was on his way to Kabul with the same aim: to suborn Dost Mohammad. Macnaghten, back in Calcutta, though, was ambivalent. He still thought Shah Shuja the rightful ruler and Dost

Mohammad and his Barakzais, usurpers. In the meantime, Dost Mohammad had declared a *jihad* (holy war) on Ranjit Singh with the aim of recovering Peshawar, the Afghans' winter capital, from the Sikhs. Like most holy wars, it was a good way of uniting the people behind him. Success in the battle of Jamrud boosted Dost Mohammad's prestige and confidence. Burnes reached Peshawar from which, although still in Sikh hands, it was proving difficult to maintain order in the surrounding countryside. Burnes thought there might be some sort of possible compromise whereby a deal could be brokered between the Company, the Sikhs and the Afghans with the aim of keeping the Russians out. Dost Mohammad got on very well with Burnes, although being well aware of the British duplicity in supporting Shah Shuja; not unusual in Afghan politics, he probably thought par for the course. However, Burnes's confidence in striking a deal was soon to be seriously displaced.

Lord Auckland, the Governor General, and Dost Mohammad were at two ends of the widest imaginable spectrum. Auckland, was a bored, complacent Whig nobleman, who cared little for India and even less for Afghanistan, of which he knew little; compared to Dost Mohammad, who was alert, intelligent, charming and aggressive. And Afghanistan was *his* Country. Auckland, guided by the pedantic and patronising Macnaghten, had no intention of involving himself with Dost Mohammad's problems with the Sikhs, or anyone else. He relied heavily on briefings from his civil servants who put whatever spin they felt inclined on their submissions. The anti-Burnes gang were in fine fettle. Totally against the evidence, they maintained that the usurper, Dost Mohammad, had a feeble grip on power, was unpopular with the people and his troops rebellious. Macnaghten disliked Burnes and briefed against him preferring to listen to the veteran spy, Wade. Not only were their opinions biased but their facts were actually wrong, leading to serious misjudgements.

Burnes was getting desperate. If the British did not move swiftly to ally Dost Mohammad, then the Russians would do so. He suggested that the British could be friends with *both* Ranjit Singh and Dost Mohammad. This was not, however, Macnaghten's view. He saw leaving the Sikhs in Peshawar and putting Shah Shuja back on the throne the best solution. He was backed by the myopic Auckland. This was not going to end well.

Ominously, towards the end of 1837, the Persians invaded western Afghanistan and besieged Herat. At the same time, to Burnes's chagrin, the Russian envoy arrived in Kabul. Burnes believed that he himself had arrived at Kabul in the nick of time, for an envoy from the Shah of Persia was already at Kandahar, bearing presents and assurances of support. The Dost made it clear to Burnes that his approaches to Persia and Russia were only at his despair of the lack of British support, and was desperate for assistance from any source to meet the Sikh threat. He maintained he was prepared to abandon his negotiations with the Russians and Persians if he was given assistance from the Anglo-Indian Government. Burnes communicated these friendly proposals to the Government, supporting them by his own strong representations. Meanwhile, carried away by enthusiasm, he exceeded his powers by making efforts to dissuade the Kandahar chiefs from the Persian alliance by offering to support them with money. For this unauthorised negotiation Burnes was severely reprimanded by Auckland, and was directed to retract his offers to the Kandahar men.

Burnes's then increasingly anxious letters direct to Auckland were met, eventually, with lack of interest and disdain. As a last resort, Dost Mohammad lowered his pride so far as to write himself to the Governor General imploring him 'to remedy the grievances of the Afghans, and afford them some little encouragement and power.' This heartfelt representation had no effect. The tone of Lord Auckland's reply, addressed to the Dost, was so dictatorial and supercilious as to look as though it was written deliberately to cause offence. Burnes was told, effectively, to stop consorting with Dost Mohammad. If Dost Mohammad continued to liaise with the Russians, the British would support the Sikhs' invasion of Afghanistan and he would be ordered to relinquish all claims to Peshawar and Kashmir. Burnes himself would be withdrawn from Kabul.

It was getting worse; the Russians were pouring gold into the Kabul coffers, suborning those close to Dost Mohammad and 'advising' the Persians at Herat. The real sadness in all this is that Dost Mohammad preferred the British to the Russians and could easily have been brought into the fold, following Burnes's advice to Calcutta. In April though, Dost Mohammad formally received the Russian envoy in great splendour. There were promises from the Russians of support to fight Ranjit Singh, trade deals between the countries would be endorsed and Afghan rights over Peshawar and Kashmir recognised. On his return journey the Russian envoy negotiated a treaty with the Kandahar chiefs, which was immediately ratified by the Russian minister at the Persian Court. All was lost. On 25 April 1838 Burnes left Kabul in despair.

Meanwhile, Auckland was relaxing in the Simla hill station. However, was the penny beginning to drop? Whig grandees don't panic but alarm and anxiety was rising. Did he really expect Ranjit Singh or Shah Shuja to deal with Dost Mohammad without help? He hoped so. Macnaghten was therefore dispatched to sound out Ranjit Singh, who, with practised ease, soon had the envoy round his little finger. The Sikh chieftain had no intention of invading Afghanistan and, while always keen to increase his assets, tangling with Dost Mohammad was unattractive. However, Ranjit Singh, the crafty bargainer that he was, said he could be persuaded to join an expedition to punish Dost Mohammad if his sovereign rights over Peshawar and Kashmir were recognised, the British pay him a large sum of money and he receive annual tributes from various rulers, including Shah Shuja. Macnaghten promptly agreed to this, the boot now being well on the other foot. It was looking like British-supported Sikh piracy rather than Sikh-supported British armed diplomacy. At this stage, no one had bothered to tell Shah Shuja of this little operation to put him back on his throne as a British puppet. Macnaghten then met him for the first time and told him what the deal was. He was given some flattering assurances but the reality was that he was in no position to bargain; he wanted his throne back at any cost. On 16 July, he signed what was called the Simla Agreement.

Auckland was racked by anxiety and indecision. Old India hands could see it all ending in trouble. Getting an army into Afghanistan, filing it through the easily ambushed narrow passes, then maintaining it in hostile territory, fighting a ruthless enemy, well versed in the terrain and adept at hit and run, was going to be extremely difficult.

Supposing, however, there was success. How was the next phase of occupation in a conquered Country going to work? What, then, was going to be what is nowadays called the 'exit strategy'? How were they going to get out? Serious political, financial and military problems would have to be faced in the long term. Had Britain properly supported Dost Mohammad against the Russians, as he wished, there would have been no question of 'invasion' and peace and calm would have prevailed. Now the opposite was going to happen; the neutral Afghans would turn against the 'invader' and be thrown into the arms of the Russians.

With much gloom in some quarters, the wheels for the expedition inexorably began to turn; 20,000 troops were mobilised and Macnaghten was given political command of the force. On 1 October 1838, Auckland declared war and announced the intention to restore Shah Shuja to his throne by force. Mountstuart Elphinstone, who had been the head of the mission to Kabul thirty years earlier, maintained that 'if an army was sent up the passes, and if we could feed it, no doubt we might take Kabul and set up Shah Shuja; but it was hopeless to maintain him in a poor, cold, strong and remote country, among so turbulent a people.' Lord William Bentinck, Lord Auckland's predecessor, denounced the project as an act of incredible folly. Marquis Wellesley regarded 'this wild expedition into a distant region of rocks and deserts, of sands and ice and snow,' as an act of infatuation. How right they were.

Hearts sank. It was Voltaire who, in 1761, quipped that the Holy Roman Empire was 'neither Holy, nor Roman nor an Empire.' It could equally be true of Conolly's description, in 1840, of the entanglements over Afghanistan as 'The Great Game.' In correspondence with Major Henry

Rawlinson, who had been recently appointed as the new political agent in Kandahar, Conolly wrote, "You've a great game, a noble game, before you."

It was to be no 'Game' and it certainly wasn't 'Great' for the majority of those involved.

CHAPTER 2

Memsahib

In the 19th Century, fathers, anxious to have their daughters suitably married off and having failed to do so at home, sent them out to India. There, where there was a grave shortage of European ladies, the girls could pick up some dashing young army officer or, better still, someone who had already started to make serious amounts of money. This was, unkindly, called the Fishing Fleet.

Not for Florentia, however. She was born into an old East India Company family in Madras in 1790. Her grandfather was Alexander Wynch, who had left for India aged 13 and started work as an unpaid 'writer' or clerk in the Company. Evidence of his skill still exists in the transcript on parchment which he made of the Parish Registers of St. Mary's Church, the oldest English church in India. Working his way up, he was admitted to the Council of Fort St. David in 1744. He married twice, firstly to Sophia Croke who died in 1754, then, secondly, to Florentia Cradock, aged 17, in 1755. He was Deputy Governor of Madras when, in July 1758, the French captured Fort St. David and he was made a prisoner-of-war. Released in October, he resigned from the Company on 'health grounds' and sailed for England. On his way via the Cape of Good Hope, he gathered significant intelligence from French sailors harbouring in Cape Town on French future plans for attacks on British possessions in India. He passed these on to a grateful Government. In 1768 he was re-appointed Chief in Masulipatam and, at this stage, started to make a great deal of money, particularly in financial transactions with the Nawab of Arcot, who became his major debtor. In 1773 he was made Governor of Madras but relieved of his post two years later in questionable circumstances, resulting in his resignation from the Company and retirement to England. However, true to the Nabob style of repatriated India hands, he was not short of money and initially, took up residence in Upper Harley Street. It was from here, in May 1786, that his daughter, Frances, aged 15, eloped to Gretna Green with the unreliable son and heir of Sir William Jervis Twisden of Roydon. Immediately afterwards, the spendthrift fled to France to avoid his creditors. However, all was not lost for Frances as her father left her and another daughter, Margery, £10,000 in his Will to be given to them on marriage or on attaining the age of 21, whichever came first. In today's money, that equates to something more than £12 million. No wonder he could afford to live subsequently in Gifford Lodge, Twickenham, before dying in Westhorpe House, Marlow, in December 1781.

Alexander's son, George, by his marriage to his second wife, was Florentia's father. Like his father, George entered the Madras Civil Service becoming Collector in 1791 and a Justice of the Peace two years later. He retired to England in 1798, no doubt, also having made a considerable amount of money, dying in 1838.

For Florentia, India was a wonderful place to live if you were, like her family, well-to-do. Surrounded by servants, life was a round of parties, picnics, polo matches, race meetings and riding expeditions with ever-present young officers from the British regiments or those, perhaps more raffish, of the Company's army. But, in the background, was the pervasive poverty and squalor of the Indians and their fabulously wealthy Maharajas, plotting and counter-plotting, sometimes for the British and sometimes against.

Then, in 1809, Captain Robert Sale of the British Army stepped into her life.

Robert was born in September 1782, the second son of Colonel Sale of the East India Company army. He was commissioned into the 36th Foot (later the Worcester Regiment) in 1795 and in January 1798, was posted to the 12th Foot (later the Suffolk Regiment) then stationed at Fort George, Madras. He took part in the campaign against Tipu Sultan and was present at the siege and storming of Seringapatam, which fell on 4 May 1799, for which he was awarded the silver medal. Later he took part in the campaign commanded by Colonel Arthur Wellesley (later Duke of Wellington) against the notorious Dhundia Wagh, and in the operations in Malabar and Wynaad.

The 12th spent more than four years at Trichinopoly, Robert being promoted captain on 23 March 1806. He accompanied his Regiment in the operations against the Rajah of Travancore in 1809, and fought in the battles of Quilon and Killimanur in January and February 1809, before returning to Trichinopoly.

On 16 May, he married Florentia. It was to be the start of a happy and steadfast marriage of 36 years. Robert was a high quality professional soldier, not called 'Fighting Bob' for nothing but not blessed with great brain or, sometimes, good judgement. This was amply made up for by Florentia who had the intelligence and shrewdness that her husband lacked. With this, coupled with her courage and dedication, she was able to give her husband enormous support over his long career. Her loyalty and jealousy for his reputation was very apparent. Their marriage then was one of long periods of garrison life in India, punctuated by periods of active service. Their first child, Mary Harriet, was born in Walajabad in February 1810.

That year Robert was involved in the expedition against the French in Mauritius, landing at Mapon Bay on 28 November 1810. After some bitter fighting, the Island surrendered on 3 December 1810. Joined by Florentia, the Sales spent the next three years in Mauritius, having another three children, until the 12th Foot were moved to Bourbon (later La Reunion). Naturally, Florentia followed the drum. Promoted major on 30 December 1813, Robert returned to Mauritius after Bourbon was given back to France in April 1815. Three more children were born there. The 12th left Mauritius joining their 2nd Battalion at Athlone in Ireland in 1818. There, as part of the reduction of the army, the 2nd Battalion was disbanded and Robert, as a junior major, was placed on half pay on 25 March 1818.

Life cannot have been financially easy on half-pay with seven children under the age of eleven but in 1821 Robert secured a commission by purchase in the 13th Foot (later the Somerset Light Infantry), later leaving, again, for India with the Regiment. On 2 January 1823, Florentia gave birth, in Calcutta, to Alexandrina, who was to be so significant later. Overall, the Sales had twelve children, three of whom died in infancy, Julia Catherine aged 3 and one, the eldest son, George, died aged 10.

In recognition of their distinguished record the 13th had been redesignated Light Infantry in 1822 and, in 1824, the Regiment formed part of the expedition to Burma, commanded by Major General Sir Archibald Campbell. Robert now commanded the 13th, his commanding officer having been promoted brigadier general. Leading from the front, he was wounded on a number of occasions. Soldiers like their officers to lead from the front as long as they don't take them into trouble. The story goes, though, that Robert's disciplinary methods were so tough that he used to receive unsigned letters from soldiers saying that they had sworn to kill him. His response was to have a parade and make the troops fire at him with blanks. When the smoke died away their colonel would roar with laughter and shout, "Ah, it's not my fault if you don't shoot me!" Since it was highly unlikely a soldier would shoot him on a parade and even less likely that a professional soldier would mistake a blank for live ball, the story is apocryphal.

In the storming of the Burmese stockade at Kemmendine on 19 June 1824, he was the first man to appear on top of the parapet, and on 8 July he led his Regiment in the assault on the seven stockades at Kamarut, engaging in personal combat the commander, whom he killed, acquiring thereby a valuable gold-hilted sword and scabbard. To his soldiers he was becoming a legend. Florentia remained in Calcùtta with the children and, given her quality, made it her business, as wife of the commanding officer, to look after the wives of men in the Regiment while their husbands were away on operations.

At the end of November 1824 the Burmese made a determined attempt to drive the British into the sea. There was heavy fighting around the Shwedagon Pagoda, the Burmese being driven off to Kokine where they constructed a strong stockade which Campbell attacked with two columns on 15 December 1824. Robert, as usual, led the assault and was severely wounded in the head for which he was compensated with a year's pay. The 13th lost eleven officers and fifty-one men killed or wounded. General Campbell, in his dispatch, praised Robert as 'an officer whose gallantry has been most conspicuous.'

The Burmese army having retreated to Danubyu, Campbell decided to advance to Prome. Robert was sent with a column to reduce the province of Bassein. After successfully overcoming *en route* a succession of stockades, he found Bassein abandoned and burning. He advanced for some 120 miles up the Irrawaddy River without encountering any resistance, after which he re-embarked his troops and sailed back to Rangoon. On 2 June 1825 he was, at last, promoted lieutenant colonel. On the same day his brother George, in the 4th Dragoons, was promoted lieutenant colonel, and for some years their names appeared together in the Army List.

Robert rejoined Campbell at Prome on 25 August 1825 and was given command of the 1st Brigade and repulsed an attack by the Shans and Burmese at Simbike on 1 December. On the following day he stormed the position at Napadi and by the end of that month the Burmese were suing for peace. They were, however, being very slow about it and Campbell, losing patience, renounced the armistice and attacked the stronghold of Minhla. The place was taken by assault from the Irrawaddy; Robert was again wounded while still embarked but received another year's pay in compensation. The fighting continued, although the Burmese had lost heart. In February they accepted Campbell's terms, which included the surrender of the Arakan and Tenasserim provinces, and on 24 February 1826 a treaty was signed. The First Anglo-Burmese War was over. Robert's name was mentioned yet again in dispatches, and he was made Companion of the Order of the Bath (CB) for his services. In the middle of April he returned with the 13th Light Infantry to Calcutta and the loving arms of Florentia, having been away for two years.

For the next twelve years he commanded his Regiment in a succession of Indian garrisons. For a man of action, he was no doubt bored stiff but British policy in India then was one of peace and improvement of the lives of the Indians. In Agra, the Sales had a large house, in ample grounds, with the luxury of a 60 by 30 foot swimming pool. Robert spent much time gardening and playing chess. With his closest confidants, he whiled away some frustration by 'war gaming' possible situations with map models. Despite relishing the cut and thrust of action, like many of his ilk, he had a calm and quiet disposition. He adored his wife and children. Florentia was a clever woman who, somewhat surprisingly, had been mainly brought up by her uncles who gave her an aptitude for writing and an education unusual for women of her time. She entered wholly into garrison life and all the fun it provided for her and the children. Their last child, Henry, was born in June 1829. Although she had a stern look about her, she was warm, generous and very popular in a world governed by protocols and precedent; a nightmare for some of the younger wives. Florentia was the senior Memsahib in the best possible way.

By 1838, the clouds were gathering in Afghanistan to bring this peace to an end.

CHAPTER 3

The March to Kabul

The border between the Punjab part of India and Afghanistan lay along the rivers Indus and Sutlej, dominated by the Sulaiman mountain range with an average height about that of the Pyrenees. There were four principal passes through the mountains.

The direct route from Peshawar to Kabul lay through the Khyber Pass, a distance of 190 miles. The pass itself is 33 miles long and was defended, 8 miles from its eastern entrance, by the fort of Ali Masjid. 67 miles beyond that was Jalalabad, 1,960 feet above sea level. Thence to Kabul through a series of difficult passes; Gandamak, Jagdalak, Tezeen, Haft Kotal and Khurd Kabul; the latter a mere 10 miles from Kabul. This pass was the fiefdom of the Khybari tribe. They would levy tolls on every traveller from the head of an invading force down to the solitary wayfarer with his little stock of merchandise destined for a distant market.

The second was the Kuram Pass which was approached from Thal, 66 miles from the British fort of Kohat. 50 miles along the river led to Fort Kuram and a further 60 miles beyond was the Paiwar Pass at 8,000 feet. There were further minor passes leading through the Logar valley to Kabul.

The Gomal Pass cuts through the Sulaiman Mountains, about 16 miles west of Tank, via a narrow defile to Kotal-i-Sarmand at 7,500 feet. Following the course of the river another easy pass led to the final ascent of a steep mountain range beyond which lay the town of Ghazni. There was a particular tribe, the Porindahs, which had traversed this route throughout the centuries, dealing with brigands and paying tolls with equanimity.

The Bolan Pass was 500 miles south of the Khyber and was entered through the town of Dadar. There was a continuous ascent through the Hala Mountains for some 60 miles to the summit at 5,800 feet, then to Quetta. The Bolan River flowed through most of it but the last three miles were very narrow, dominated by precipitous cliffs. While Ludhiana, back on the Sutlej, tended to be the main centre of British activity, Quetta had become an advanced British frontier post, leading to Kandahar via the Khojak Pass, which was invariably blocked by snow in winter.

These passes were jealously guarded by well-established tribes whose livelihood depended not only on extracting tolls from wayfarers transiting their passes but subsidies from the rulers in Kabul to keep them sweet. However, there was never any guarantee that a previous agreement would be honoured. They were fickle and treacherous and the temptation of easy plunder was often irresistible, backed by their deadly marksmanship. Using a bipod to rest the barrel of their muskets or *jazails*, they could pick a man off at 800 yards.

There is no doubt that the physical difficulty of getting through the passes, together with the ease that a defender could dominate the routes, made the mountains a major obstacle to an invader from either side of the range. The obsession with putting a puppet on the throne in Kabul and, through him, controlling Afghanistan against Russian advances, blinded the British hierarchy to another, sounder, option. This was to dominate the passes with British military manned forts and suitably bribed local tribes, stiffened by attached British officers. Heights had to be patrolled and observation posts established to give early warning. Then hold the main line of defence against any enemy that managed to struggle through the passes, on the Indus and Sutlej Rivers with artillery covering fire and cavalry in immediate reserve to counter-attack any incursion. Then leave the Afghans, happily, to sort themselves out. There were officers like Burnes and Pottinger who, doubtless, recognised this, but they were sidelined and ignored.

On 8 November 1838, news came that the Persians had given up besieging Herat and retired, with their Russian 'advisers.' At a stroke, the immediate threat to Afghanistan was removed and the reason for Auckland's invasion effectively nullified. However, not to be put off, he pressed on. Ostensibly, the operation was to be led by Shah Shuja, to take back his rightful throne, supported by British arms. Once achieved, the British would leave Afghanistan. Suitable financial arrangements would be made with the Sikhs and the Sindh warlords to keep the eastern ends of the Khyber and Bolan Passes open. Sadly, the plan, like so many others, was not properly thought through, let alone the exit strategy. Here was an army, of some considerable strength, crossing very hard and inhospitable territory, through highly dangerous and suspect passes, with a very long and fragile line of communication and administrative support. No one had any idea of what they were going to do once they had got there. Did they really think the tribes were going to welcome them with open arms? Anyway, could Shah Shuja hold his throne after the British withdrew?

What thought had been given to that by the bright young policy advisers in Calcutta?

Shah Shuja's force was made up of local levies and disenchanted exiled Afghans, whose loyalty to the Shah momentarily rested on recovering their lands and property and meting out a good deal of revenge. There were some British officers attached to his force to give it some professional steel. To give it further status and legitimacy, the British provided an Envoy and Minister to the Court of Shah Shuja with 'political' officers in the field. This Envoy was, unsurprisingly, Sir William Macnaghten. So power was to rest in the hands of civilians to whom the military answered. This can work in peace-keeping operations but where suspicion, distrust and contempt are rife, it is a recipe for disaster which can only be rescued by outstanding leadership which, here, was sadly lacking. Burnes, now Sir Alexander, was in the team but was a disappointed and bitter man who had seen himself as the Envoy.

Having earmarked three columns for the invasion in the expectation of having to take on the Persians and the Russians, Auckland reduced the strength to two, now Herat was back in Afghan hands. Sir Harry Fane was to be the military head of the expedition, pretentiously called the 'Army of the Indus,' with carefully selected and well-seasoned troops who constituted his Bengal contingent. The force consisted of two infantry divisions, of which the first, commanded by Major General Sir Willoughby Cotton, contained three brigades, commanded respectively by Colonels Sale, Nott, and Dennis. Major General Duncan commanded the second infantry division of two brigades, of which one was commanded by Colonel Roberts, the other by Colonel Worsley. The Bombay Presidency was to provide a third force under the command of General Sir John Keane. The 6000 troops raised for Shah Shuja, who were also under Fane's orders, and were officered from the army in India, had been recently and hurriedly recruited, and although rapidly improving, were not yet up to scratch.

The plan was for the Bombay Division, numbering some 5,600 men, to go by sea and land near the Indus River and then to link up with the Bengal Division which had concentrated at Ferozepore. As there now seemed no proper reason for invasion, Sir Harry Fane, who had never liked the plan in the first place, resigned and overall command of the force then fell to Sir John Keane.

The quickest route to Kabul was to cross the Punjab and enter Afghanistan through Peshawar and the Khyber Pass, but Ranjit Singh, the ruler of the Punjab, refused to allow a force of this size, quite rightly given the administrative weight it would have had locally, to cross his territory. Had Burnes's plan of a British/Sikh/Shah Shuja triumvirate succeeded, it might have been very different. The invasion route therefore had to be through the southern passes, with the approach to Kabul via Kandahar and Ghazni; a journey three times the distance of the direct route.

The Bengal Division, which now numbered some 9,500 men, would march inland towards Quetta after assembling in Ferozepore. On the way the column would link up with the Bombay force at Vikkur about 800 miles from Ferozepore. The total size of the invasion force now numbered some 20,500 men, with twice that amount of camp followers and upwards of thirty thousand camels. The Bombay Division landed near the Indus river and made its way up-river to Rohri where both Divisions crossed the Indus in January 1839. The army was now faced with a 150 mile march through the blistering wastes of Baluchistan with inadequate supplies of food and water. 'Political' officers had been sent ahead to secure local administration but managed to fail abysmally. Men went on half rations and camels, oxen and horses, carrying supplies, died in droves. The column was harassed by the mountain tribes, which picked off stragglers and stole anything they could get their hands on. The word soon got round that there was no shortage of British gold; you only had to raise a few threats and Macnaghten would give it to you. He was unable to see any other way out of the problem.

However, Keane pressed on with the advance through the Bolan and Khojak passes. Some of the passes were so narrow and steep that the draught bullocks couldn't operate and artillery, including a heavy battering-train, had to be manhandled, taking five days. The force marched 147 miles into Afghanistan and reached Kandahar on 25 April 1839. The local city leaders, including a brother of Dost Mohammad, escaped to Western Afghanistan and the city was captured without a shot being fired. The force remained there for the next three months, recovering from the ravages of the march through the mountains.

On 27 June Ranjit Singh, the old Lion of the Punjab, died. His loss, as a reasonably reliable ally of the British, would be sorely felt. On that day, leaving behind his heavy siege train, which he simply couldn't mobilise, Keane set off for the army's next objective; the fortress city of Ghazni as it dominated the route to Kabul. The alternative to taking Ghazni was to mask it, i.e. leave a small force merely to dominate it, and press on. However, Keane was so low in rations and administrative support, this option was quickly discarded. He needed the city in which to halt, consolidate and replenish his supplies.

The Army arrived at Ghazni on 21 July. Initial reconnaissance showed the city to be heavily fortified with a 70-foot wall and a flooded moat. The defence of the city was led by Ghulam Haidar, a son of Dost Mohammad. Lacking heavy wall-blasting siege equipment meant that the only way for the British to capture the city was a frontal attack through gates, potentially resulting in heavy casualties.

However, captured Afghan soldiers revealed that all the gates into Ghazni had been sealed with rocks and debris except the Kabul Gate which was in the north. The gate appeared to be lightly guarded and inadequately defended. Major George Thomson of the Bengal Engineers suggested he could blow open the gate sufficiently wide for an assaulting force to get through. With the British besieging the city, Shah Shuja set up a position a few miles away to prevent any Afghan forces from attempting to lift the blockade. On 22 July his force was attacked by thousands of Ghilzai tribesmen, who, luckily, were beaten off. The way was now clear to attack the city.

In the darkness of the early morning of 23 July, a battery of the field artillery was positioned on the heights opposite the northern face of the fortress. The 13th Regiment was extended in skirmishing order in the gardens under the wall of this face, and a detachment of sepoys was detailed to make a false attack on the eastern face. Near the centre of the northern side was the Kabul Gate, in front of which lay, waiting for the signal, a storming party consisting of the light companies of the four European regiments, under command of Colonel Dennie of the 13th. The main column consisted of two European regiments and the support of a third under Robert Sale; the native regiments constituted the reserve. All managed to deploy without alarming the garrison.

At 3am, Indian engineers of the Bengal and Bombay Sappers and Miners, led by Lieutenant Durand, approached the gate. As artillery bombarded the city to give them cover, they blew it. The assaulting troops rushed through the shattered gate and bitter hand-to-hand fighting took place during the darkness. The Afghan defenders launched a counterattack which cut off the leading troops from Sale's supporting forces. A body of fierce Afghan swordsmen charged into the gap between the storming party and the main column. Sale, at the head of the latter, was cut down by a sword stroke to the face. With the effort of his blow, the assailant fell with him, and they rolled together among the shattered timbers of the gate. Sale, wounded again on the ground, and faint with loss of blood, called to one of his officers for help. One of them promptly ran the Afghan through the body with his sword, but he still struggled with the Brigadier. At last, in the grapple, Robert got the upper hand, and then dealt his adversary a sabre cut which sliced him through the head.

With heavy fighting, Sale managed, despite severe loss of blood, to link up with his men. The British then fought their way into the centre of the city and by dawn it was theirs. They suffered 200 men killed and wounded while the Afghans lost nearly 500 men, with an unknown number wounded. 1,600 were taken prisoner, including Ghulam Haidar. The loot consisted of numerous horses, camels and mules, ordnance and military weapons of various descriptions, and a vast quantity of supplies of all kinds.

Keane, garrisoned Ghazni, replenished his forces and, leaving behind his sick and wounded, resumed his advance on Kabul on 30 July. Within twenty-four hours Dost Mohammad had heard of the fall of the city. He gathered his chiefs together, hopefully, to receive their backing and loyalty. However, having little confidence, probably rightly, in their assurances, he sent his brother Nawab Jabar Khan to ask what terms Shah Shuja and his British allies were prepared to offer him, and recalled his son Akbar Khan from Jalalabad, with all the force he could put together. The Dost's emissary to the allied camp was informed that 'an honourable asylum' in British India was at the service of his brother, an offer which Jabar Khan summarily declined in his name without further thought. Before he left, the Nawab is reported to have asked Macnaghten, 'If Shah Shuja is really our king, what need has he of your army and name? You have brought him here with your money and arms. Well, leave him now with us Afghans, and let him rule us if he can.' When Jabar Khan returned to Kabul, the Dost, having been joined by Akbar Khan, concentrated his army of 13,000 men and thirty guns but realised that, without the full support of his followers, he was in severe trouble. Nevertheless, he marched out along the Ghazni road, and drew up his force at Arghandi to face Keane. From here, he could secure a safe withdrawal to the hill country of Bamiyan if his people failed him or were defeated.

As he had, sadly, anticipated there was no fight left in his men. The Dost, Koran in hand, rode among his downcast troops, and exhorted them in the name of God and the Prophet not to dishonour themselves by transferring their allegiance to one who had filled Afghanistan with infidels and blasphemers. 'If,' he shouted, 'you are resolved to be traitors to me, at least enable me to die with honour. Support the brother of Fatteh Khan [a brother of his] in one last charge against these Feringhee dogs. If in that charge he will fall; then go and make your own terms with Shah Shuja.' This appeal had no effect whatsoever. Furthermore, it was reported by a soldier-of-fortune called Harlan that his guards deserted the Dost, and that a rabble plundered his pavilion, snatched from under him the pillows of his divan, seized his prayer carpet, and finally hacked into pieces the tent and its trappings. On the evening of 2 August he finally gave up and rode away toward Bamiyan, his son Akbar Khan, with a handful of loyal men, covering his back. News of Dost Mohammad's flight reached Keane on the 3rd, at Sheikabad, where he had halted to concentrate. James Outram volunteered to head a pursuing party, to consist of some British officers as volunteers, some cavalry and about 2000 Afghan horsemen under a notorious turncoat named Haji Khan Kakar, who undertook to act as guide. They should have overtaken Dost Mohammad but for the wily Haji obstructing progress at every point. The Dost was, therefore, able to escape to Bokhara.

As Keane moved forward, he captured the guns which the Dost had left in the Arghandi position. On 6 August he camped close to Kabul and on the following day Shah Shuja triumphantly entered Kabul at the head of his forces, supported by British regiments and with Sir William Macnaghten close at hand. Neither the new Shah nor his pageant kindled any enthusiasm from the Kabulees. There were no shouts of welcome and the citizens did not bother to make him even a gesture of a *salaam*. They stared at the European strangers with hatred in their eyes. The Shah took up residence in the citadel, the Bala Hissar, where he was joined by his son, Timur, who had crossed the Khyber Pass from Peshawar with a Sikh escort provided by Ranjit Singh, accompanied by Claude Wade, Macnaghten's old crony. A contemporary described the Shah as, 'A stout person of the middle height, his chin covered with a long thick and neatly trimmed beard, dyed black to conceal the encroachments of time. His manner toward the English is gentle, calm and dignified, without haughtiness, but his own subjects have invariably complained of his reception of them as cold and repulsive, even to rudeness. His complexion is darker than that of the generality of Afghans, and his features, if not decidedly handsome, are not the reverse of pleasing; but the expression of his countenance would betray to a skilful physiognomist (sic) that mixture of timidity and duplicity so often observable in the character of the higher order of men in Southern Asia.'[7]

Sir John Keane was made Baron Keane of Ghazni and all looked well for the peaceful occupation of Afghanistan and the deterrence of the Russians and Persians.

What could possibly go wrong?

---

[7] *Henry Havelock, (1840). Narrative of the war in Affghanistan on 1838-39. London:* Henry Colburn.

CHAPTER 4

Kabul

Kabul lay in a gorge, between two steep and rocky ridged hills. At the eastern end of the town, on the spur of a hill, dominating it was the Bala Hissar, or citadel, with high stone walls, bastions and high-rise dwellings within. Flowing from the town towards the north-east was the Kabul River in a beautiful valley of between eight and twelve miles wide. The river and its tributaries irrigated the various orchards and cultivated terraces in the small settlements surrounding the town. Dotted among the fields and orchards were small square forts and towers.

The obvious place to house the Kabul garrison was in the citadel, the Bala Hissar. It was a substantial fort on high ground and reasonably impregnable. However, Shah Shuja refused to allow it, reserving the place for himself and his retinue. Macnaghten and Cotton, now the commander of troops in Afghanistan, gave in and bought some land from the Shah north of the city.

Despite advice from military engineers and artillerymen, the British constructed their cantonments to house their forces and the Mission Residence (B)[8] for the Envoy and officers' quarters, on this land, flanking the canal, which flowed to the west of the river. Even worse was the decision to establish the commissariat depot, containing all their

---

[8] Letters refer to places on the map of Kabul City and Cantonments.

supplies and ammunition, isolated to the south of the compound in a disused old fort (E). The ground was swampy and liable to flooding from the Kabul River and intersected with irrigation channels, making any cavalry or artillery deployment extremely difficult. It was dominated by high ground on both flanks and several forts. The perimeter of some 1500 by 600 yards was almost impossible to defend properly. An enemy could, effectively, get to within 200 yards under cover and, from the forts, fire upon any troops exiting from the compound gates. There was a military camp between the Seeah Sung hills and the Jalalabad road well to the east of the cantonments across the canal and the river, over which a bridge had been built; hardly a position for a quick reaction force to come to the aid of those in the cantonments. The village of Beymaroo (M) was just to the north of the cantonments, dominated to the north-west by the Beymaroo Heights. To crown it all, the Treasury (Z), in which all the pay and cash was kept, was in a building in the city opposite Burnes's house (W). All in all, it was about as militarily incompetent as one could imagine. One can only think that the military hierarchy thought they weren't going to be there for long and therefore the tactical aspects of the position didn't really matter. Additionally, they may have thought that it was politically unacceptable to bully the Shah out of his citadel.

Kabul town was not particularly well laid out; streets were narrow, flanked by high houses with flat roofs. Most of the town was on the right bank of the river with, opposite, houses of the richer residents. There was a covered bazaar, consisting of five open squares, connected by four arcades, down the centre of which was a marble aqueduct running with a small stream. The sides were lined with shops selling everything from fruit to leather goods.

With a good deal of relief that they had achieved their object, the 'politicals', and officers and men of the Army of the Indus settled down in the town and its surroundings to enjoy themselves in the certainty that they would soon be marching back to India. A number of officers' wives joined them, including Florentia and her youngest daughter, Alexandrina, aged 17. Typically, sporting events took place with horse racing, wrestling matches and even cricket although what the Afghans made of the latter is not recorded.[9] A Major Daly of the 4th Light Dragoons won a race in which the prize was a valuable sword presented by Shah Shuja. The Afghans, on their side, introduced the soldiery to the gambling delights of cock-fighting and, no doubt, relieved them of several rupees in bets. Relations appeared to be cordial between the residents and their new occupiers. The warning of General Sir Henry Fane as to the difficulties the British would face once the Shah was back on the throne, failed to register. The reality, of course, was that while the British remained in Afghanistan, propping up an unpopular ruler, they would be despised and hated, whereas if they left, the Shah would undoubtedly fall.

With the complacency which had dogged earlier decisions, the Bombay Division was dispatched back to India with a contingent of Bengal troops in September 1839. Sir Willoughby Cotton had about 10,000 men left. Kabul, Jalalabad, Kandahar and Ghazni were to be garrisoned. The

---

[9] Maybe the forerunners of the Afghan cricket team defeated by England in the 2019 World Cup; nothing to be ashamed of, being beaten by the Champions.

Sales spent the winter of 1839 in the Shah's so-called palace in Jalalabad, returning early in 1840 to Kabul where Robert, now 'Sir Robert' and a Brigadier General in recognition of his part in the capture of Ghazni, took over command of the garrison consisting of the 13th Foot, 35th Native Infantry, some light artillery and an element of the Shah's Levies. The situation was, though, far from satisfactory. The Army was now separated from its main base in Ludhiana several hundred miles through the lawless and often snow blocked passes of the Khyber and Bolan, with their two main outposts, Jalalabad and Kandahar three hundred miles apart; hardly what nowadays would be called 'in mutual support.' To make matters worse, with the death of Ranjit Singh in June 1839, the Punjab started to sink into anarchy and any agreement allowing the British free access across the state was quickly forgotten. In the Khyber itself, things were no better where the tribes were being troublesome. They were dissatisfied with the amount of annual blackmail paid them for the right of way through their passes. When Shah Shuja had been a fugitive thirty years previously, they had concealed and protected him and, in return, he had promised them, unknown to Macnaghten, the augmentation of their subsidy to the old scale from which it had gradually dwindled. Wade, returning from Kabul, did not bring them the assurances they expected, whereupon they rose up and occupied the strategic fort Ali Masjid, the key to accessing the Pass from the east. Mackeson, the Peshawar political officer, threw them out and reinforced the fort. However, the relieving force, on its return to base, was attacked by the bandits. The Sikhs were routed, and the sepoys lost men and transport. The emboldened Khyberees now turned on Ali Masjid in earnest but the garrison, having been strengthened, held out until a couple of regiments marched down from Jalalabad. It was then announced that Mackeson had hatched a deal with the chiefs for the payment of an annual subsidy which they considered adequate. It was the classic of how things worked; if the tribes felt in need of gold, they'd rise up, close the passes and cut throats until they were paid off with further funds. A few months later, the cycle would begin again. The only real way to deal with it was a heavy imposition of efficient troops and some exemplary punishment; this cost money and force deployment.

The Sales had a comfortable house in the cantonments near the Envoy's and now as 'Lady' Sale, Florentia was number two only to Lady Macnaghten in the wives pecking order. Life was fun and certainly for Alexandrina, who must have ruined many young officers' hearts. There was hunting, amateur theatricals and ice-skating in the winter. The whole edifice of Society was propped up a by a vast army of servants brought from India. It was not unusual for a battalion of infantry to be accompanied by some 5,000 camp followers. The Sales themselves shared, with another officer, nearly 40 servants, whom they had brought from India. The upshot of this was to raise jealousy and resentment from the local Afghans as employment opportunities were not open to them. Secondly, it restricted information which would have been useful coming from local servants to the more perceptive of the British. The Envoy, though, employed an Afghan journalist at 150 rupees a month and an old mullah at 200 rupees who, between them, concocted 'splendid untruths' as Florentia put it. These men had Sir William's confidence and would flatter him into believing what they told him. An early 'fake truth' perhaps?

1840 dawned with an abortive attempt by the Russians, worried about the British success in Afghanistan, launching an expedition into Central Asia towards Khiva. Happily for those in Kabul and Calcutta, this failed and the Russians withdrew by March. More worryingly, Dost Mohammad and his sons escaped from captivity in Bokhara and, easily gathering adherents, appeared in the hills above Bamiyan, being rapidly joined by loyal tribesmen, including deserters from a complete Afghan regiment.

Macnaghten reinforced Bamiyan by sending a force there under Colonel Dennie. On 18 September, Dennie moved out with two guns and 800 men against the Dost's advance parties raiding in an adjacent valley. Unnervingly, his detachments driven back, Dennie suddenly found himself facing the irregular mass of horse and foot which constituted the Dost's army. Mackenzie's cannon fire shook the undisciplined ranks and his infantry pressed home their advantage, and soon the Dost's men were fleeing in panic, with Dennie's cavalry in eager pursuit. Dost Mohammad himself escaped with difficulty, losing his entire personal equipment. He was once more a fugitive.

But the Envoy's elation was short-lived. Dost Mohammad was yet to cause him further anxiety. Defeated in Bamiyan, he was ready for another attempt in the Kohistan country to the north of Kabul. Disaffection was rife everywhere throughout the kingdom, but it was perhaps most in the Kohistan, which was seething with intrigues in favour of Dost Mohammad, while the local chiefs were infuriated by the exactions of the Shah's revenue collectors. Macnaghten summoned the chiefs to Kabul. They came, did homage to

Shah Shuja and swore allegiance to him but went away from the capital pledging his overthrow, and jeering at the scantiness of the force they had seen at Kabul. Intercepted letters disclosed their schemes, and by the end of September, Sale, with a considerable force, marched out to punish the disaffected Kohistanees. For three weeks Robert marched to and fro through the Kohistan, pursuing will-o'-the-wisp rumours as to the whereabouts of the Dost, destroying forts on the course of his weary pilgrimage, and being subjected occasionally to hit-and-run attacks.

Meanwhile, in the belief that Dost Mohammad was close to Kabul, and highly conscious that the capital and surrounding country were ripe for a rising, Macnaghten descended into nervous gloom. The troops at Bamiyan were urgently recalled. Cannon were mounted on the Bala Hissar to overawe the city, the concentration of the troops in the fortress was under discussion, and men were talking of preparing for a siege. Macnaghten's confidence was deteriorating under the strain of events as shown by his writing of the Dost: 'Would it be justifiable to set a price on this fellow's head?' How his judgement was failing was further evidenced by his talking of 'showing no mercy to the man who has been the author of all the evil now distracting the country,' and by his complaining of Sale and Burnes that, 'with 2000 good infantry, they are sitting down before a fortified place, and are afraid to attack it.'

From his reconnaissance patrols, Robert learnt that the Dost had crossed the Hindoo Kush into the Kohistan and that he was now in the Purwan Durrah valley, stretching down from the Hindoo Kush to the Gorebund river. The British force set off in pursuit. As they neared a village, the Dost's people were seen evacuating it and the adjacent forts, and making for the hills. Robert's cavalry was some distance in advance of his leading infantry, but time was precious. Anderson's horse went to the left, to cut off retreat down the Gorebund valley. Fraser took his two squadrons of Bengal cavalry to the right, advanced along the foothills, and gained the head of the valley. He was too late to intercept a small body of Afghan horsemen, who were already climbing the heights but, badly mounted as he was, he could effectively pursue them. However, the Afghans turned to fight rather than run. The Dost himself was in command of the little party, and he was certainly not a man to run away. He wheeled his handful of men so that his horsemen faced Fraser's troop down below them. Then the Dost pointed to his banner, bared his head, called on his supporters in the name of God and the Prophet to follow him against the unbelievers, and led them down the slope.

Fraser had formed up his troopers when recall orders reached him. Ignoring the command, he gave the order to charge. As the Afghans came slowly down the slope, they fired occasionally. Either because of the rounds, or because they were just terrified, Fraser's troopers broke and fled. The British officers galloped back unsupported. Broadfoot, Crispin and Lord were killed; Ponsonby, severely wounded and his reins cut, was carried out of the *mêlée* by his charger; Fraser, covered with blood and wounds, broke through his assailants, and brought his report of the disgrace of his troopers to Robert. After a sharp pursuit of the deserters, the Dost and his followers leisurely quitted the field.

Burnes wrote to the Envoy that there was no alternative for the force but to fall back on Kabul, and entreated Macnaghten to order an immediate concentration of all troops there. Macnaghten received Burnes's letter the day after the disaster in the Kohistan, when he was taking his afternoon ride on the Kabul plain. He must have been deeply depressed as he rode, when suddenly a horseman galloped up to him and announced that the Ameer was approaching. 'What Ameer?' asked Macnaghten. 'Dost Mohammad Khan,' was the reply, and sure enough there was the Dost close at hand, with a single orderly. Dismounting, the Afghan chief saluted the Envoy, and offered him his sword, which Macnaghten declined to take. Dost and Envoy then rode into Kabul together, and such was the impression the former made on him that Macnaghten, who a month before had permitted himself to think of putting a price on 'the fellow's' head, begged now of the Governor General 'that the Dost be treated more handsomely than was Shah Shuja, who had no claim on us.' This was followed by a strange confession from the man who had initiated the tripartite treaty, and approved the Simla manifesto: 'We had no hand in depriving the Shah of his kingdom, *whereas we ejected the Dost, who never offended us, in support of our policy, of which he was the victim.*' [Author's italics] Despite his recent successes, Dost Mohammad's self-confidence had deteriorated into utter despondency. He was well treated and was soon on his way into exile in Ludhiana, an (almost) honoured guest as a pensioner of the East India Company.

In April 1841 Sir Willoughby Cotton was replaced as Army commander by Major General William Elphinstone. This was not one of the better decisions by Auckland. Elphinstone had fought well at Waterloo but was now 59, unfit and riddled with painful gout, and, while personally affable, had no liking for India, let alone the Afghans. He was past it; incompetent and indecisive. Bluntly, a disaster waiting to happen. At the same time, the Kabul garrison was reinforced with a brigade from India with a view, at some stage, to relieve Robert Sale's men. It was commanded by Brigadier General John Shelton. Shelton had fought in the Peninsular War, losing an arm. He was a particularly nasty bit of work; rude, cantankerous, obstructive and highly unpopular. The last man to be any use to poor Elphinstone.

The Sales firmly established themselves in a house in the cantonments and developed a garden to Robert's taste. Then on 9 August 1841, Alexandrina married one of the better officers of the Royal Engineers, Lieutenant John Sturt much to the happiness of her parents.

By the summer of 1841, Macnaghten, virtually running things in the absence of any direction from Elphinstone, was continuing to delude himself that all was well and provided rosy reports to Calcutta. He was backed by a complacent Burnes, who most certainly knew better, but hoped that Macnaghten would achieve his aim of being posted to Bombay as Governor and he could step into his shoes. A contemporary wrote of him, 'Sometimes sanguine, sometimes despondent, sometimes confident, sometimes credulous, Burnes gave to fleeting impressions all the importance and seeming permanency of settled convictions, and imbued surrounding objects with the colours of his own varying mind.'[10] Even if Burnes had been a discreet and steadfast man, he could have exercised no influence on the autocratic Macnaghten, since between the two men there

---

[10] John William Kaye: *History of the War in Afghanistan* London, 1851.

was neither empathy nor confidence. Burnes had, indeed, no specific duties of any kind. In his own words, he was in 'the most nondescript situation.' Macnaghten gave him no responsibility, and while Burnes waited for the promise of the office of Envoy, he chiefly employed himself in writing long memorials on the situation and prospects of affairs, on which Macnaghten's marginal comments were brusque, and occasionally contemptuous. The resolute and clear-headed Pottinger, who, if the opportunity had been given him, might have supported and steadied Macnaghten, was relegated to provincial service. Throughout his career in Afghanistan the Envoy could not look for much advice from the successive commanders of the Kabul force, even if he had cared to consult them.

More and more money was now needed to back up the regime. It was now costing £1 million per year. Calcutta was increasingly reluctant to provide it and told Macnaghten to find it himself. Taxes were, not unnaturally, always difficult to extract from the locals and, with the unpopularity of their new ruler, almost impossible to raise. Troops had to be used to enforce it thereby further reinforcing the hatred of the British overlords. On the other hand, Macnaghten's only solution to pacify the tribes was to bribe them. They were no fools and realised all they had to do was to threaten and gold would drop into their hands. This situation simply could not continue, so what was he to do? In desperation he then cancelled the subsidies (bribes) paid to the Eastern Ghilzais to keep open the passes between Kabul and Jalalabad. These were the people who, in essence, kept the lines of communication open through to Ludhiana. At a stroke, Macnaghten alienated them and their sympathisers in other tribes, closed the passes and created turmoil and insurrection elsewhere.

No wonder he dreamed of Bombay.

CHAPTER 5

Insurrection

In addition to the disaffection of the Ghilzais, there were a number of disturbances and local insurrections throughout 1841. On the whole these were suppressed and hostages taken to ensure future good faith. Nevertheless, in Afghan eyes, the British were weak in their response and this encouraged malcontents within the Army who stirred up trouble, including, on one occasion, butchering their own commander, Lieutenant Maule of the Bengal Artillery. Early in October, three Ghilzai chiefs suddenly left Kabul and, after plundering a settlement at Tezeen, established a defensive position, blocking the Khurd-Kabul Pass, some ten miles from Kabul. To make matters worse, intelligence was received that Dost Mohammad's fourth and most capable son, Mohammad Akbar Khan, was at large and had never forgiven the British for the treatment of his father. A charismatic leader, it is highly likely that he influenced the Ghilzais. He was going to be trouble.

As part of the reduction of forces, Sale's Brigade had been earmarked to return to India but, as a result of the uprising, the Brigade was ordered to deploy to winter quarters in Jalalabad, forcing the five mile long Khurd-Kabul Pass on the way, via Gandamak, in ferocious fighting in which Robert was (again!) shot in the leg. He had agreed that Florentia should remain in Kabul with Alexandrina and her husband, Captain Sturt, and rejoin him later, travelling with

Elphinstone who was to be replaced by General Nott – not a moment too soon.

Meanwhile, in Kabul, things were not going well. There were instances of officers being insulted and attempts made to kill them. These actions were brushed aside as mere expressions of local anger and no effort was made to find out what was really happening. One particular individual, Abdullah Khan, a man previously trusted, turned out to be an inveterate enemy. As an example of his style, he had a brother, who stood between him and his inheritance, buried up to his chin in the ground. A noose was then fastened tight around his head and tied to a wild horse which was driven round in a circle until his head was twisted off. This Khan and his cronies put it about in Kabul that it was the intention of the Envoy to seize the rebel chiefs and send them to England.

Florentia, perceptive as ever, was highly critical of Elphinstone's weakness in refusing to occupy the Bala Hissar on the grounds that it was too far from the cantonments (A). How, she thought, they could manage a week's march to Jalalabad if they couldn't make the one and half miles to the Bala Hissar? To her utter scorn, she found out that Shelton would appear for a conference with Elphinstone and Macnaghten and roll out his sleeping bag on the floor and feign sleep. Other officers were obstructive or merely withdrew in exasperation. One can imagine the curl of her lip. Elphinstone should have had her on his committee. Macnaghten vacillated. Earlier he had demanded an extra five regiments from the Government in India; two of them European. However, having now been appointed Governor of Bombay, he looked for a quick exit from Kabul. To do so, he changed his mind about troop reinforcements and declared that the Country was so peaceful that those presently garrisoning the towns could be withdrawn once the Shah had raised five regiments of his own. Moral courage was not Macnaghten's strongest suite.

Florentia related the story of the unfortunate Mrs Smith who was travelling, lightly guarded, through the Bolan Pass to Kandahar when she was set upon by Baluch brigands. Her escort fled and she was killed. When her assailants found out she was a woman, they left her body intact with all her rings and earrings in place. Amongst these tribes there was a superstition that killing a woman was unlucky.

At this stage Florentia was fully expecting to leave Kabul within days. There was some tiresomeness from Shelton who complained that he should be accommodated in a proper house in the cantonments. Florentia pointed out that his place was in the Seeah Sung camp, with his men. Her diary doesn't disclose whether she told him that to his face but, if she did so, it wouldn't have been surprising. Her house, one of the best, was to be renovated for the occupation of General Nott on his arrival. It had a particularly good kitchen garden, which was one of Robert's hobbies, and the fruit was much admired by the locals. Nott was expected to take over command from Elphinstone on 1 November but quite how was anyone's guess.

In the early hours of 2 November 1841, serious insurrection broke out in Kabul. The rebels rapidly plundered the Treasury (Z), massacred the guard of 40 men and slew Sir Alexander Burnes and two other officers, who lived, not in the cantonments, but in a house in the city. There were reports that Captain Sturt was also wounded but only lightly. Pandemonium reigned; the Shah sent some of his troops down from Bala Hissar to disperse the mobs but they were summarily repulsed with the loss of some 200 men and guns. From his camp to the east of the Seeah Sung hills, Shelton sent his men into the city to cover the Shah's troops back into the Bala Hissar. Macnaghten mounted his horse in the Mission, rode out to the gate and wisely rode back in again. There was nothing he could do. Had the Afghans killed or taken him prisoner, it would have done no one any good. Shelton then moved his Brigade into the cantonments. Lieutenant Vincent Eyre of the Bengal Artillery was one of those highly critical of the positioning and construction of the cantonments. In his view, they were virtually indefensible and overlooked from the hills and nearby forts. To make matters worse, the commissariat, containing all their stores, was in an old fort, detached from the cantonments and therefore almost impossible to defend, he noted. How could anyone allow that to happen? He was quite clear that the only proper place for their forces was in the Bala Hissar. He was only too right. Florentia cynically commented that the laid back and fanciful sense of security in the cantonments was a direct result of Lord Auckland's view from Calcutta that all was tranquil in Afghanistan and its inhabitants as peaceful as the citizens of London. The Shah, in an extreme state of anxiety, gathered a number of British officers around him and sought their advice. Florentia coyly redacted in her diary the name of one, whom she described as pitiful and childish in the extreme, not having a word to say or an opinion to offer. It can only have been Shelton.

Florentia's immediate worry was over her son-in-law, John Sturt. She had him brought to her house where she could see that he was certainly not 'slightly' wounded which is what she had been told. He had been stabbed deeply in the shoulder and the side, and in the face, just missing his temple. He was covered in blood and unable to speak, with blood coming out of his mouth. His tongue was paralysed, and the nerves in his throat were affected preventing him from swallowing or speaking. Dr Harcourt dressed his wounds and made him as comfortable as possible. Later that evening he improved somewhat and was just able to say he felt better. One of Florentia's servants, Mohammad Ali, who lived in the city, arrived in a great state, having been threatened and reviled as a *chuprassy* (a highly valued servant) of the foreign General, whom, his detractors said, had been beaten at Tezeen and that all his troops had run away and he with them. Anyone knowing Fighting Bob Sale would have collapsed with laughter at the thought. Although it wasn't particularly funny for his wife.

At three in the morning on 3 November, drums beat the call to arms in the cantonments. This was in response to a large body of men coming from Seeah Sung hills direction; however, they turned out to be the 37th Native Infantry coming from Khurd-Kabul, hotly pursued by 3000 Ghilzais. They made it safely and were a significant asset to the defence. There was now considerable nervousness about attacks thought to be imminent from the tribesmen of Kohistan, the mountainous region fifty miles north of Kabul. In the afternoon, a large body of rebels drew up in extended line 900 yards south-east of the cantonments, displaying a green religious flag. After they were engaged with cannon fire, they eventually withdrew. That evening a considerable number of rebels penetrated the area between the commissariat fort and the cantonments. Florentia was rightly worried that if the commissariat fell, they only had provisions for three days in the cantonments and, additionally, they would be cut off from the city. She heaped sarcasm onto the Shah, Macnaghten and Elphinstone whom she accused of being paralysed by the outbreak of the insurrection. She maintained that there were chiefs loyal to the regime but who were ignored, just as the Afghan who warned Burnes of his imminent attack was rebuffed with scorn. One such was Syud Mohammad Khan, a staunch loyalist to the Shah and the British. For his support, he was given the honorary title of *Jan Fishan Khan*, the 'exterminator of his sovereign's enemies.'

Orders were sent down to Kandahar to send reinforcements to Kabul. Sale, reorganising at Gandamak, which he had reached on 30 October, was ordered by Macnaghten to return immediately to Kabul. However, with some 300 casualties and very little transport and only one day's supply of rations and water, he rightly refused. Furthermore, as he was unable to hold Gandamak, he decided to press on for Jalalabad which he reckoned could be made into a substantial fort and a main strongpoint on the route to India. He reached there on 15 November.

On 4 November, the enemy occupied the King's Garden (K) and the Mohammad Shereef fort (F) to its south, covering the road from the cantonments into the city. They then attacked the commissariat fort (E) cutting it off from the cantonments. It was being held by Lieutenant Warren and some 100 men. He was hard pressed and in grave danger of being overrun. Elphinstone ordered a rescue attempt to be made to cover the evacuation of the fort, despite the fact that the loss of provisions in it would have severe repercussions. The first attempt was driven off and then a second was made with two companies of 44th Foot. As they left the cantonments, they came under highly effective fire from the Mohammad Shereef fort and the King's Garden, killing the commander, another officer and wounding three others. There was nothing for it but to withdraw back into the cantonments. During the evening another attempt was made by the 5th Light Cavalry but it too was repulsed with heavy losses. Elphinstone was again briefed on the catastrophe of giving up the commissariat; not only would they lose a large quantity of food, medicine and clothing but its loss would thoroughly encourage the enemy. The provisions in the cantonments were now down to two days' worth and there was no prospect of obtaining any more from anywhere else. Consequently, Elphinstone sent orders to Warren to hold out as long as possible. Warren denied ever having received this order which was hardly surprising. Given the circumstances it is difficult to imagine how the order could have been got through. Nevertheless, Warren did manage to send a message later on that night that the enemy were mining one of the towers and several of his men had deserted. Unless reinforced, he could not hold out much longer. He was told he would be reinforced by 2 am. At 9 pm, Elphinstone held a conference at which Macnaghten stated unless Mohammad Shereef's fort was taken that night, they would lose the commissariat. Elphinstone was reluctant, given the earlier lack of success, to commit any more troops to the operation, however, he was told that a night attack might be possible given the Afghans were slack about sentries after dark. A reconnaissance revealed that the guard on the fort consisted of only about twenty to thirty men, sitting outside the gate, smoking and talking. Another patrol confirmed this. More time was lost as the General dithered. Eyre consulted Sturt, who was recovering from his wounds, and they recommended an attack in the early hours of the morning to which, after further procrastination, the General agreed. Accordingly, orders were given for a force to be ready at 4 am to blow open the Kohistan gate (the one from the city to the immediate south of the cantonments) (P) and a party of the 44th to exit via a breach in the north wall of the city, and to assault the commissariat. However, daylight came before this could happen and when they were on the point of getting under way, Warren and his men arrived at the cantonments having evacuated the commissariat. As the enemy were setting fire to one of the towers, Warren got out through a hole cut in the wall. Unsurprisingly, he was formally told to give his reasons for abandoning his post. He replied that he would only do so in front of a Court of Inquiry. This then seemed to be conveniently forgotten. There was no doubt that this was the first really major nail in the British Kabul coffin; the loss of the commissariat in terms of provisioning was enormous, coupled with the overwhelming encouragement and morale boost it gave the rebels. Some of the more neutral chiefs were, accordingly, throwing in their lot with the rebels.

What now began was full-blown street fighting in the city and major battles in the countryside among the forts and the cantonments, embroiling infantry, artillery and cavalry. The reality was that there were simply not enough well-trained troops to deal with the rebels and the leadership, apart from relatively junior officers, was sadly lacking. Elphinstone was ill, old and dithery, incapable of making up his mind. Macnaghten was out his depth, militarily, and all he wanted was to get out as soon as possible to Bombay.

Shelton was difficult, abrasive and downright insubordinate. Sale, brave that he was, had not the brain to handle it and, anyway, was out of it at Gandamak on his way to Jalalabad. The best people around were Florentia; Sturt, her Engineer wounded son-in-law, and Eyre the Gunner, plus some very brave young officers, a number of whom quickly lost their lives. Shah Shuja sat at a window in one of the Bala Hissar bastions, anxiously watching, through a telescope, the events happening around the cantonments. He was *gobrowed*, a rather apt Eastern expression meaning something between being dumbfounded and at one's wits' end.

Eyre made a good effort bringing guns to bear on the rebel-held Mohammad Shereef fort but the fleeting chance of a well-timed infantry assault was missed. Trying again on 6 November, a well-planned attack on the fort was launched with three infantry companies of about 150 men, supported by Eyre's guns. The fort was taken with Ensign Raban shot through the heart when waving a flag of success in the breach. Trying to move on to take the King's Garden area adjacent to the fort was too difficult and there was fierce hand-to-hand fighting. With a considerable number of enemy massing to the west, it was considered sensible to withdraw back into the cantonments. The main worry now was the lack of supplies after the loss of the commissariat. Some had been obtained from the village of Beymaroo, half a mile north of the cantonments but, clearly, its inhabitants were now under the influence of the rebel chiefs and it would be a brave man to supply the British. Starving out the occupants of the cantonments was a good option for the insurgents.

Lady Macnaghten told Florentia that her husband had drafted a letter for General Elphinstone to send to Robert Sale, recalling him from Gandamak, entreating him to leave his sick and wounded there and come to their aid. Elphinstone agreed but then changed his mind, saying he was not prepared for Sale to desert his wounded. Florentia was well aware that if Robert left his wounded, arrived at the cantonments and saved the day, he would be highly praised but if the worst happened, his wounded slaughtered and he failed to relieve those in the cantonments, he would have been severely condemned. Florentia wanted to send him a letter under Macnaghten's authority (via a messenger in the Envoy's 'secret service') but to her disgust was turned down. It was rumoured that Nott's Kandahar force, on its way to India, was to return if it had not yet crossed the Khojak Pass. Another rumour was that the Shah was to vacate the Bala Hissar and move into the cantonments. With his 800 entourage of wives, daughters and servants, they would soon starve, as Florentia icily pointed out. With an analysis that would have pleased an instructor at the Staff College, Florentia concluded, and she was not alone, that the Bala Hissar citadel was the only sensible place for the British force to maintain its power. Florentia's grasp of the differences between 9 pounder guns (iron 'nines'), brass 6-pounders, 18 pounders, their relative accuracy, firepower and transport problems would have earned her place in the Mountain Artillery, an elite band. A further idea from some lunatic was to kick all the Afghans out of the Bala Hissar garrison, and those in the cantonments, and to live off the rations they left behind. But no one really knew anything and gloom and low morale set in.

The cantankerous Shelton was now summoned by Macnaghten, effectively to take command, although not in so many words, from the decrepit Elphinstone. Florentia generously gave him the benefit of being a brave man but heartily disliked by his troops and fellow officers; 'his arrival is a dark cloud overshadowing us.' She had been told that the moment he arrived in Bala Hissar earlier, he had had ammunition boxes filled with flour to provide for an eventual withdrawal from Afghanistan. It soon became clear that Shelton had grave misgivings that the Kabul garrison would last the winter. This, of course, became widely known, and despondency became infectious. Macnaghten, however, was surprisingly robust and maintained that the British should remain whatever the cost. Having this major difference of opinion at the decision making level was unhelpful to say the least. Sadly, some of the British soldiers, who were meant to set an example to their Indian comrades, also started to despair after their considerable losses. The Shah's confidence completely evaporated and he told the females of his harem, about 860 of them, that if the enemy took the cantonments, he would poison them all.

On 10 November, the enemy lined the hills either side of the cantonments, attacked the Rikabashee Fort (G), between the river and the canal, within musket shot of the cantonments, and plundered the village of Beymaroo at will. Shelton bravely led a counter attack onto the fort where there was some fierce fighting including Colonel Mackrell of the 44th being wounded in both legs, three cuts to his back, two toes cut off and three or four cuts to the arm which was amputated on recovery to the cantonments. Unsurprisingly, he later died. Florentia assessed that at least

150 enemy had been killed, with 26 of the 44th and 50 of the 37th. Shelton then pursued the enemy into the Seeah Sung Hills, covered by Eyre's guns. Returning after dark, it was decided to blow up some of the forts to deny them to the enemy but the Rikabashee and Zoolficar's (I) were kept intact. Some grain was recovered from the forts, boosting the cantonments store with another three days' worth. Their success did have an effect on the head man of Beymaroo who sent a grovelling *salaam* to the Envoy, wishing to know his pleasure. The curt response was, 'If you wish to keep your two forts, sell us grain.'

Morale took an upward turn and Shelton, as a successful leader, became more popular with the soldiery. Florentia reckoned they could occupy Bala Hissar by night, providing sufficient ammunition had been pre-positioned there. She admitted this would not be comfortable but they could purchase the stores of the departing Afghans and last out the winter come what may. She realised, however, this was far from the minds of Macnaghten and Shelton who would not abandon the cantonments to the enemy. She was buoyed up by Sturt's remarkable recovery; no doubt benefitting from his wife's and mother-in-law's nursing.

Rumours were rife. Would Nott be with them in three weeks? Was Sale returning from Gandamak? Had Lieutenant Crawford, Captain Sanders and Captain Skinner been hacked to pieces in Kandahar? Had the enemy obtained the necessary scaling ladders and fascines for crossing the ditches to attack the cantonments by night? Had the Ghilzais been bought off by the Envoy? It was very stressful for everyone, including a robust a person as Florentia.

On the 13th, the enemy appeared in large numbers on the Beymaroo Heights to the west of the cantonments and opened fire with two canon. There was further argument between Elphinstone, Macnaghten and Shelton about taking a force out to deal with them. Elphinstone would only agree if Macnaghten took full responsibility, so it was late before the force was ready. Shelton led the troops consisting of some 16 infantry companies, cavalry and artillery under Eyre's command. The leading elements quickly reached the foot of the hills but as contact was made with the enemy, there was no covering fire from Eyre's guns which had bogged down in the irrigation ditches. Seeing this, the enemy were encouraged and fierce hand-to-hand took place before Eyre could bring his guns to bear with grapeshot and shrapnel. Anderson's cavalry then charged, driving the enemy back up the hill, pursued closely by infantry. Eyre got his guns into the gorge between the hills where he could bring fire down on the enemy in the plain to the west. Some enemy guns were recovered and those that weren't were spiked. It was not an option to occupy the heights that night, so Shelton withdrew his men into the cantonments while still in contact with the enemy. Eyre was pretty critical of the British marksmanship compared with the Afghans. He maintained that the Afghans take a deliberate aimed shot compared with the British who fire off at random without bothering to take aim. He observed Afghan horsemen braving British fire up to twelve yards with impunity. Anyway, all went quiet later that night. Florentia moved into Sturt's house and gave hers up to Shelton who was grumbling about being cold in his tent.

Little did they know it but this was to be the last British success; it was going to be the road to disaster from now on.

CHAPTER 6

Defeat

On 15 November, two surviving officers of the siege of Charikar, a town in the Kohistan region some 40 miles north of Kabul, staggered into the cantonment, completely exhausted. They were the famous Eldred Pottinger[11], hero of Herat, who was wounded in the leg, and Lieutenant Haughton, adjutant of the Shah's 4th Gurkha Regiment, who had had his right hand amputated and was severely cut about the neck and left arm. Dr Grant, who had performed the operation, disappeared and was never seen again. They had been down to one glass of water per day for the last four days and their horses had not drunk for ten days nor eaten for five. The saga of the siege of Charikar was one of bravery in the face of vastly superior numbers and treachery and panic by their own troops. The escape by the two

---

[11] Eldred Pottinger was a man worth his salt. In 1837 he had travelled through Afghanistan in disguise. Arriving at Herat, he found it besieged by the Persians, supported by Russian 'advisers' and immediately made himself known to the Afghan commander, offering his services. The siege lasted a year and was unsuccessful, owing much to Pottinger's help. For this, he was promoted brevet-major and awarded the CB. By 1841 he was political officer in Kohistan when the revolt broke out. Taking refuge with the **Gurkha** garrison of **Charikar**, he withstood yet another siege, this time of fourteen days, and then made the hazardous journey to Kabul.

officers and a small band, which gradually dwindled by desertion and death, to just themselves, a loyal Gurkha, a clerk and a trader, was a tale of fortitude and survival against all odds. They should never have made it.

In the cantonments, camels were dying by the day; their carcasses littering the area outside the walls, creating an odious stench. Water was short and there was the constant unease of being overlooked by enemy on the commanding hills. The long line of the cantonment walls needed a large number of sentries to guard it which took its toll on the resilience and strength of the men. It was getting unusually cold and an early fall of snow was expected with apprehension. Again there were rumours of an imminent night attack by the enemy. However, it was the first night of the new moon and locals maintained, therefore, there would be no attack for three nights as everyone was feasting.

Ammunition was transferred stealthily by night into the Bala Hissar citadel to give the option of withdrawing into it if the opportunity arose. The move was, again, discussed with the benefit of hindsight, that occupation of the Bala Hissar was the right plan all along. To give him his due, Macnaghten had favoured this from the start but had been overruled by the military and then gradually came round to their view. The disadvantages of a move now were that it would be difficult to transfer the sick and wounded; there was little firewood and lack of forage for the horses in Bala Hissar; the jubilation of the enemy at the abandonment of the cantonments and, finally, the high risk of annihilation *en route*. To officers like Eyre, this was defeatist. Yes, conveying the sick would be difficult but not impossible; for the short distance, two or three men could be carried in a palanquin, some might manage to walk and others could ride camels on top of their loads. Firewood was scarce in the Bala Hissar but there was enough for cooking, and the relative comfort of the accommodation in the citadel would make up for it. Starving horses would have to be shot and the enemy's triumph would be short lived as anything of value in the cantonments would have been destroyed before departure. Additionally, dismay would soon set in with the enemy when they realised what a strong position the British were now in. Finally, the distance was less than two miles, so half that distance could be covered by guns from the Bala Hissar and, if the Seeah Sung Hills were occupied by a strong force, with guns, it could cover much of the plain in the immediate vicinity of the route out of the cantonments. While a move like this, with the number of camp followers, was bound to lead to losses, it was, in the long run, the best option. From there, troops could deal with the enemy in the city and surrounding forts from a firm, impregnable base. However, Shelton being dead against it, it was a lost cause. On top of that, Shah Shuja was wavering and wrote to Macnaghten that he favoured doing a deal with the rebels. He was told, sharply, that there was no chance unless Macnaghten approved the terms.

Reports were received that Sale had reached Jalalabad although there was hope, especially from Florentia of course, that this was an enemy ruse to lower spirits in the cantonments that there was to be no rescue by Sale's men. Florentia thought that it was unlikely that Sale had ever received the order to return. He had, as we know, but ignored it. On 18 November, it was apparent that Sale had indeed reached Jalalabad (on the 15th). The news came by hand of a messenger who had torn the paper into four to conceal it. Running into the enemy, he swallowed one part of it but escaped, and brought in the other pieces. Sale had arrived at Jalalabad and had been attacked by 40,000 enemy. Sallying out, he beat them and pursued them for eight to ten miles before returning. Florentia's letter to him covering events from 2 to 8 November had reached him and was the only news he received. It was copied on to the Commander-in-Chief and Lord Auckland to Florentia's evident satisfaction. Interestingly, her letters to her beloved husband start, formally, 'Dear Sale.'

There was discussion about the need to attack Mahmood Khan's fort (H), to the south-east of the cantonments, their side of the river. The problem was that the enemy had set up a battery of two guns under its walls from where they could engage the British foraging parties and target the south-east bastion. It also covered the road to the Bala Hissar. At 900 yards it was too far for their 9 pounders but there was an irrigation canal which afforded 'dead' ground up to within 300 yards of the enemy. Capture of the fort would give the British a good outpost from the Bala Hissar and boost their morale. Shelton agreed to the attack but, for some reason it was vetoed, surprisingly, by Sturt. Florentia was quick to defend him suggesting that they would suffer heavy losses in taking it, then could ill-afford the manpower, subsequently, to garrison it.

Elphinstone should have had Florentia on his administrative staff. She realised he had no idea what grain was being acquired and how the indents were being falsified – the Shah's 6th were asking for six *maunds* daily (about 80lbs) but the 37th, with many less men, twenty. She knew exactly what ration a man was entitled to and was well up to knowing what dishonesty was going on. She was also highly critical of soldiers uselessly firing off their weapons.

She was astonished that one unit, during the night, had loosed off 350 rounds at imagined enemy or, as she put it, their own shadows. She reckoned they had 13 *lakhs* (100,000) of ball, and 900 barrels of powder and shot. She also thought laterally. Why not follow Sturt's idea of sending out a detachment to the Seeah Sung hills to cut off the supplies going into the city, then do a deal with the traders to supply the cantonments rather than the city? She had no patience with people who said they weren't carrying flour but only charcoal. Well, the enemy needed charcoal with which to make gunpowder as much as those in the cantonments needed food, so it still needed to be stopped, whatever it was, from going into the city.

Macnaghten now drafted an analysis for Elphinstone as to their future, realising that no help would be forthcoming from Jalalabad. He suggested that if everyone would eat meat – they now had enough fuel and water – they could last the winter. A retreat to Jalalabad would be disastrous and dishonourable and should not be contemplated until the very last moment. If they did withdraw, they would be sacrificing not only their valuable property but, importantly, Shah Shuja, whom they were committed to protect. Even if they made it to Jalalabad, there would be no accommodation for the troops and the camp followers would be annihilated. It was deemed impossible to negotiate from a position of weakness. Withdrawal to Bala Hissar was an option but, again, much would be lost in doing so. Guns captured by the enemy could be turned upon them. It was still just possible reinforcement could arrive from Kandahar or something might turn up. Anyway, it would be a decision for the military in eight to ten days' time.

It was a masterly civil service draft; outlining all the unsavoury disadvantages of a course of action and then, with a metaphorical shrug of the shoulders, saying, of course, ultimately it was a decision for the General. The whiff of umbrellas being raised came unpleasantly in the wind.

This appreciation of the situation cannot have done Elphinstone's blood pressure or gout any good. The newest rumour was that the enemy had sent for the captured guns from Charikar and were to use them in a night attack on the cantonments. There was also a suggestion that the Shah's troops in Bala Hissar might sally forth to the Ghazni gate in the city to eliminate two snipers – a blacksmith and a barber, the best shots in Kabul – who were taking great toll of any soldier exposed at 300 yards. But, as Florentia commented, it was merely the subject of speculation and conversation. She deplored officers whom she called 'croakers'; those going about dejectedly spreading alarm, despondency and wild gossip. Heading the croakers, in her view, was Shelton. She had absolutely no time for this arrogant, disloyal officer. At dinner one night he suggested that the Envoy had information that 80,000 foot and 10,000 horse were on their way to set fire to their magazine with red hot shot. Quite how these balls were to be conveyed, red hot, when the enemy had no furnaces to heat them was a mystery. Where did he get this vast number of enemy from anyway? But any hare-brained story was quite likely to be believed in the panic-stricken garrison.

The British had an on-off relationship with the elders of the village of Beymaroo about half a mile north of the cantonments. Sometimes they would agree to supply the cantonments but, at others, not unnaturally, when the enemy occupied the village, refused. What worried them most, and, indeed, the occupants of the cantonments, was when the enemy occupied the high buildings on the forward slope of the hill to the south-west of the village which was within range of the Mission Compound. On 22 November a large number of enemy from Kabul city took up a position on the crest of this hill. Determined that they should not occupy the village, Major Swayne of the 5th Native Infantry was tasked to take control of the village with a detachment of soldiers including Eyre and some guns. On arrival, however, he found it to be already occupied by the enemy. Fire was opened by both sides and a stand-off ensued. Eyre managed to get his guns under the lee of Zoolficar's Fort (I) from where they could bear on the enemy on the hill. Swayne, basically, did nothing, leaving his men with virtually little cover for most of the day. Late in the evening Afghan horsemen got round the rear of their position, threatening to cut them off from the cantonments. Shelton then appeared with some reinforcements and withdrawal back to the cantonments was accomplished having achieved absolutely nothing. Eyre was shot in the hand.

Colonel Oliver joined Florentia's list of 'croakers.' Having been told by some of his men that, at last, grain had been brought in to the cantonments, he replied, 'It was needless, for they would never live to eat it.' Rightly, she despised such men and commented, 'Whatever we think ourselves, it is best to put a good face on the business.' She knew more about the maintenance of morale than half the commissioned officers around her. She had much more time for men like Captain Bygrave, the Paymaster General. By nature of his appointment he was on the Staff in the Headquarters, yet he took his place on the ramparts night after night, together with the men. Florentia realised only too well that officers had to share the same discomfort and danger as their men, and be seen to do so; she had little respect for those who didn't.

Ominously, Mohammad Akbar Khan, Dost Mohammad's charismatic fourth son, appeared in Kabul city.

At a conference in the General's house, it was decided that they could not put up with enemy occupying the Beymaroo village and the hill – the Heights – above it any more. Accordingly, in the early hours of the 23rd, Shelton led a force out of the cantonments consisting of seventeen infantry companies, three cavalry troops, some sappers and a single horse artillery gun. They managed to get the gun up the hill overlooking the village and brought fire down on the main enemy bivouac area. This caused the enemy to clear the area and return fire from the shelter of the houses. A number of officers suggested to Shelton that they take advantage of the enemy's disruption and put in a quick assault while it was still dark. He refused. As day broke, many of the enemy were seen evacuating the village westwards across the plain to a distant fort having run out of ammunition. An assault force of some two companies was then ordered to take the village under the command of Major Swayne. Unfortunately, he missed the main gate and tried to get in through a barricaded wicket gate without success. The attack was held up and Swayne himself was shot through the neck. As Shelton saw a large number of enemy coming towards them from Kabul, he withdrew his force onto the hill. Lieutenant Walker was sent with some irregular cavalry to the west of the knoll to cut off enemy fleeing from the village. Meanwhile, leaving three companies on the knoll, Shelton moved the rest to the south-west of the hill overlooking the gorge between the two hills. Enemy from the city were now in considerable strength on the south-west summit and had re-occupied the village with fresh men with full ammunition scales. They also sent a large group of cavalry to deal with Walker and his men. Under very heavy fire, Shelton's men were loath to expose themselves but encouraged by the bravery of Colonel Oliver, redeeming himself from being one of Florentia's arch 'croakers,' a handful followed him into the fray. Sadly, the one gun Shelton had, was firing so much its mechanism became too hot to handle. Walker was recalled under pressure from enemy cavalry. Shelton's force was now surrounded except for the flank facing the cantonments. His single gun had run out of ammunition, he had sustained considerable losses and men were dying of thirst. Things were looking bleak.

Some intrepid enemy had crawled up the edge of the knoll from the gorge and engaged the British at close hand. At the same time Shelton's men were engaging enemy trying to cut his force off from the cantonments. At one point he offered a reward to any man who could capture an enemy flag planted on a tumulus thirty yards to their front. Not a man volunteered. In fact, alarm and despondency was setting in; men were reluctant to follow their officers and some were slipping away. The enemy overran the gun crew, taking the limber and horses. However, the enemy had lost one of their leaders and a certain amount of confusion resulted. Taking advantage of the lull in the enemy's attacks, Shelton's men recaptured the gun and fresh ammunition was sent up from the cantonments. Bodies were recovered, including those of Captain Macintosh and Lieutenant Laing and the courageous gun crew. The British cavalry were exhausted and reluctant to move, and the infantry were worn out and disheartened. Florentia, who could see all this from a vantage point on the roof of a house, dodging behind a chimney to avoid the rounds whizzing past her, must have had her heart in her mouth. Given half a chance, she would have been in the mayhem with her troops.

Shelton sent a message to Major Kershaw, whom he had left, in reserve, with three companies on the rising ground overlooking the village, to bring his men forward. Kershaw was worried that if he did so, their route back to the cantonments would be compromised and therefore, in the well-worn way in which a subordinate disagrees with an order given by a superior, without being rude or insubordinate, replied, 'he begged to suggest' that Shelton fell back on his position. Before this response could be delivered, however, the front rank of Shelton's square at the other end of the hill broke. The mass of enemy simply overwhelmed them. Entreaties and orders from officers were ignored and an utter rout took place with men running for their lives towards the cantonments. Enemy cavalry and occupiers of the village took a heavy toll of the fugitives. Heavy supporting fire was unleashed from the Mission Compound by the 5th Infantry and a fresh troop of cavalry charged across the plain, joined by Lieutenant Walker who had galvanised some of his own men and was, subsequently, mortally wounded. In the cantonments, there was a great effort made to get the Mountain-train gun into position where it could give supporting fire to the gun out on the hill. But it was too late. However, for whatever reason, the counter-attack had some effect. The commander of the leading enemy group, Osman Khan, stopped his men and pulled them off the pursuit but not before they had captured the gun for the second time.

Vincent Eyre, no doubt still nursing his wounded hand, was highly critical of the operation. The aim had been to occupy the village. Given the relative strength of the British over the Afghans in the village at the time, it should have had a reasonable chance of success. As a Gunner, he deplored the taking out of the single gun. Well-learnt lessons of the past showed that a second gun must support the first; when one fires, the other is being reloaded. Secondly, the village should have been attacked by night when the enemy were slack in their defence and low on ammunition. The sappers, who were there expressly to raise a protective *sangar* of rocks, were not used, hence men were unnecessarily exposed to enemy small arms fire. Skelton formed squares which may have worked against cavalry at Waterloo but here presented an ideal target to the sharpshooters of Afghanistan, probably the best marksmen in the world. The British cavalry were hemmed in by the squares and had little space to manoeuvre to their best advantage. Finally, when the outcome was obvious, Shelton, instead of conducting an orderly fighting withdrawal to the cantonments, hung on far too long, resulting in ultimate headlong flight in complete disarray.

The British were now at their lowest ebb. They had been, effectively, defeated. They were in the wrong place, barely provisioned and badly led from the top. Morale and confidence had evaporated. What options were now left?

CHAPTER 7

Surrender

November 24th dawned unhappily for those in the cantonments. Even now, thought Eyre, a real leader could grip the situation and steer them out of trouble but no one was there. The soldiers' spirit had gone, and desertion and insubordination was rife. The enemy became bolder by the hour, creeping up to the walls of the cantonments and dismantling the bridge over the river. There had been a small unfinished fort to house the bridge guard but it was never completed, so that possible route out had now gone. The Bala Hissar evacuation option was raised yet again and, once more, demolished for the same reasons. Elphinstone wrote a lengthy memo to Macnaghten emphasising all the difficulties, which were fully endorsed by Shelton. Eyre privately thought that even with all the disadvantages, this was the honourable way to go. What else were they to do?

Gloomy news came in that Colonel Oliver's body had been found, minus his head and a finger. The finger probably was taken for the diamond ring he always wore. No heads were left on the Europeans. Doubtless they were now adorning the ramparts of the city on spikes.

An emissary from Osman Khan, a nephew of Dost Mohammad, arrived to offer terms. The Khan took the credit for calling off his men from annihilating the British the day before because he felt no rancour against them but they were to leave the country and leave hostages to ensure

Dost Mohammad's return. The hostages were to be the officers, their wives and families: in his power, he promised they would be safe. He wished no harm but leaving the country was non-negotiable. Akbar Khan was to appear the next day with 6,000 men and if terms were not agreed he would take the cantonments even if it meant sacrificing some of his men. This was seriously bad news.

The Envoy sought the advice of the General, who responded, 'We have now been in a state of siege for three weeks. Our provisions are nearly expended and our forage nearly consumed, without the prospect of procuring a fresh supply. Our troops are much reduced by casualties and the large number of sick and wounded increases daily. Considering the difficulty of defending the extensive and ill-situated cantonment, the near approach of winter, the fact that our communications are cut off and we have no prospect of reinforcement, I do not think it possible to retain our present position in the country. You therefore ought to avail yourself of the offer to negotiate which has been made to you.'

Not much room for manoeuvre then.

A day later two Afghans arrived at the cantonment, demanding to see the Envoy. They turned out to be Sultan Khan and his secretary. The Envoy saw them in the officers' guardroom. The terms were totally unacceptable and the visitors left. That night a letter was received from the Afghan chiefs spelling out the detail. It stipulated that Shah Shuja and his family were to be handed over; the British lay down their arms and unconditionally surrender, then they might have their lives spared and be allowed to leave the country never to return. Sale's force was to proceed to Peshawar before Elphinstone's men were allowed to leave the cantonments. This was too much for Macnaghten. He remonstrated that this was not in the good faith he had expected for a peaceful resolution to the situation and the terms were so dishonourable that if they persisted he must again 'appeal to arms, leaving the result to the God of battles.' In other words, a fight to the death.

Life now in the cantonments was full of stress and anxiety. Akbar Khan reportedly brought with him 6,000 men, adding to the 10,000 horse and 15,000 foot already in the city. Florentia, sniffily, remarked that they were probably Uzbeck rabble but the numbers were, nevertheless, overwhelming. That evening a great crowd of Afghans approached the walls of the cantonments. They appeared unarmed and friendly saying the battle is over. Men of the 44th went out and exchanged greetings whereupon the Afghans gave them cabbages. At that point, the Adjutant ordered his men back into camp, suspecting that the cabbages might be drugged in some way to render the soldiers insensible. However, on inspection, nothing was found. If the situation wasn't so desperate, it would have been quite funny. Nevertheless, there were undoubtedly spies among the many servants in the cantonments, relaying everything that was going on back to their masters in the city. Men were seen prowling round the perimeter of the camp in highly suspicious circumstances. Florentia's views on security were not difficult to imagine. She had her own ideas which, if she'd had her husband there to transmit them to the hierarchy, might have worked. Her only sounding-board was her son-in-law, Sturt. He tried his best but was really too junior to be properly heard. The lesson of senior officers listening properly to clever Sappers, however junior, had not been learned by the

General, and certainly not by Shelton. It was now becoming much colder but, despite this, fires, except for cooking, were not allowed leading to much dissatisfaction amongst the men.

The Afghans were now becoming more aggressive and insolent, knowing full well it was all going their way. On the 26th, thousands lined the hills overlooking the cantonments, then came down onto the plain and approached the cantonments. They appeared, mostly, unarmed but a number had sticks with two-foot long knives bound to the ends. One cheeky man asked if the 37th were there? Yes. Could I have my horse back then, please, which I lost to them the other day? Sturt told him, in Persian, to push off in suitably barrack-room language or he would turn the guns on them. He was implored not to do so, they had only come, they said, to see the sights and amuse themselves. There was even a ludicrous rumour that the Afghans were going to return the gun, with the horses, that they had taken on the 23rd. People will believe anything, sourly thought Florentia.

Even though negotiations were still possible, when the enemy occupied Beymaroo village, it was shelled. This was in retaliation for having ponies of the foragers fired on but hardly helpful, one would have thought, given the extreme predicament of the British. Shah Shuja was in a state. He thought the British were going to sell him out for five lakhs of rupees (£50,000) and an unimpeded exit from the country. He had one remaining chief stand by him; Jan Fishan Khan. The Khan had had his forts and property destroyed and his wives and family dispersed. He had no knowledge of their fate except that a son was burnt alive. One of Shah Shuja's wives, when urged to flee, to

Florentia's admiration, told him, 'I will not leave you; if you fall, we die together; and if you are victorious, we will rejoice together!'

A constant worry was the lack of grain, both for humans and animals. The artillery horses, in particular, were badly looked after since Lieutenant Walker's death. The braver traders, out to make a killing, sold their grain at exorbitant prices but, of course, ran the risk of alienating, with dire consequences, their Afghan colleagues. If caught, they could expect a, literally, sticky end. One of them received 50 rupees daily whether he produced anything or not; termed '*buckshees*' by Florentia, a word very much alive today. Florentia's son-in-law, Sturt, as she always addressed him, was ever full of ideas, unlike his superiors. Put men permanently on the ramparts, with fires allowed, he suggested, and shell the city from time to time, from the cantonments and from the Bala Hissar, with particular aim at the quarter where the gunpowder makers operate. He accepted this was all a bit of a show but a good two-fingered salute to the Afghans and good for their own morale.

Ever perceptive, Florentia reckoned she could gauge the level of morale by how the Envoy and his wife were addressed. In bad times they were 'The Macnaghtens' in the better, they were 'Sir William and my Lady.' They also returned to their grand house in the Mission Compound from their emergency tent in the cantonments. This seemed to boost morale though the reality was very hollow. Florentia suspected the 'politicals' doing deals but couldn't find out what. Without any real evidence, except that one chief in the city sent all his wives away, Florentia thought there was argument and dissension among the leaders of the rebels – what she called the 'confederacy' – in the city and morale was low due to the lack of firewood, but that was more likely wishful thinking. With Akbar Khan at the helm, there was grip and coordination.

On 1 December, Eyre reported that there had been a deliberate night attack on the Bourge-i-lakh, a tower forming an outwork to the Bala Hissar fortress. This tower, although isolated, was important in that it dominated much of the defensive walls. The attack failed due to the efforts of Major Ewart, commanding the garrison, who reinforced the defenders of the tower and, despite, repeated assaults, the enemy were driven back with much loss.

Florentia counted exactly 49 enemy horsemen on the Seeah Sung hills, which were ludicrously reported to the General as 300. They were not shot at as it was thought they came from Mohammad Khan's fort (H), now occupied by the Ghilzais, with whom there appeared to be some sort of negotiations going on. This was curious; the Ghilzais were not the men to negotiate with anyone unless at the end of a knife or musket. Nevertheless, constant exchanges of fire, and minor skirmishes went on the whole time. The enemy moved a strong force out from the city, lined the crest of the Beymaroo hills and put two guns into the gorge, from where they kept up desultory fire on the cantonments but with little effect. There was an attempt to blow up the gate of Mohammad Shereef's fort (F) without success mainly due to Sturt destroying the mine the enemy had placed under the tower.

An interesting man, in Florentia's view, was Khojeh Meer, the head man of Beymaroo village. He said the priests had been round a number of the local villages, warning the inhabitants not to support the British on pain of death. He himself was in a precarious position, playing a double game; he had to let the enemy occupy the village yet, at the same time, provide grain for the cantonments. Gloomily, he predicted that, when the British left, he'll have to run for his life to Peshawar. A messenger arrived from Jalalabad and Florentia hoped he brought a letter from her husband but, sadly, not. The man had spent five days in the city before coming to the cantonments – why, she doesn't explain – and his information from Jalalabad was out of date being only up to 21 November. Florentia noted that, at last, some order and discipline was being imposed and the 5th were even cleaning their muskets. Previously, they merely stacked them allowing the barrels to rust and the powder become damp. Sturt was sent off by Shelton to investigate one of the captured forts on fire. He returned, fuming with anger, having discovered the troops were burning the defences he had put up. A committee was organised to assess the useless horses they had. Once condemned, there would be plenty of cheap meat, including that of the redundant camels. According to Florentia, the heart of the latter was as tasteful as that of a bullock but she hadn't been tempted by this delicacy.

To their infuriation, those in the cantonments could see the enemy finally destroying what was left of the bridge over the river (Q). It had never been properly protected from the start and any suggestion that it was vital for any withdrawal and access to the camp to the east of the Seeah Sung hills was met with indifference. The frustration of men like Eyre and Sturt, and then to Florentia, who understood the tactical importance of something like this, was palpable. Too late, Elphinstone asked Sturt whether it could be rebuilt? Not a chance, was Sturt's rejoinder, without materials, labourers and with the enemy on site.

It was vitally important for the British to hold the forts that, if occupied by the enemy, could threaten the cantonments; particularly Mohammad Shereef's (F), very near the south-west cantonment bastion, and Mohammad Khan's (H), about 750 yards from the south-east. There was a disgraceful episode on 6 December when, under attack from Afghans, who had crept up through the King's Garden, the garrison of the Mohammad Shereef fort panicked and fled back to the cantonments, leaving it, and 6,000 rounds of ammunition, in the hands of the enemy. The garrison consisted of Europeans of the 44th and Indian sepoys of the 37th. The flight was initiated by men of the 44th whose officer had been wounded and, pathetically, had returned to the cantonments to have it dressed. Everyone blamed each other, but it was clear that the 44th had let their comrades down. Infuriated, Shelton paraded the men, who had vacated the fort, in the snow, until three or four in the morning, on the basis that it was their job to retake the fort. In the end, they were not deployed but their reliability now in question. The 44th guard on the cantonment bazaar, was replaced by sepoys of the 37th.

Unbelievably, it was again discovered that the cantonment forces were now down to one day's rations. Accordingly, Captain Hay was despatched, with ponies carrying stores, to the Bala Hissar, with orders to return with grain. Needless to say, the convoy was attacked, the ponies and their handlers scattered and yet more stores lost. No one appeared to be able to make their minds up whether a withdrawal into the Bala Hissar was a realistic option or not. These half measures of sending stores into the citadel and, at the same time, taking out grain was the epitome of indecision.

Returning to the Mohammad Shereef fort, it was Sturt's intention to have it retaken and, if not, to blow it up to deny it to the enemy. (It is extraordinary how much influence this officer had. Even accepting Florentia's bias in that he was her son-in-law, he constantly features in the saga to the extent, at one point, Florentia observed how stupid it was to risk the life of the only engineer officer). An example of the dysfunctioning command was the conversations related to Florentia by Sturt. He had suggested to Shelton that a reliable commander for the fort would be Captain Layton, an officer of steadiness and courage. Sneeringly, Shelton asked if Layton wanted the job? Sturt replied that he didn't know but he, Sturt, wanted him to do so. Shelton's dislike of Layton arose through his lack of polished manners and ungrammatical language; basically, he wasn't a gentleman. When it had all gone wrong, Shelton told Sturt he had ordered him to tell Layton he was to remain. Sturt denied ever having been told this and Shelton then appealed to Elphinstone who supported Shelton. Sturt maintained his recollections of the conversation were different; Shelton was lying on the floor rolled up in his bedding either asleep or pretending to be while he, Sturt, was wide awake. Elphinstone hedged by replying that he did not think what was said amounted to an order. Florentia's view was Elphinstone, totally unsettled, delegated his power to Shelton who tried to throw responsibility back onto Elphinstone's shoulders or anyone else's. The General (Elphinstone) was too gentlemanly to refuse, and accepted blame. Sturt's exasperated comment was to the effect that if there weren't his nearest and dearest in the cantonments, he'd blow them sky-high. In reply to the General's query as to whether the fort was practicable and tenable, Sturt's understandably sarcastic response was, 'Practicable if the men will fight: tenable if they do not run away!'

On 8 December, Macnaghten, again, wrote one of his curiously public letters to Elphinstone, requesting him to state whether, in his opinion, any further attempt to hold out against the enemy would merely have the effect of sacrificing Shah Shuja and themselves and, whether, supposing this to be so, the only alternative left was to negotiate a safe retreat out of the country? Florentia reported that it was the other way round in that the General wrote to the Envoy, reiterating his view on the badly placed cantonments, lack of provisions and the need to negotiate with the enemy. Whichever way the letters went, the result was the same; the General was concerned over lack of sustenance, the inadvisability of waiting for a possible rescue from Kandahar, the amount of sick and wounded, lack of transport animals, and the inability to defend the cantonments adequately. He could, therefore, only repeat his opinion that no time should be lost in entering into negotiations. A frustrated Florentia repeated her view that if Sturt's advice (and, to be fair, others') that they should have withdrawn into the Bala Hissar ages ago, they'd now be in a position to last until relieved by reinforcements from elsewhere.

Good news came from Jalalabad that Sale had sallied forth from the town and defeated an enemy force but he warned that greater reinforcements than those on their way would be needed. The whole country was in insurrection and a strong siege train, engineer officers, light infantry, British infantry and dragoons were required. Meanwhile in the cantonments, apathy prevailed and Shelton, who should have been organising bridging equipment, issuing preparatory orders for evacuation and a movement order, did nothing. As Eyre pointed out, 'the expedition was suffered to die a natural death.'

Surprisingly, there was no letter from Sale to his wife. She occupied her time by paying attention to Sturt's pony which had been knocked down by a nine-pounder. The ball had ricocheted off the ramparts and hit the horse in the neck but, having the shaggiest mane in the country, it was not the worse for wear. The company of the 44th, involved in the Mohammad Shereef farrago, anxious to clear their names, wanted a Court of Inquiry. This was refused in that everyone knew they were the first to run away. The rest of the Regiment 'cut' the company; men being good judges of their comrades' conduct.

Macnaghten sent an officer to meet several Ghilzai chiefs who were prepared to negotiate on the payment of two lakhs of rupees. The officer took the money but was only met by one man; the remainder having reneged on the deal and would not accept the cash. Although related to Akbar Khan, they had no love for him and would bring the Envoy the Khan's head if he wished, so they said. Despite the desperate straits the British were in, the offer was somewhat sanctimoniously turned down on the basis that assassination was not the British custom. It was more likely that Macnaghten, rightly, had absolutely no trust in the Ghilzais. At the same time a message was sent to Shah Shuja in Bala Hissar by hand of an intrepid officer, Captain Hay, accompanied by an escort of fifty cavalrymen. They made it there and back under considerable fire and while, on return, there were ten horses without riders, only one man was missing. Florentia was unclear as to the exact contents of the message but guessed it was an invitation to the Shah to come to the cantonments to accompany the Army out of the country.

On 11 December the rebel chiefs indicated they were willing to negotiate. Macnaghten, accompanied by Captains Lawrence, Mackenzie and Trevor, met them on the plain the cantonment side of the Seeah Sung hills. The enemy were led by Akbar Khan, with a number of Barakzai and Ghilzai tribal elders. Macnaghten smoothly addressed them in terms of friendship and cordiality. He lamented that these feelings had been so rudely interrupted but professed himself ignorant of the causes. He expressed the view that all the British wanted to do was to restore to the seat of his ancestors a king, who, notwithstanding his misfortunes, had ever reigned in the hearts of his people and that his restoration had apparently given the utmost satisfaction to all classes throughout his dominions. If, however, this satisfaction had passed away and given way to contrary emotions (and he supposed that the assembled Sirdars and Khans spoke for the people) then it was no longer the British Government's wish to persist in displeasing those chiefs. He was therefore willing to negotiate a smoothing over of present difficulties and adopt such measures most likely to be conducive to the establishment of mutual friendship between the British and Afghan governments, the maintenance of which, he felt assured, must be earnestly desired by both parties.

Akbar Khan and his colleagues expressed their hearty consent, adding their personal esteem for the Envoy and their gratitude for the way in which the exiled Dost had been treated. The Envoy then read a draft of the general articles of a proposed treaty. In essence they were that the British should evacuate Afghanistan, including Kandahar, Ghazni,

Kabul, Jalalabad and all other stations. They should be allowed not only to return unmolested to India but to be provided for on their way there with conveyance for baggage and stores etc. They should be accompanied by hostages and Dost Mohammad, his family and other Afghans in exile would be allowed to return. Shah Shuja should be offered the option of remaining in Kabul or accompanying the British to Ludhiana; receiving from the Afghan government a pension of one lakh of rupees (£10,000) per annum in either case. An amnesty should be granted to all those who had attached themselves to Shah Shuja or his allies, the British. All prisoners should be released. No British forces would be sent to Afghanistan again unless called for by the Afghan government between whom and the British nation perpetual friendship and mutual good offices should be established.

To all these terms the chiefs, with the exception of Akbar Khan, cordially agreed. He cavilled at several, particularly the amnesty, but was overruled by his colleagues. He vehemently refused to allow the garrison to be supplied with provisions until it had quitted the cantonments, which he demanded should take place the following morning. There was some confusion amongst the delegates resulting in an agreement that the cantonments should be evacuated in three days' time and provisions would be allowed in. It was agreed to put the terms in writing and the chiefs returned to the city accompanied by Captain Trevor as a hostage. As can be imagined, anxiety was felt in the cantonments while negotiations were under way, particularly for the safety of the Envoy. There was, indeed, a thought that Akbar Khan intended to seize Macnaghten at the meeting but was restrained by the other chiefs. The Envoy had, deliberately, only taken a few troopers as bodyguard in order to give an air of confidence to his opponents and his outward expression of good faith. While it has been easy to criticise Macnaghten for his judgement in the early stages of this saga, there is no doubt that he, personally, behaved with courage and a sense of responsibility which was not reflected by his military counterparts. It should not be forgotten that he was also dealing with a perfidious people whose word was not to be trusted, whose avarice was legendary and whose respect for human life was baseless.

To everyone's surprise, the following day no troops from Bala Hissar arrived in the cantonments and the chiefs now decided they would like Shah Shuja to remain and, to strengthen their allegiance, hand over his daughters to them in marriage. They also insisted he drop his absurd attachment to ceremony, which they heartily disliked, such as keeping important chiefs waiting to see him, hanging about for hours outside his doors. This did not nullify the terms of the treaty, nor did their demand for British ladies to be hostages, which was refused. Through grated teeth, the Shah agreed, given the only alternative was exile yet again. The fact that the chiefs wanted to retain the Shah puzzled the Envoy who knew full well the hatred they had for him and his family. Evil was afoot.

Things were not going well in the cantonments. As retreat was now firmly on the cards, the General was determined that the well-stocked magazine of arms and ammunition should not be left behind for the enemy. He therefore ordered that certain of the camp followers should be armed and company commanders should exchange their men's old muskets for new ones. This then appeared to be signal for all and sundry to raid the magazine and help themselves to whatever they wanted. For some hours pandemonium reigned and any semblance of discipline and order completely failed. It was indicative of the level of unsteadiness and recklessness to which the troops had descended and the lack of control by their officers and non-commissioned-officers.

The troops that were, earlier, meant to leave the Bala Hissar for the cantonments, inevitably, got delayed. Part of the reason, to be fair, was that they were encumbered with an iron nine-pounder gun and a 24 pounder brass howitzer, drawn by bullocks. It was the General's wish that the latter should be left behind but in the age-old ploy, when a subordinate is not keen to comply with his senior's instructions, Vincent Eyre commented, 'His order to that effect had by some accident missed its destination.' Additionally, one of the better commissariat officers (a Quartermaster in today's army), Captain Kirby, realising the dire straits of those in the cantonments, loaded up a considerable amount of wheat and flour on the wagons.

Outside the gate of the Bala Hissar, the officer commanding, Major Ewart, found Akbar Khan and a small body of followers, waiting to 'escort' him to the cantonments. Ominously, a much larger number of Afghans were lining the crest of the Seeah Sung hills, along the base of which Ewart's convoy had to pass. It was difficult not to expect treachery, particularly when some of the Khan's men tried to push their way into the Bala Hissar as the rear-guard were leaving. Luckily the guards were alert and slammed the gate in their faces, loosing off a round or two of grapeshot. Unfortunately, they accidentally hit some of their own men trying to get back in, including Connolly, who had a horse shot under him. Clearly, it was the intention to take the Bala Hissar with the troops on the hills once the Khan's men had forced the gate. The sinuous Akbar Khan then suggested to Ewart that, in view of how late it was, he should re-enter the citadel with his party and await dawn before proceeding to the cantonments. Ewart, accordingly, applied to Shah Shuja to do so but his request was refused on the grounds of suspected foul play. So there was nothing for it but to bed down for the night under the walls in low marshy ground, without tents, bedding, firewood or food. For most, a nervous, sleepless night with the close vicinity of the Khan's men and watch-fires very obvious on the hills.

In the morning, Akbar Khan allowed them to set off and all was fine until the rear-guard, passing the Seeah Sung hills were fired on. The nine-pounder accidently separated from the column when crossing an irrigation ditch was rushed by the Afghans. A luckless artilleryman, strapped to the barrel since he was ill, was immediately butchered. The enemy were driven off with rounds of grapeshot from the mountain train howitzer and the arrival of a furious Akbar Khan, on his horse, threatening to cut down anyone who interfered with the detachment. They reached the cantonments, with relief, at nine o'clock that night.

Shah Shuja still appeared to be undecided as to which option to go for; remain and take his chance with the Barakzais or leave with the British into exile. The perceptive Sturt could see, clearly, that a retreat had a distinct possibility of being harassed all the way, leading to bloodshed and disaster. He suggested to Florentia that if he could see Osman Khan, who, as head of the Barakzais was due to remain in Kabul, on a personal basis, he might be able to negotiate a deal. He thought that if he offered himself, wife and mother-in-law (!) as hostages in exchange for their own safety and that of the retreating British, that might work. He authorised Captain Lawrence to broach this with Macnaghten. To his astonishment, he discovered his name had already been put forward, under rather different and uncomfortably vague circumstances. It was said that Shah Shuja was now alienated from the British and was siding with the Ghilzais and that Osman Khan, therefore, was to accompany the Envoy and not remain in Kabul. This embarrassed Sturt considerably and felt he could not press his case further but not so Florentia, who felt not in the least prejudiced. She, therefore, represented to the General the folly of leaving their only engineer officer (Sturt) behind as a hostage when they faced the perils of the Khyber and the Punjab and would surely need his services. The General concurred, it having, he said, slipped his mind. Sturt, now determined not to leave his wife and mother-in-law behind, wrote a letter to Macnaghten:

'My dear Sir William,

Within the last hour a report has reached me, that myself, Lady Sale, and Mrs Sturt, had been proposed to the Cabul chiefs as hostages, in exchange for Captain Trevor.

I have a very distinct recollection of having told Lawrence to mention to you that I had no objection to such an arrangement *under certain terms*; but not having been made acquainted with the fact of such a proposition having been made, or further consulted on the subject, I write in much anxiety to inquire if there is any foundation for the report, and if there is, to be made acquainted with the arrangements proposed, under which I can be expected to acquiesce in them as far as regards Lady Sale and Mrs Sturt; for myself I am ready for any circumstances likely to benefit or aid in bringing negotiations to a satisfactory conclusion. I trust you will ease my mind upon that point, for reports have reached me from several quarters, all of which are more vague than satisfactory.

Very

truly yours,

J. L.D. STURT.

15th December, 1841.'

A slightly evasive reply came from Macnaghten which stated that he had been terribly busy and couldn't remember whether Sturt's name had been mentioned to the chiefs or not but it didn't matter as no ladies were to be left as hostages. What the response did not say, however, was whether Sturt was to be a hostage or not. Was the Envoy keeping his options open?

The Afghans continued to be difficult, refusing to supply any food or forage unless every fort in the vicinity of the cantonments were given up. This was totally unacceptable as a number of them dominated the cantonments and would put the British in serious jeopardy. Horses were now having to eat bark off trees and their own dung; the camp-followers were down to eating the flesh of animals which died daily through cold or starvation. Sturt was standing by one of the cantonment gates when approached by an Afghan who asked if he was an officer. When Sturt said he was and why he wished to know and what did he want? The man half drew his sword and said, 'to fight.' Sturt told him to push off in soldierly language.

There was nothing for it but to concede to the Afghans' demands; the Rikabashee (G), Magazine (D), Zoolficar (I) and Musjeed (L) forts were handed over. The Afghans handed over Nussuroollah Khan as a hostage and a considerable amount of provisions together with 2000 camels and 400 ponies for the march to Jalalabad. Florentia, rightly, was full of foreboding and commented that 'our allies', as they were now called, would be uncharacteristically magnanimous if the British were allowed to escape having got them in their net. She reckoned they'd be attacked all the way to Khoord Kabul but would be safe thereafter as they would then have, as hostage, the son of the chief who controlled that part of the country. She heard, indirectly, from her husband that all was well in Jalalabad but the Sikhs were being tiresome which boded ill for the journey through the Punjab; another reason to keep their favourite Engineer at hand. Florentia caught an Afghan servant of Akbar Khan's trying to strip bits off her veranda. Sturt took him by the scruff of the neck and gave him a kick in the pants. Onlookers were astonished at the indignity being meted out to the servant of a Sirdar. Maybe he was lucky; any problems at Kandahar, they were told, were dealt with by strapping the miscreant to the muzzle of a gun and blowing him apart. This undoubtedly concentrated the minds of the rest.

There was a heavy snowfall of up to five inches on the 18th, which added to the woes of those in the cantonments. There was further delay to any departure due to the Shah's continuing indecision and the failure of the chiefs to produce adequate transport. The Envoy gave orders for Ghazni to be evacuated by the 27th Native Infantry who were to proceed through the Doormat Valley and the Gomel Pass to India. The 22nd December was fixed as the date to leave the cantonments.

Shelton was caught entering a private deal with Akbar Khan to obtain forage for his own animals. He'd asked Macnaghten for a small gift to give a 'respectable native' and, when out of his room to collect the gift, the emissary from the Khan stole the sword which the Shah had given Shelton. When Shelton applied to the Envoy to retrieve it, the story came out. Shelton was given an admonishment from the General for engaging in private correspondence with a chief. Curiously, the General, hearing only the first part of the story asked Macnaghten whether he too could get some forage direct from Akbar. Macnaghten indignantly refused to allow individual correspondence with a chief but assured the General if he, Macnaghten, obtained any, he'd let the General have some. A convoluted and, slightly, distasteful episode which reflected badly on all concerned.

Further pressure was exerted by the chiefs, who now demanded a share of the British guns and ammunition and Shelton as a hostage. The General desperately considered breaking the treaty as things were looking very ill and treachery was in the air. One way of doing it would be to carry out a simultaneous attack on the forts they had just given up, plus Mohammad Khan's fort (H). He hoped this would sufficiently alarm some Afghans into siding with the British. Sturt produced a plan to assault Mohammad Khan's fort but advised that the troops were too weak and dispirited to have any real chance of success. He then suggested to the General that they break the treaty and march forthwith to Jalalabad, using the only available transport for the sick and wounded, and emergency stores. Florentia realised what a public spirited gesture this was as Sturt had acquired, at considerable personal expense, a carriage for all his and his wife's (and, presumably,

Florentia's) most valuable possessions. This would have to be left behind. The General couldn't bring himself to do so and risk sacrificing the whole force.

Tajo Mohammad Khan, an Afghan who had always quietly been on the side of the British – it he who had warned Burnes of his imminent assassination – clandestinely came to see Florentia and James Sturt. He told them of Akbar Khan's intended treachery and said the force would be annihilated. He was anxious that Florentia and the Sturts should accept his protection and he could hide them in the hills until the British inevitably reappeared to take vengeance on the killers. They thanked him but tried to make him understand that they were what Florentia called 'military subjects' which meant that, honourably, they had loyalty to their comrades and must stay with the force although their realised they had little hope of saving their lives.

On 21 December, Macnaghten met Osman Khan and Akbar Khan on the plain to nominate four hostages. Skelton was understandably reluctant to be one and was not forced, although there were, perhaps, some who would have happily seen him becoming one. The four handed over were Captains Connolly, Airey, Warburton and Pottinger. Captains Trevor and Drummond were allowed to return from the city to the cantonments. Drummond had been hidden in the city since 2 November. The next day an Afghan officer arrived to take over guns and ammunition. Vincent Eyre, of course, supervised. Craftily, he suggested they could have a large pile of 8-inch shells which he knew would be useless as the mortars to which they belonged were with Captain Abbott's battery in Jalalabad. The Afghan departed with great glee, with his prize laden on some old ammunition wagons. Sleight of hand was, clearly, not solely the province of the Afghans though Lady Macnaghten's carriage and horses were given up to Akbar Khan. As some cavalry horses were being taken out to be shot, a few Afghans appeared to take them away alive. The guard of the 37th bayoneted one thief and shot another, which sent them on their way.

Florentia reported the Afghans saying that if Shelton had pressed forward his attack, when recovering the gun on 23 November, right up to the city gates, they would never have come out again. Since he didn't, they realised they had nothing to fear from the British and could do what they liked. Nevertheless, there were those who were taking care to preserve their letters of thanks and praise from the British as they had a good idea that a force would be sent against them in due course. There also seemed to be argument in the ranks of the chiefs in the city. Some were saying the British should just be killed before any departure. Others, like the Anwar Zeeman Shah Khan, were dead against this and said he was going into the cantonments and would never be party to acting in anything but good faith. Furthermore, if difficulties were put in the way of the British on their way to Jalalabad, he would go with them. It was said that, later, Akbar Khan swore on the Koran that he would do whatever the Anwar wanted. Florentia made it clear, however, that since the Envoy had given Akbar Khan money and taken his side, the Sirdar had become more self-confident and influential than he deserved. This was not a good sign.

It was decided that the departure would begin on Tuesday 4 January. Osman Khan was to accompany the British together with the son of the Anwar.

Captain Skinner, currently under the protection of Akbar Khan, and two senior Afghans, brought new proposals to the Envoy. Macnaghten should, they said, the following day, meet Akbar Khan and the chiefs of the Eastern Ghilzais outside the cantonments when the following agreements could be ratified. The Envoy was told to hold a considerable force, which, on a given signal, should join Akbar Khan's and the Ghilzais' troops in attacking Mahmood Khan's fort (H). They were to seize Amenoollah Khan and, for a certain sum of money, Amenoollah's head would be presented to the Envoy. Macnaghten shrank from this, protesting that the British did not deal in blood money. The fort was then to be occupied by a British regiment and the Bala Hissar by another one. Furthermore, once the Khans had been subdued, the British would be allowed to remain in the country, to save face, for another eight months. They would then be allowed to leave as if it were on their own accord. Shah Shuja would remain on the throne with Akbar Khan his chief Vizier. As an additional reward for his support, Akbar Khan would be paid 30 lakhs of rupees (£300,000) now and 4 lakhs (£40,000) for life.

Macnaghten should have seen this charade for what it was. Nevertheless, he ordered the 54th, Shah's 6th and some guns for a 'secret service.' Clearly, this was the assault force for attacking the fort. It was so totally alien to the rebels' plans that he should have detected some treacherous ploy. Instead, blinded by a drive to recover some of the ground lost, he agreed to the arrangement. He saw it as a way of being able to evacuate the country with as much credit as possible and give the Government time to negotiate a treaty with the Russians defining the areas in influence in Central Asia. His state of mind can be sympathetically understood. He had been the architect of the policy to replace Dost Mohammad with Shah Shuja and maintain his position with British arms. This policy was now in abject ruins and he felt, largely, to blame although badly let down by the inept military. He should have seen the trap for what it was.

On 23 December, the Envoy, accompanied by Captains Lawrence, Trevor and Mackenzie left to meet Akbar Khan on the Seeah Sung plain. Lieutenant Le Geyt was in command of the escort. Before leaving, he encouraged the General to have the ramparts fully manned and to ensure everyone was on high alert. The troops earmarked for the 'secret service' were to be held at immediate notice. On the way, Macnaghten briefed those accompanying him on what was happening and warned Captain Lawrence to be ready to gallop to the Bala Hissar to prepare the Shah for the arrival of the regiment. His escorting officers expressed their apprehension of the scheme and the distinct possibility of treachery on the part of Akbar Khan. Macnaghten said, 'Dangerous it is; but if it succeeds, it is worth all the risks: the rebels have not fulfilled even one article of the treaty, and I have no confidence in them; and if by it we can only save our honour, all will be well. At any rate, I would rather suffer a hundred deaths, than live the last six weeks again.'

Meanwhile, crowds of Afghans were seen hovering, ominously, near the cantonments and Mohammad Khan's fort, causing anxiety in everyone's minds, except the Envoy's. The British delegation was met near the bridge by a number of chiefs led by Akbar Khan but also including Amenoollah Khan's brother, which should have immediately alerted the Envoy that something was wrong. What was he doing here when he was just about to arrest his brother? Anyway, the usual courtesies were exchanged and Macnaghten presented Akbar Khan with a valuable Arab stallion. The Khan thanked the Envoy and for the brace of double-barrelled pistols, coach and horses he had sent the day before. The parties then sat down on ground, carpets covering the snow, partially concealed from the cantonments.

Captain Lawrence remarked that there were a number of hangers-on, armed to the teeth, far too close to the delegates, upon which he was told by Akbar Khan that they 'were all in the secret.' Akbar Khan then shouted, 'Seize, Seize,' and grasped the Envoy's left hand with an expression of diabolical ferocity. Sultan Jan grabbed his right hand and they pulled him down a slope. Macnaghten's face registered horror and astonishment and cried, 'For God's sake.' The three captains were seized and brusquely disarmed. They were then forced to mount horses, each behind a Ghilzai chief, protected with difficulty by an armed guard, against a vicious rabble wielding swords and long knives screaming for blood. On approaching Mohammad Khan's fort, there were further attempts to kill the three officers. Trevor fell from the back of the horse carrying him and was immediately cut to pieces. The other two made it into the fort, much bruised and cut about. At the entrance, a furious cut was aimed at Mackenzie's head which was parried by the chief on whose horse he was riding, the blow hitting him on the shoulder. They were kept in a small sort of dungeon, with howling rebels trying to shoot them through the window. A severed human hand was held up in the window for the captives to see; unaware at the time that it was actually Macnaghten's. Amenoollah Khan arrived and gave them a torrent of abuse, threatening to have them blown from a gun. Amid all the self-congratulations of the Afghans, came one small voice of a Mullah who declared it a foul disgrace to Islam. The captives were then led to Akbar Khan's house, through a city strangely quiet after the day's excitements.

Back in the city, the captives were told by Captain Skinner of Macnaghten's and Trevor's killing. It had been Akbar Khan's intention to seize the Envoy, take him into the city and dictate terms to him, and detain him as a hostage. However, given Macnaghten's spirited defence, a furious Akbar Khan drew a pistol, ironically a gift from Macnaghten the day before, and shot him through the body, which was immediately hacked to pieces by the ferocious Ghazis (Ghazi, literally, means 'hero' but these were no heroes as we know them but merely cut-throat brigands). It was this that Florentia and others saw going on from the rear gate of the cantonments and were appalled that no cavalry had been sent out to recover the body. The corpse was then taken to the city where it was hung up, together with Trevor's, in the principal bazaar. The head was delivered to Anwar Human Khan's house, having been paraded round the city, where it was triumphantly shown to Captain Connolly. Skinner and Mackenzie were issued with Afghan dress and sent back to the cantonments where Major Eldred Pottinger had assumed position of the Envoy.

Where one might ask was the Envoy's escort when they were so badly needed? Apparently Lieutenant Le Geyt, having only proceeded a few hundred yards from the cantonment gate, had his troops turned around and, with shots raining after them, had galloped back into the camp. He said the Envoy having been carried off, his men refused to get involved and he'd come back for help. Instead of rallying, this seemed to inject complete paralysis into the people in the cantonments. Even though, now, armed Afghans were patrolling around the outside of the ramparts and circulating between the meeting place and Mohammad's fort, nothing was done; no shots were fired, no sorties made and no soldier stirred from his post. Treachery was allowed to triumph; the murder of a British Envoy was perpetrated in the face, and within musket-shot, of the British army. Not a single effort was made to avenge the deed, but the mangled and insulted body was allowed to lie on the plain before it was dragged away to be paraded in the public market. When Elphinstone was asked why the two regiments held at high readiness for the 'secret service' by Macnaghten were not deployed in the emergency, he maintained that the cantonments were too lightly defended to allow them to go. Those in the cantonments, at whatever level of seniority or employment, can only have felt the utmost despair and shame.

The Afghans repeated their offer of a treaty with a few alterations, commenting that while the Envoy's breach of faith had cost him his life, they regretted his death. Additional clauses in the treaty were that (a) all guns, less six were to be left behind, (b) all treasure was immediately to be given up and (c) the hostages were to be exchanged for married men and their wives. General Sale's name was specifically mentioned. In reality, did they want Lady Sale in their power? Secretly, she was probably flattered. Elphinstone replied that he while he might give up officers as hostages, he would not allow wives and families to accompany them unless they consented. Officer hostages having their wives stay with them were offered 2,000 rupees a month in compensation. Vincent Eyre said that if it was in the public interest, then his wife would stay with him. Captain Anderson said that he'd rather put a pistol to his wife's head and shoot her. James Sturt refused to allow his wife or mother-in-law to remain except at the point of a bayonet but he'd perform any duty required of him. This was a bit of a *volte face* from his earlier plan; clearly he'd had second thoughts or maybe his mother-in-law had got wind of it. Florentia herself took no notice and busied herself, making hammocks to carry the sick; so light, she said, that two men could easily carry a heavy man in one.

It must have been about the worst Christmas Day any of them could remember or, indeed, ever. A letter was sent from Connolly in the Bala Hissar to say that the Anwar Zeeman Khan, who was very sympathetic to the British cause, had arranged for Macnaghten's and Trevor's bodies to be stolen and delivered to the cantonments at night. Trevor's had not been so mutilated. How Macnaghten's various body parts were to be reassembled was unclear. Anxiously, Florentia waited for news from her husband but although a messenger arrived from Jalalabad, he only bore news up to 7 December. It was reported that reinforcements from India had reached Peshawar and, simultaneously, Mohammad Osman Khan offered safe escort for all to Peshawar for five lakhs of rupees (£50,000). Pottinger was approached by an Afghan delegation to honour the 'promise' made by the Envoy in his agreement with Akbar Khan. This was a payment of fourteen lakhs of rupees to various chiefs. Pottinger called a conference in which he stated that no confidence could be placed in any treaty with the Afghans and, under the circumstances, to bind the hands of the Government by promising to evacuate the country, restore the deposed King and waste so much public money, merely to save their own lives was inconsistent with the duty they owed their Country. The only honourable course was to hold out to the last in Kabul or force an immediate retreat to Jalalabad. His colleagues demurred on the grounds that the lack of provisions, the surrender of the surrounding forts and the insuperable condition of the roads in the current season, made it preferable to pay any amount rather than sacrifice the whole force in prolonged hostilities.

Pottinger therefore accepted the Afghan proposal but stipulated that Captain Lawrence be released in order to deal with the financial transactions. Poor Lawrence arrived back looking ten years older and haggard with anxiety. However, there was no question of leaving behind any women as hostages which was contrary to the usages of war. (It was hardly likely that the latter featured too highly in the Afghan repertoire). Apparently, Naib Shureef had paid for Sir Alexander Burnes's burial but it never happened and parts of his body, cut in many pieces, still hung in the trees of his garden. The Envoy's head remained in a straw bag, hanging in the souk. Akbar said he was going to send it to Bokhara to show the king there what he does to foreigners here and what he'll do to him, clearly not a friend of his. Captains Drummond, Walsh, Warburton and Webb were sent to join Connolly and Airey at Anwar Human Khan's house as hostages. They were held in cramped conditions but relatively well treated and protected from the mob. A number of the sick were conveyed to the city under the protection of the chiefs and under the command of an officer of the 44th, together with a medical officer. Some of the Shah's guns and an amount of treasure were made over to the enemy. British guns, to the disgust of the soldiery, were brought to the gates of the cantonments, ready for handover. Evacuation routes were discussed. One possibility would be via Doormat (a more southerly route) but Florentia, unsurprisingly, favoured Jalalabad.

Florentia made an interesting point about the command structure. She asserted that the Envoy had planned to replace Elphinstone when General Nott arrived from India via Kandahar. This, however, would not have been necessary as Elphinstone had already contacted Nott and handed command over to him on 1 November. So, she thought, did Elphinstone, legally, have any powers to deal with the chiefs on behalf of the troops? Probably just as well they didn't know that.

On 30 December, 500 Ghazis attacked the rear gate of the compound but, luckily, the guard was alert and unleashed a considerable amount of grapeshot which repulsed them. The enemy tore up the small bridge over the canal on their withdrawal, out of spite. Sturt, according to Florentia, kept receiving contradictory instructions about making a breach in the ramparts and sloping the sides of the canal to make it easier for the camels to cross. Clearly, he did not want to make a wide enough breach in the walls to take the whole force, until as late as possible, given the enemy's ability to mount an attack and the British now woefully short of guns. Nor did he wish to deal with the canal making it easier for the enemy to cross, again, until the last minute. A quandary often faced by highly professional Sappers. The General, in his usual way, left it to Sturt, which was probably just as well. Florentia's laconic comment, 'Snow all day.'

Orders, for instance, for opening fire were now only being verbally given. Normally, they would be in writing so the responsibility would be clear. If given verbally, when things go wrong, shoulders could be easily sloped. This was typical of the malaise now pervading across the cantonments. No sign of the Envoy's or Trevor's bodies, so Sergeant Williams, who had died of wounds, was interred in the grave behind the barracks, which had been prepared for the Envoy.

The chiefs still prevaricated; some wanted the British to go immediately, some, realising the mayhem that could occur in the vacuum, wanted the evacuation postponed. As far as the Shah was concerned, the Afghans were happy to let him live but merely put his eyes out. Perhaps he didn't know this when he offered Lady Macnaghten his protection in the Bala Hissar. Sergeant Deane, who had an Afghan wife, had many friends and acquaintances in Kabul, was contacted by two men who reported that Akbar Khan was totally treacherous and had 10,000 Kohistanees ready to attack the British at Tezeen and all the Ghilzais at Sourkab on the route to Jalalabad. He was also trying to induce the soldiers of the Indian regiments to desert.

To show how totally out of touch the General was, he sent a note to Sturt which, amongst other things told him that Pottinger intended to take 250 planks of wood to cross the stream in the Khoord Kabul pass. Firstly, they had to bridge the Kabul River, the existing one having been destroyed by the enemy, then, possibly, the Logar River, if that bridge had been destroyed. The streams in the passes, which needed crossing, occurred every hundred yards or so. By Florentia's reckoning, with each camel only able to carry two planks, 125 animals would be required. Since they didn't even have enough for their ammunition, where were these to come from? Anyway, these streams, a few inches deep, would probably be frozen. She should have been on his Staff.

The exit timed for 3 January was, again, delayed. The Kohistanees now quietly changed sides since they had not been given any of the chiefs' money. An emissary told Sturt that they were happy to deliver hostages to the British, hand over provisions and try to bring up reinforcements from Jalalabad. It was their intention to attack and burn Kabul three days after the abandonment of the cantonments. Florentia, with heavy sarcasm, reported yet another thought that Pottinger and his colleagues had of, again, forcing a way into the Bala Hissar. Now? Who were going to get the guns up onto the Seeah Sung hills to give covering fire – fairies? When taxed, they thought it had been successful in some Peninsular battle, 130 years ago. 'Straws' and 'grasping' were words which uncomfortably came to her mind.

With great joy, Florentia received a letter, dated 19 December, from her husband in Jalalabad. He wrote he had received her letter giving news up to 9 December and was, understandably, anxious. He had heard that reinforcements were on their way from Kandahar and that the cantonments were well stocked with provisions. The advance guard of cavalry, with ammunition, from Peshawar had arrived at Jalalabad, to be followed by the 3rd Foot (The Buffs) and 9th Foot (Norfolks), six regiments of native Infantry and sapper officers and artillery. The news from Kabul had no effect on the chiefs around Jalalabad, whose followers were deserting daily. Sale's men were in desperate need of pay, having had none for three months. He copied her letter to the Government in Calcutta, the Commander-in-Chief and to another son-in-law, Captain Brind[12], married to their daughter Henrietta, as no one else gave them any idea of the situation in Kabul. She and Alexandrina were warned by friendly Afghans, not to travel in palanquins on the sides of camels but ride horses mixed up with the other horsemen and wear turbans and common leather sheepskin coats over their garments. Thus making themselves less identifiable as prime targets.

The chiefs were due to come to the cantonments to take them over on 4 January. Anwar Zeeman Shah Khan was to liaise with the General. Sturt asked whether he was to make the breach in the ramparts? 'Only you are the best judge of that,' was the unhelpful reply. Then a follow-up was that there was to be no move until further orders. The usual 'order, counter-order, disorder.'

A note exists from Captain Grant, an officer on Elphinstone's staff, later killed at Gandamak, to Sturt, dated 30 December:

My dear Sturt,

The General wishes to know what you have done about cutting a passage through the rampart for our exit; if the Sappers are unable to do the job, you might have an European working party, if you will let me know the number you require; and the work should be done tonight, if possible.

Yours sincerely,

W. Grant.

Sturt immediately replied:

---

[12] Another victim of the Mutiny, he was subsequently killed at Sialkot on 9 July 1857 by troopers of the 9th Light Cavalry. His brother, General Sir James, had five wives; not all at once.

My dear Grant,

A party of forty Europeans with the regular sappers will do the job in about three hours: all inside is cleared away.

I cannot help giving the warning before doing this tonight. If we do not march tomorrow, we shall want a gun and a very strong guard, to prevent the Ghazeeas (sic) entering.

Perhaps the General is not aware that about 500 men were on the point of forcing the gate today, and, being prevented, tore up the remaining portion of the canal bridge, which no longer exists. While giving this warning, I have ordered the work to be begun now; therefore, if it is desired to be stopped, send to me; if not, send the Europeans. I am not answerable if accident happens, as I now wish you to tell the General that, in my opinion, no other than concealed measures should be used for moving out, until a few hours before that event takes place. If we march tomorrow, it should be done or commenced now; if not, it is my deliberate advice – do not execute it, or you endanger cantonments.

Yours ever,

J. L. D. Sturt.

Hearing nothing more, the following day, on his own initiative, Sturt began to make the breach in the walls as the chiefs were now saying that the force should leave tomorrow.

Shah Shuja sent a plaintive message to ask if not even one officer of his force would stand by him?

Indeed, he was now abandoned to his fate and the flight of his protectors began.

CHAPTER 8
Retreat

On Thursday 6 January 1842, in a foot of snow, with the temperature well below freezing, the British army finally left Kabul for India.

There were no high spirits or jubilation at seeing the end of their time in Afghanistan as one would expect from soldiers at the end of a hard operational tour. People were very cold, undernourished and badly clothed; they had been under siege for two months and on half rations for the whole of that time. Their 2000 pack animals and bullocks were weak, thin and badly fed, mainly existing on bark from trees and twigs. There was little firewood and, before they left, Florentia and the Sturts cooked their last dinner and breakfast over the fire made of a broken-up mahogany table. The soldiers themselves were poorly armed, with scant ammunition. These were the lucky ones who had escaped the constant attacks and harassment from the Afghans and now, without a doubt in anyone's mind, faced unimaginable rigours of the mountain passes in deep winter through country controlled by tribesmen of blood-soaked ferocity and treachery. Leadership and morale were rock-bottom.

The strength of the force was as follows:

Horse Artillery one troop	90
Her Majesty's 44th foot	600
5th Regiment Light Cavalry	260
5th Shah's Irregular Light Cavalry (Anderson's)	500
Skinner's Horse one troop	70
4th Irregular Horse one troop	70
Mission Escort/ Bodyguard	70
5th Native Infantry	700
37th Native Infantry	600
54th Native Infantry	650
6th Shah's Infantry	600
Sappers and Miners	20
Shah's Sappers and Miners	240
Half the Mountain Train	30
Six Horse Artillery Guns	
Three Mountain Train Guns	
Total (fighting men)	4500

In addition were some 12,000 camp followers, including women and children.

They left the cantonments by the rear gate and a breach Sturt's men had made to right of it by collapsing part of the rampart to form a bridge over the ditch. By eight o'clock most of the baggage was outside the cantonments. There was no sign of the promised escort and there were fears that they might have to fight their way out despite negotiations being made for their safety. There were about 50 to 100 Afghans lounging around the gates but did not molest them. However, a start was made at nine o'clock and it was hoped the Afghans were actually going to honour their word.

The order of march was as follows:

Advance Guard under Brigadier Anquetil (the commander of the Shah's forces)
    Her Majesty's 44th Foot
    Sappers and Miners
    One squadron Irregular Horse
    Three Mountain Train guns

Main Body under Brigadier Shelton
    The Escort, with ladies
    The invalids and sick
    Horse Artillery two guns
    Anderson's Irregular Horse
    37th Native Infantry, with treasure
    5th Native Infantry, with baggage

Rear Guard under Colonel Chambers
    54th Native Infantry
    6th Shah's Infantry

> 5th Light Cavalry
> Horse Artillery four guns

Although the ladies were put with the main body, Florentia and Alexandrina, remembering the advice they had been given earlier, pushed themselves in amongst Captain Hay's irregular cavalry in the advance guard. At about ten o'clock, a message came from the Anwar, Jubbar Khan, requesting a delay of another day as his escort was not ready to accompany them. By this time, however, the larger part of the force had started and already villagers from Beymaroo had forced their way into the northern part of the cantonment, the Mission Compound, and started to pillage and plunder. It was too late.

The start was frustratingly slow, the first mile taking about two and a half hours. There was only one small bridge over the canal about fifty yards from the compound but the water was eight foot wide and quite deep. A half mile on from the cantonments, the Kabul River had to be crossed. Again and again, Sturt had tried to impress his masters the need to maintain, and guard, a bridge there for exactly this eventuality. The Afghans, of course, had destroyed the existing bridge some time ago, so Sturt was now ordered to build a fresh one although he maintained the river was, in places, fordable. Before it got light, Sturt improvised a bridge with gun carriages. It couldn't have been done any earlier as the Afghans would have simply made off with them. He, and his men, therefore had to work for hours up to their waists in water, knowing that when they got out, they weren't going to be able to change their sodden, and now freezing, clothes until the end of the march. The bullocks had great difficulty in dragging the gun carriages through the snow and it was all wasted work as a ford was perfectly practicable a little above the bridge where the water was quite shallow. Florentia and Alexandrina happily forded the river in preference to crossing over the planks laid on the gun carriages. Not so, however, the camp followers who were determined not to get their feet wet, so shoved and jostled to go over the bridge. Much of the stores and baggage was lost in this shambolic crossing. Alexandrina managed to save her bedding which was carried by a pony ridden by her maid, and therefore kept close to her. It was midday before the advance guard was completely across.

On paper, the order of march looked tidy and militarily efficient but it wasn't. Once the camp followers were out of the cantonments, with private and public baggage, they became mixed up and entwined with the soldiers, without any order or discipline. Control was completely lost. The main body, with its long train of weighed down camels, continued to pour out of the gate until evening. By then thousands of Afghans, the majority of whom were the fanatical Ghazis thronged the area of the cantonments, screaming with exultation. The rear guard, almost having to fight their way out, were forced to take up a defensive position outside the cantonments when faced with delay due to the damaged bridge over the canal. Baggage was plundered and lost. Bored by pilfering, Afghans now lined up on the rampart walls, taking pot shots at the rear guard which was forced to spike, and abandon, two of the horse artillery guns. Many of the camp followers threw down their packs and ran; others simply lay down in the snow and waited to die.

With night falling, the countryside was illuminated by the blazing buildings in the cantonments, set on fire by the insurgents. Even the gun carriages, which had been left, were burnt, thus depriving the Afghans of the means of handling the guns which had been handed over to them. Earlier, Elphinstone had been strongly advised to destroy them for that very reason but had demurred as not being the spirit of the treaty. Before the rear guard started off again, Lieutenant Hardyman of the 5th Light Cavalry and fifty of his men were dead in the snow. Scores of soldiers joined camp followers just sitting at the side of the road, worn out, freezing and having completely given up. The rear guard straggled into the camp at Begramee, a mere five miles from the cantonments near the Logar River, at two o'clock in the morning. Here confusion reigned. Tents had been randomly pitched with no order, regiments being mixed with others, huddled together with camp followers, camels, horses and baggage. The thin canvas was a poor insulation against the freezing temperature which plummeted as night wore on. Many were not even afforded that protection and had to lie in the snow with no food or fire. Several died of frostbite during the night including a senior European ordnance officer. The more experienced soldiers, such as Captain Mackenzie's riflemen, cleared a space in the snow to expose the earth, lay down in a circle, with their feet in the centre, then spread as much clothing as they could muster over the whole group to generate sufficient animal warmth to keep them alive. Captain Johnson rigged up a groundsheet shelter for Florentia and the Sturts but it was dark, there were no pegs and the wind blew under it, gradually stiffening Florentia's limbs. She left the bedding to the Sturts and curled up in a straw chair, covering herself with her sheepskin coat.

Florentia had what she was convinced to be a premonition. Earlier on, her son-in-law, keen to preserve some of his most valuable books, sent a number to a friend in the city for safe keeping. She found, amongst those thrown aside, a book of Campbell's Poems, which fell open at *Hohenlinden*. This verse haunted her day and night:

'Few, few shall part where many meet,

The snow shall be their winding sheet;

And every turf beneath their feet

Shall be a soldier's sepulchre'.

Florentia was a robust woman, not given to sentiment, but this, though, was never far from her thoughts. Even at this early stage, her common sense told her that the chances of reaching their goal were looking decidedly unlikely. Overnight, nearly the whole of the Shah's 6th, and all the Shah's sappers and miners deserted, many returning to Kabul.

The next morning this rabble started off with no order given or bugle sounded. In theory, it was the reverse order, with the rear guard taking over the advance guard duty but, in reality, a mangled mass of soldiers, camp followers and baggage-cattle. Arrayed like this, without any conformity or discipline, there was no prospect of fighting back properly if attacked by the enemy. Half the Indian infantry soldiers were, anyway, unfit for duty through sheer inability to keep their ranks, and so joined the non-combatants with increasing confusion. Compacted snow and ice had to be chiselled off the horse hooves and breath froze in the air, forming icicles on beards and moustaches.

The advance guard had to force its way through a mob of camp followers and baggage animals, which had, on their own account, started earlier. As they progressed, they could see numerous small bodies of Afghans on horse and foot, following them from the flanks, running parallel. They were not molested, so perhaps they were the escort? No, they weren't because they soon attacked the rear guard of the 44th, the 3-pounder mountain train guns and a squadron of irregular horse. Much baggage was lost but the enemy were largely checked by the guns. Yet, nevertheless, they presented a bold front and kept up desultory sniping from a distance. Hampered by the multitude in front of them, the soldiers found fire and movement extremely difficult and, at one stage, when halted by a deep water cut, the guns tried a detour. In doing so, they became separated from the protective infantry and the enemy, sallying forth from a small fort, seized them. An effort to recapture them might have worked if the artillery officer, Lieutenant Green, and his gunners had been supported by the infantry, but they weren't, and had, out of desperation, to spike the guns. Brigadier Anquetil called for reinforcements from the front but it was impossible for any to force their way through the rabble. A group of Afghan cavalry charged into the middle of the column and rode off with considerable plunder. Two 6-pounder horse artillery guns had to be spiked as the horses were simply too exhausted to pull them.

It had been Elphinstone's intention to push on to Khoord Kabul through the pass but with only the advance guard arriving at Boothak at 1pm, he decided, much to Florentia's dismay, to call a halt there. She realised that they had left Kabul with five and a half day's rations to take them to Jalalabad, with no forage for the cattle and no likelihood of procuring any *en route*. Her view was that with unnecessary halts, the snow being a foot deep and having no cover for the troops, who were paralyzed with cold, they weren't going to make it. Perhaps a little unfairly, she blamed the General's staff, who warned him that by going on, he risked the safety of the army.

Elphinstone had been made aware that the rear of the column was in danger of being entirely cut off, so sent back as many troops as he could spare, with the two remaining guns. The enemy had now grown in number and were dominating the road from the heights on the right. Captain Skinner, who appears to have been a sort of liaison officer with the Afghans, had fallen in with a follower of Akbar Khan and learned that the Khan was camped nearby. Going to see him, Akbar Khan told him that he had been sent by the chiefs to escort the column to Jalalabad but it had been attacked as the army had set off contrary to their wishes. He insisted that the force remained at Boothak until the following morning when he would provide food, forage and firewood for the troops. However, he demanded six hostages to insure against the column not marching beyond Tezeen, before General Sale's evacuation of Jalalabad, in compliance with the terms of the treaty.

Florentia and another eight slept under a rudimentary tent erected by Captain Johnson, all touching one another; sensible, given the cold, but not what ladies were used to. They shared a few Kabul cakes and some tea. No ground had been allocated to the troops, so many of the sepoys merely huddled up with the camp followers. Water was difficult to obtain from the river as people were fired on when they approached it. Numbers were falling by the hour through cold and enemy sniper fire. Scornfully, Florentia reported that they were told that the chiefs were faithful and Akbar Khan was their friend. The reason for the delay was that the Afghans were going to clear the passes for them. Believe that and you'll believe anything, thought Florentia.

The latest terms from Akbar Khan having been agreed, the force made it to the entrance of the Khoord Kabul pass, ten miles from Kabul in two days. Chaos was indescribable with some 14,000 to 16,000 men, with several hundred cavalry horses and baggage cattle, jammed together in one heaving mass, suffering from starvation, cold, exhaustion and, inevitably, death.

By sunrise on the 8th, confusion reigned as no orders for any move had been given out. Men were so cold, they could hardly handle their weapons. A number of sepoys burnt their caps, accoutrements and clothes to keep warm. With enemy appearing to the rear of the position, camp followers rushed to the front, seizing cattle in their way and leaving the ground strewn with boxes of ammunition, plate and various bits of property. A cask of spirits was quickly broached by some artillery men, which may have done them good in the short term but would have dire consequences in the cold later. As the enemy looked as though they were preparing to attack, Major Thain, seizing the initiative, led a group of the 44th in a quick assault. This so surprised the opposition that they beat a retreat leaving Thain and his men in possession of some critical high ground. Florentia reckoned if they had taken this sort of action right from the start, it would have made the Afghans, who disliked being charged, think twice before attacking. Bullets whizzed round Florentia's head while she sat on her horse. Brandy, which appeared to be available to all, was being issued from the 54th stores. Some inebriated cavalrymen mounted up and swore they'd attack the enemy. Held, properly, in check by one of their officers, he roundly abused them as drunkards and talked of punishment. Ashamed of themselves they appealed to Sturt, who told them they were good men who had served him well in the cantonments but their lives were now too valuable to risk in a foolhardy, but brave, jaunt. If their services were required, he'd go with them. They respected Sturt who had been with them when on sentry and in places of extreme danger. When on the ramparts in the cantonments, at night, in the cold, Sturt had gone round with a glass of brandy for them from his very small personal stock. As for Florentia, she drank a tumbler of sherry, while sitting on her horse; not very ladylike, she thought, but so be it. She noticed three or four year old children being given cupfuls of it without any ill effect.

Captain Skinner again went to see Akbar Khan who demanded Major Pottinger and Captains Lawrence and Mackenzie be handed over to him as hostages, plus 15,000 rupees. This was done and hostilities ceased for the time being with promises that 'influential men' would be sent forward to clear the passes of Ghilzais who were in ambush positions. The column lumbered off at about midday with the 5th Native Infantry in the lead. An attempt was made, at the mouth of the pass, to separate troops from the non-combatants, which was only partially successful and created yet more delay with camp followers trying to get in front. Due to the cold and two nights' exposure, the force was really now down to a few hundred fighting men; even the cavalry had to be lifted onto their horses. Florentia and Alexandrina pushed themselves into the advance guard and Lieutenant Mein, 13th Light Infantry, who had been with Sale's brigade on the way to Jalalabad in October, pointed out to them where the fighting had taken place, including where Sale and he had been wounded. (He had returned to Kabul to recover from his wounds and had been looked after by Florentia).

The whole idea of threading through the passes ahead of them, with bloodthirsty tribesmen waiting for them, filled everyone with increased foreboding. This seething mass of uncontrolled people trying to pass through the defile of about five miles in length defied imagination. The pass was shut in on either side by high crags and the sun only momentarily reached the bottom through which a mountain torrent ran. The stream was frozen at the edges and, combined with the snow on the banks, made footing precipitous for man and beast. This stream had to be crossed and re-crossed twenty-eight times. Some chiefs did actually ride with the advance party and made their followers shout to the enemy on the heights not to fire. Although the chiefs ran the same dangers as the force, they were, in Florentia's view, so keen to be rid of the British they were prepared to take that risk. Despite the chiefs' presence, as the defile narrowed, heavy fire rained down on the column from above.

Trying to push on ahead to clear the pass, Florentia and Alexandrina came upon Captain Thain's horse, shot through the rear quarters. As they did so, Sturt came back, to find them or Thain, and immediately his horse was shot from under him. Before he could get up, he was hit severely in the abdomen. Lieutenant Mein stood over him, protecting him from the cutthroats, while entreating passers-by for help. He was joined by Sergeant Deane of the Sappers and between them, they dragged his body on a quilt through the rest of the pass, then found a pony on which they carried him to the camp at Khoord Kabul. Alexandrina's horse was wounded in the ear and neck and Florentia was hit in the arm, with three other rounds going through her sheepskin coat. With the enemy only fifty yards away, they galloped their horses flat out, over a very rough road. The main effort of the enemy was, luckily, against the column and rear guard and not the chiefs (of course) where Florentia was. The other ladies were travelling in panniers on either side of camels, mixed up with the baggage animals and main body of the column. Here the onslaught was heaviest. On one camel, in a pannier, was Mrs Boyd and her youngest boy, Hugh, and on the other side, Mrs Mainwaring and her three month old infant. The camel was shot. Mrs Boyd mounted a horse and her boy on another behind a man. The man was promptly shot dead and the boy carried off by the Afghans. Mrs Mainwaring, now on foot, carried her baby in her arms. She grabbed a pony laden with baggage and tried to sit on the boxes but fell off. A passing Afghan asked if she was wounded and told her to mount behind him. Suspecting treachery, she refused on the grounds that it would be too difficult with her baby in her arms. Annoyed, the man ripped the shawl from her shoulders and made off, leaving her to her fate. She then had to walk, through the snow, picking her way over dead and dying men and animals, crossing the stream, wet up to the waist, constantly under fire, with men being killed either side of her. She made it, exhausted to the camp but, even then, no chance to change her sodden clothes. Mrs Bourke, little Seymour Stoker, his mother, and Mrs Cunningham; all soldiers' wives, and the child of a man in the 13th were carried off by the Afghans. There is an unlikely story that a child, John Campbell, was abducted, aged two, by the

Afghans. He was allegedly brought up by an Afghan family until he escaped after 15 years.[13]

Panic ensued with mindless slaughter; people pushing and shoving to get to the front and through the defile, abandoning women and children, baggage, arms and ammunition, in an effort to save their lives. The rear guard of the 44th, 54th, and 37th suffered most and another gun had to be spiked. The 37th were paralyzed with cold, to such an extent they gave up obeying their officers and refused to grapple with the enemy who, nonchalantly, removed their weapons and even clothing off their backs. The 44th helped themselves to their ammunition. Major Scott and Captain Swinton of the 44th had gone to the front, severely wounded, so Captain Souter took over command. Lieutenant Steer of the 37th managed to shove a pony, with boxes of ammunition, to the rear to re-supply the 44th but the weight of fire was such that he had to abandon them. The 44th, fighting a rear guard action were being hampered by stragglers getting between them and the enemy. They were joined by Elphinstone, Colonel Chambers of the 5th Cavalry with Captain Hay and some troopers of the Irregular Cavalry, with the one remaining gun. They managed to check the Afghan follow-up, allowing the 37th to pass through. After holding the position for a good hour, they then pressed on through deep snow, manhandling the gun

---

[13] 'Lost Among the Afghans: Being the Adventures of John Campbell, otherwise known as 'Feringhee Bacha,' Amongst the Wild Tribes of Central Asia' as told to Hubert Oswald Fry (London 1862). Author's Note: a Dr Campbell was one of the survivors with Florentia. There is no evidence that he lost a baby son to kidnappers.

as the horses were unable to do so. They reached the camp without further sniping from the enemy. A number of officers had been killed and probably a further 500 regular troops and 2,500 camp followers. On leaving Kabul, each sepoy had about forty rounds of musket ammunition in pouches, with 100 in reserve. No sepoy now had a single round and there were a mere three ammunition camels left alive. The light company of the 54th, having left Kabul thirty-six hours before, with a strength of eighty, was now down to eighteen men.

On reaching Khoord Kabul, snow began to fall heavily and continued until dawn. There were only four small tents; one for the General, two for the ladies and one for the sick. Florentia and Alexandria laid Sturt on a bank between them. Johnson and Bygrave grabbed some coarse blankets which they threw over the three of them. Doctor Bryce came and examined Sturt's wound and dressed it but, from the expression on his face, there was little hope. He cut the ball out of Florentia's arm, without, of course, any anaesthetic, and dressed both her other wounds. Captain Johnson and Lieutenant Mein carried Sturt over to the ladies' tent and then came back for Florentia and Alexandrina. Sturt was in agony and dying of thirst. Mein heroically spent all night on trips to the stream for water in a tiny cup, the only drinking vessel they had. With thirty of them packed in, sleep was impossible. A number of wretched wounded wandered around and perished in the night. There was no food, firewood or dry clothing. It was a wonder anyone survived at all.

Dawn came with the General's intention to set off at 10 o'clock. However, the camp followers and a large number of troops moved off at about 8 o'clock, under no orders, taking as many ponies and camels as they could. They were followed by many more of the regular troops as they felt like it. They had gone, perhaps, a mile when the whole lot were ordered back. Akbar Khan had sent a message to the General, through Captain Skinner, that they were to stay in the camp for the day as he had not yet made arrangements for security or provisions for the force. Captain Skinner urged the General to accept the Sirdar's (as he was now known – the General) wishes. Not having too many options, he did so and sent Captain Anderson to recall everyone. This was highly unpopular, particularly with the native troops, who saw delay extending their devastation and the only way out was to move as fast as they possibly could. Ideas of desertion rose in their minds, specifically in the Shah's cavalry, mainly young men, who could see the fatal results of these useless and unnecessary delays.

Mrs Trevor kindly gave up her camel pannier to Sturt who, otherwise, would have been left to die on the ground. Sadly, the rough movement increased his suffering and accelerated his death but he was conscious enough to know that he had his wife and Florentia with him when he died. Even amongst the snow, they managed to give him a Christian burial; more or less a shallow scrape with rocks piled on top. Thus perished one of the real heroes of the Kabul disaster; a man of courage and resource, good ideas and not afraid to voice them. Also a leader, highly respected by his men. A great physical and emotional loss to Alexandrina, pregnant with their child, and to Florentia.

What was to become of them now?

CHAPTER 9

Kidnapped

At about midday on 9 January, Akbar Khan, together with the hostages Pottinger, Mackenzie and Lawrence, arrived in Khoord Kabul. He told Lawrence that he had a proposal to make but was nervous that, in doing so, his motives might be misconstrued. He said that he was prepared to take under his protection all the married men and their families, and guarantee them honourable treatment and a safe journey to Jalalabad. He added that Lawrence had seen for himself from the previous day's events – the loss of Captain Boyd's and Captain Anderson's children – that the camp was no place for ladies and children. He intended that the wounded officers also should have the opportunity to take advantage of this. They would be escorted a day's march in rear of the Army. Lawrence thought this an acceptable offer and, at that moment, Captain Skinner arrived, and wholeheartedly endorsed the scheme. With Pottinger's agreement, Skinner went off to persuade the General.

Up to now, scarcely any of the ladies had eaten a proper meal since leaving Kabul. Some had infants a few days old at their breasts and could barely stand. Others, heavily pregnant, could have hardly walked across a drawing-room floor let alone roughed it on the backs of broken down ponies and in panniers on the sides of camels, or perched on the top of boxes on baggage animals. Most had been without shelter and abandoned by their servants. All, with the exception of Lady Macnaghten and Mrs Trevor, had lost their possessions and merely had the clothes they stood up in. Invalids were in the nightdresses they had left Kabul in, carried in litters. It was to have been hours rather than days before they died. The husbands would, not unnaturally, have preferred to stay with their men but their role in protecting the women and children was more important. It, rightly, didn't take much to make the General see what sense Akbar Khan's offer made, although the Sirdars's potential for treachery was never far from his mind, and he told Skinner to warn everyone for an immediate departure with a troop of Afghan cavalry which was waiting for them. No one, of course, knew what was in Akbar Khan's mind. Perhaps he didn't really himself? At the time he was the professed friend of the Army, and the General had effectively little option but to trust his good faith and to give him the confidence that he did so. Later, it was discovered that troopers of the Shah's irregular cavalry and those of the Mission escort, were being enticed away in large numbers by the Khan's men. In response to the General's remonstrance, Akbar Khan loudly protested that this was false and, on the contrary, anyone deserting would be shot. Hypocrisy and perfidy came easily to the Khan.

The families were then escorted by a very circuitous route to a fort about two miles away where Akbar Khan had taken up temporary residence. The three hostages were already there. With the group were Captain Troup, Brigade Major of the Shah's force and Lieutenant Mein, the wounded officer who had been taken under Florentia's wing. Lieutenants Waller and Vincent Eyre, the Gunner, who were also recovering from wounds, joined them. Florentia and Alexandrina were not given much choice but if there was a faint hope of reaching Jalalabad, they had to seize it. The Boyd child was restored to his parents, having been picked up in the Khoord Kabul pass the previous day. Mrs Burnes and young Stoker, a child of a soldier of the 13th, were there. The Anderson little girl had been taken to Kabul to Nawab Zeman Shah Khan, so was probably safe. Three dark and dirty rooms were made over to them. Florentia's was fourteen foot by ten and contained Alexandrina, Mrs Trevor and seven children, Lieutenant and Mrs Waller and child, Lieutenant Mein, Mrs Smith and Mrs Burnes, two soldiers' wives, and young Stoker, who had been saved from people who were carrying him off to the hills. He was covered with what was probably his mother's blood; her whereabouts were unknown, nor of Mrs Cunningham of the 13th. At midnight they were given some mutton bones and greasy rice. All they possessed were the clothes they had been wearing since they left Kabul. They lay on the floor, covered with the odd sheepskin coat. Even so, this was better than being in the snow, with no protection from the cold.

The following day, the small courtyard of the fort was thronged with supporters of Akbar Khan's. On the whole they were kind and courteous but, in accordance with their custom, the ladies had to remain in their rooms, to Florentia's annoyance. In the afternoon the Khan appeared and had a conversation with Lady Macnaghten in which he expressed his sorrow at having been instrumental in her present predicament and his desire to make her as comfortable as possible. He stopped short of telling her he'd actually killed her husband himself. The captives, for that was, effectively, now what they were, soon learned that the Afghans' idea of good manners did not extend to spoons and forks, considered effeminate luxuries, and dived their fingers into shared bowls of greasy pillau. For the first time in many days, though, they enjoyed the warmth of a wood fire, although blinded by the smoke.

There was typical order, counter-order, disorder on the General's part. Initially, he sent an order that Captains Anderson and Boyd were to return to their troops, having been told that their officers being taken away had a bad effect on the soldiers, despite now being commanded by Lieutenant Le Geyt. However, he was then persuaded that removing them from the captive party would cast doubts in the mind of Akbar Khan that his trust was being betrayed. They stayed.

On 11 January, at about 11 o'clock they started for Tezeen, with an escort of fifty cavalrymen. The officers were warned, nevertheless, to have their swords and pistols at hand for fear of attack by the bloodthirsty Ghazis. Their servants, who could not walk, were left behind with a promise from the Sirdar that they would be fed. Dreadful scenes awaited them for it was the same route that the army had tramped along the previous day. The snow was streaked red with blood and the mangled bodies of British and Indian soldiers littered the way. Helpless camp followers lay beside them, blood seeping from ghastly open wounds. Here and there, small groups of miserable, starving and frostbitten wretches, many of them women and children, clung to the last sparks of life. The bodies of Majors Scott, 44th, and Ewart, 54th, together with that of Doctor Bryce were recognised by the party. There was nothing they could do. There were bands of truculent Ghazis about, weighed down with booty, and swords running with blood. They shouted curses at the prisoners, infuriated that they weren't allowed a chance to kill them. Subsequently, the party arrived at the Tezeen fort to find Lieutenant Melville of the 54th, who had given himself up to Akbar Khan after receiving five wounds in protecting his Regimental Colour. (Eyre sniffily said 'some slight sword cuts'). He'd given his last five rupees to an Afghan to take him to the Sirdar who, on arrival, personally dressed his wounds with burnt rags. They were distressed to see 400 of the irregular Indian cavalry, mainly Anderson's and the Mission bodyguard, camped outside the fort, having deserted on the 9th and 10th. It was rumoured that the Sirdar had offered to escort the army if they laid down their arms, but the General was having none of it.

The following day they set off for Seh Baba in the Tezeen valley, preceded by the cavalry deserters. At Seh Baba, they branched off to the Surroobee Fort belonging to Abdoolah Khan, passing the sad sight of Doctor Cardew's body, lying with some artillerymen and the last abandoned horse artillery gun. Further on was Doctor Duff's body. He had been the chief surgeon to the force and had the unenviable distinction of having his left hand amputated with a penknife by another doctor. They were overtaken by Doctor Macgrath, the medical officer of the 37th, and, with him, six men of the 44th. So, at least, they had a doctor to deal with their own casualties. Macgrath had been wounded when rallying forty or fifty irregular cavalry to come to the help of some wounded who were being butchered at the bottom of the Huft Kotul Pass. Nearly killed himself, he was rescued by an Afghan horseman who recognised him as having been kind to a sick friend of his in Kabul. To his disgust, he found, with the party, Khoda Bukh Khan, a Ghilzai chief, to whom the cavalrymen with him now grovelled and apologised for not deserting with their comrades the previous day. They spent the night all together in one room, where an old woman cooked chapattis for them at three for a rupee but, when she discovered the demand, raised it to a rupee each, to Florentia's scorn.

They now headed south-east towards Jagdalak over narrow mountain paths which the camels found difficult with their loads. At one point they were exposed on a high plateau with no signs of cultivation or human habitation but soon descended back onto a road recently used by the army. Again, it was strewn with the dead and dying and wretches, just alive, crying out to them for clothing, food or water which they couldn't give them. They reached Jagdalak late in the evening to find a ruined enclosure full of bloodied corpses, mainly European. One easily recognised was Captain Skinner's, the officer who had been so instrumental in conveying messages between the warring chiefs and the British commanders. They were allowed to give him a decent burial. There were three ragged tents erected for them where they found General Elphinstone, Brigadier Shelton and Captain Johnson.

These officers were now hostages of the Sirdar and this is their story.

CHAPTER 10

Destruction of an Army

Returning now to the 9th of January at Khoord Kabul, Florentia recounts the last days of Elphinstone's Army, with the help of Doctor Brydon's[14] story.

After the ladies and officers had left under the protection of Akbar Khan, the irregular cavalry, less, about 80 men, deserted and went over to the enemy. Later they were seen in the company of some Afghan horsemen and there was a thought that they may attack the column. Several more ordinary soldiers and camp followers went over to the other side. Was the Sirdar going to honour his pledge to shoot deserters? Probably not, but one of the messengers from the Mission was caught running away and was promptly shot *pour encourager les autres*. All the bearers of the palanquins for the sick either deserted or were slaughtered. The camels and ponies had either been taken by the enemy or the lawless camp followers. The force was now down to about 300 of the 44th, 100 of the Irregular Horse and 70 of the 5th Cavalry, with a number of men from the assorted Indian regiments.

Enormous apprehension and stress pervaded the army. What was going to happen to them? Were they going to

---

[14] William Brydon was born in 1811 and entered the East India Company's Medical Service. He was seconded to Shah Shuja's service in Afghanistan.

survive the hunger, cold and lack of shelter and warmth or be merely butchered by the Afghans? Some could hardly hold a weapon and even snow blindness took its toll. Brydon still had a couple of his servants, one of whom had secreted away a bag of barley for his horse and filled his water-skin with pistachio nuts. So the animal had a feed of corn and the good doctor feasted, with his two servants, on the nuts.

No sooner than it was light on the 10th, there was the usual rush to the front by the camp followers. No one wanted to be in the rear which was the most vulnerable to attack. The weaker ones were left at the roadside to die. The advance guard of the 44th and about fifty of the 5th cavalry, with the one and only remaining gun, managed to struggle to the front. The Afghans were already on the crests of the hills bringing down fire onto the column trying to get through the ten foot wide Tarakie Tungie gorge, from where there was gradual ascent to the Huft Kotul pass. A sergeant major in Doctor Brydon's regiment had acquired some eggs and a bottle of wine from a box left behind by the ladies. Shared out between four officers, the eggs were found to be frozen hard and only just edible. The wine was the texture of honey with only a little liquid in the middle. Snow blindness was becoming widespread and the Doctor urged people to rub snow in their eyes which afforded some relief. Stragglers from the rear guard of the 54th now caught up with them and reported that they were the sole survivors; almost every man had been killed or wounded. Some had thrown away their arms and accoutrements and were massacred on the spot. Sick and wounded were butchered where they lay. The commander, Major Ewart, had both arms broken by musket balls and two other officers were wounded. Lieutenant Melville, seeing the Indian officer carrying the Regimental Colour wounded, seized it. Vainly trying to detach it from its pike, he made his way on foot, his horse having been shot under him. With the Colour, he was clearly a marked man, and, as soon as he exited the pass, he was felled with a spear thrust to the back. He received more sword cuts to the head as he was on the ground but managed to crawl as far as the retreating column. Now surrounded by the enemy and being further wounded by a spear in the chin and a knife cut to the neck, he thought his days were numbered. However, at that moment, his assailants saw what they thought was a box of treasure the other side of the pass and left him to take what they could. Finding a riderless pony without a saddle, he climbed on and somehow caught up with the main column. On arrival, he was strapped to the only gun they had and the General told him he would be handed over to Akbar Khan with the other wounded officers and the women and children. He was unceremoniously dumped at the side of the road when the gun had to be brought into action against the immediate enemy. Again, he thought this is where he would meet his end but he was gathered up by a horseman he had known in the cantonments who delivered him to the Sirdar who kindly welcomed him and had his wounds bound up. He gave seven rupees, all he had, to the horseman who had rescued him. He was presented with a turban, his cap having been cut to pieces. The Colour was lost in the mayhem.

The fighting element of the army was now down to 200 men of the 44th and 50 of the 5th Cavalry, and the solitary gun. Seeing enemy to their rear, they brought the gun to bear. However, it turned out to be Akbar Khan and his men. The General therefore sent Captain Skinner, with an escort, over to him to remonstrate that attacks had been made against them in violation of the treaty. The Sirdar smoothly replied that he could not control the local inhabitants, the Ghilzais, with a mere 300 of his own men. However, as the remnants of the army now amounted only to a few Europeans, he would guarantee their safety to Jalalabad if they handed over their arms to his soldiers. He maintained that he suggested this so that his own followers would not be afraid of treachery. Unsurprisingly, the General refused. Earlier, Captain Mackay had approached the Sirdar with a draft letter, presumably initiated by the General, to General Sale, ordering him to evacuate Jalalabad in accordance with the treaty. Akbar Khan now rejected it on the realisation that a journey by Mackay to Jalalabad was too dangerous.

It was a long and difficult 2000 foot descent from the Huft Kotul to the Tezeen valley. Under constant sniping fire from Afghans in the hills, many more were killed and those who could not walk were left to their fate. The wounded Doctors Duff and Cardew were put on a gun carriage but were not to last long. The dying Doctor Bryce, who had been shot through the chest, handed his will to Captain Marshall. The column reached Tezeen at about 4pm. Akbar Khan, resting in his father-in-law's fort close by, sent emissaries to the General. Captain Skinner accompanied them back to the Sirdar to find some way of saving the rest of the column which now amounted to about 4,000 people of every description, although an exact number was too difficult to assess. Skinner returned with the same disarmament offer as before, and, as previously, the General refused. The latter then decided, weak and famished as they were, with no prospect of re-provisioning in Tezeen, they would push on. So, they set off at about 7pm in the hope that, in darkness, they would beat the Afghans to the next pass, the two-mile long Jagdalak, about fifteen to twenty miles distant. It was, gloomily, pointed out to the General that, even starting after them, the Afghans, by a short cut over the mountains, could arrive before them and dominate the pass from the heights. Leaving the remaining gun behind, they marched all night, abandoning many of the camp followers who simply refused to move.

By midnight, they had reached Seh Baba. A few shots were fired at them and the rear of the column attacked, so the main body of the 44th, less 30 men, was moved back to protect it. Brydon was given a biscuit and a sardine by another officer, which he warmly welcomed having had nothing to eat since the frozen eggs the morning before. From Seh Baba the road turned sharp right over the mountains to Jagdalak, and across the river was a short cut back to Kabul but not negotiable by camels or guns. The one-handed Doctor Duff was too wounded to continue and was left behind, to be murdered two days later. About three miles on was Bareekub, with a stream of fresh water to replenish water bottles. There were inhabitants in caves among the rocks but they left the troops alone. By dawn, they arrived at Killa Sung, which was about seven miles from Seh Baba, but uncomfortably dominated by enemy on the surrounding hills preventing anyone getting to the water in the stream. There they had to wait for two hours, under desultory fire, for the rear guard, which had been under much pressure, to catch up. Any stragglers were swiftly murdered. Brydon was able to treat Captain Grant, whose jaw had been shattered, and Captain Marshall, who had been shot through the chest. Previously, they had managed to cook, over some brushwood, slices of an Arab charger which had been shot.

Two miles from Jagdalak, the descent into the valley starts and the hills were now fully manned by the enemy, who poured well aimed long shots from the rocks. With very few Europeans now in the advance guard, the General ordered the officers, numbering about twenty, to form a line in front to boost morale of the troops. Predictably, a number were killed and wounded. During a brief respite, the General ordered the slaughter of three bullocks and the flesh given to the starving troops, which they ate without cooking. The General then sent a message, at about half past three, to Akbar Khan to ask, yet again, why they were being attacked? The Sirdar replied that he wished to talk to Captain Skinner. Scarcely had he left, when a heavy weight of fire was brought down on the exhausted troops. Wearily, they tried, in the confusion, to take what cover they could. A courageous group of twenty men of the 44th galvanised themselves and charged a hill occupied by the enemy. Such was the surprise and effect on the Afghans, that they ran before the troops could reach the summit. Sadly, the 44th men were unable to hold the position though, and had to be recalled to the main body. The force reaching Jagdalak was now down to 150 men of the 44th, 16 dismounted horse artillery men and 25 of the 5th Cavalry. Not a single Indian soldier had a weapon or ammunition.

At about five, the Sirdar sent a message that he wanted to see the General, Brigadier Shelton and Captain Johnson, who acted as interpreter. If they came, he would stop any further killing and provide food for the column. An additional condition was that they should remain as hostages dependent on General Sale evacuating Jalalabad.

He would then escort the remaining party to safety. At dusk, Mohammad Shah Khan, the Sirdar's father-in-law and one of the principal Ghilzai chiefs, came with an escort to take them to the Sirdar. They started with the confidence that, at last, Akbar Khan meant what he said. They met him at the top of the valley, about two miles away, and were greeted with warmth. Food was provided; a large dish of pillau, laid out on a cloth spread on the ground, out of which they all ate. It was the first meal they had had for forty-eight hours. They gathered round a roaring fire and discussed the situation. The General was, understandably, anxious that the Sirdar should keep his word and provide food and water for the column in the morning. He faithfully promised to do so.

The General was also keen to return to his men and offered to be replaced by Brigadier Anquetil. It was pointed out to the Sirdar the stigma that would be attached to a senior officer enjoying the safety and hospitality of the enemy while his soldiers suffered privation and danger, but the Sirdar would not agree. However, he promised that, in the morning, he would summon the chiefs controlling the Jagdalak Pass, to ensure safe conduct. With that, he showed them to a tent, in which, wrapped in their cloaks, they fell into an exhausted sleep.

On 12 January, they rose with the dawn and were attended by two of the Sirdar's servants and were told not to leave their tent without one of them since the camp was now flooded with Ghilzais, anxious to pay their respects to the Sirdar and would like nothing more than to kill one of them to demonstrate their loyalty. At nine, the Pass chiefs and those controlling Sourkab arrived. Sourkab is about thirteen miles from Jagdalak on the road to Jalalabad and is a standard stopping off place. The chiefs were bitter and would entertain no lessening of their hatred of the British. They refused to accept any money and nothing would satisfy them but the extermination of the column, or what remained of it. The Sirdar tried his best to persuade them and reminded them that his father and family were in the power of the British in Ludhiana and vengeance would be extracted if mercy was not now shown. Mohammad Shah Khan offered them 60,000 rupees on condition that the column would not be attacked. They left to consult their followers. Mohammad Shah Khan mentioned to Captain Johnson that he feared the chiefs, without some great inducement, could not resist the temptation of plunder and murder that was now on the cards. He wound up by asking if the General would be prepared to give them two lakhs of rupees (£20,000) for a safe passage? The General acceded with alacrity and Mohammad Shah Khan went away, promising to return shortly. Again, the General pleaded to be allowed to return to his troops, without success. Johnson was asked to write a note to Captain Skinner to summon him to meet the Sirdar. Sadly, Skinner never received it, and two others, because he had been shot in the face and died the same day. The Sirdar, expressed much sorrow, since he had been very fond of him.

All morning, crowds of Ghilzais, and their chiefs poured into the encampment, to make their salaams to Akbar Khan and to participate in the plunder and massacre of the Europeans. They appeared to achieve more satisfaction in slitting throats than acquiring booty. On a hint from the Sirdar, they changed from speaking Persian to Pushtu, which was not understood by the British. Akbar Khan, all the while, looked as though he was trying to conciliate, but was he not really hiding his true feelings? He was told by the chiefs, 'When Burnes came into this country, was not your father entreated by us to kill him; or he would go back to Hindostan, and at some future day bring an army and take our country from us? He would not listen to our advice, and what is the consequence? Let us now that we have the opportunity, take advantage of it and kill those infidel dogs.' The Sirdar left at about midday for a hill to the rear of the British bivouac and did not return until sunset. In reply to anxious queries as to the return of Mohammad Shah Khan, the reply was always 'immediately.' Frequent assurances were given that the troops had been provided with food and water but, subsequently, it was found not to be the case. The Sirdar returned, accompanied by Mohammad Shah Khan, bringing the news that all was finally and amicably arranged for the troops to be given safe conduct to Jalalabad. He went on to say that he would accompany them early in the morning. Captain Johnson was instructed to write to Brigadier Anquetil to have the troops ready to move at 8 am and to General Sale at Jalalabad to commence evacuation under the terms of the treaty. Before the note could be sent, firing was heard from the valley where the troops were and a report was brought in to say that the Europeans had moved off through the Jagdalak Pass, followed by the Ghilzais. Pandemonium ensued; the Sirdar suggested he and the officers should follow them and the General agreed. The chief then changed his mind saying that in doing so it might jeopardise the troops by bringing with him the horde of Ghilzais in the valley. He promised to send a confidential messenger to Meer Afzul Khan at Gandamak, two or three miles beyond Sourkab, to ensure their safety. If they started at midnight, mounted on horses, they would overtake the column by daybreak. As they were about to separate for the night, the Sirdar again changed his mind and delayed their departure until daybreak. Argument fell on deaf ears.

Akbar Khan told Johnson, after Mohammad Shah Khan went to parley with the Pass chiefs, that the latter were dogs and no trust could be placed in them. He urged Johnson to summon three or four of his closest friends to accompany him in the event of the troops being betrayed. Johnson appreciated the chief's advice but explained that the officers would not desert their men in this time of great danger. The Sirdar then proposed that, in the event of the Ghilzais not agreeing to the terms, he would, himself, with a party of men ride to the foot of the hills where the troops were, at dusk, and bring away every European, mounted behind each of his men. The Ghilzais would not fire for fear of hitting his followers. He would not, though, allow a single Indian soldier to be rescued as he could not protect 2000 (sic) men. Johnson interpreted this for the General who deemed it impracticable as, from past experience, he knew how impossible it was to separate the soldiers from the camp followers. From time to time they heard firing from the valley but were assured all fighting had ceased. This was inaccurate in that ever since the officers had left for the Sirdar's camp, the troops had constantly been under fire, several hundred being killed and wounded.

The remainder, starving, cold and dying of thirst determined to make one last desperate effort to leave Jagdalak. Anxiety and nervousness was increased by the absence of Elphinstone and Shelton. Decisions had, therefore, to be made by Brigadier Anquetil, the commander on the spot. Ordering them to fall in at 8 o'clock in the evening, they were harried by the camp followers and did not therefore leave Jagdalak until about 9. Heartrendingly, they had to leave their wounded behind, well knowing that they would be slaughtered by the first party of Ghilzais coming upon them. Discipline was at low ebb, compounded by the enemy constantly attacking the rear of the column. However, because of the relatively unexpected departure, the road blocks that the column came across in the Pass were only lightly guarded and therefore pushed through but with difficulty as the road was flooded with ice and the sides in deep snow. Brydon was riding a horse, with some other wounded officers close by on a camel, when his orderly rushed up, saying he had lost his pony and implored him to take him up behind. There was no time to do so as, at that moment, he was pulled off his horse and knocked down by a blow on the head from an Afghan knife, which might have killed him had he not had a copy of *Blackwood's Magazine* in his forage cap. As it was, a piece of bone about the size of a wafer was cut from his skull. Stunned, he scrambled to his knees, seeing a second blow coming. He parried it with the edge of his sword, cutting off some of his assailant's fingers. The knife fell to the ground and the attacker made off. Brydon had lost his horse, cap and a shoe. His orderly was dead and he never saw the other officers again.

About two miles out of Jagdalak, the leading troops came across another barricade of trees and bushes across a narrow gorge with low steep hills on either side. The ambushing enemy attacked in considerable force, with knife in hand. The camp followers and wounded men fell back on the handful of soldiers for protection, which caused confusion and hampering the troops trying to tackle the enemy. The odds were heavily against them. Brydon, scrambling over the obstacle, received a sharp blow on the shoulder from an Afghan running at him from the hill. He managed to grab hold of Captain Hopkins's stirrup leather and walked with him for some distance. He was met by a saddler from the Shah's cavalry on horseback, who told him he was wounded and dying, so implored Brydon to take his pony or someone else would. Brydon tried to encourage him but he fell off, shot through the chest, dead. Mounting the pony, Brydon pushed on to the front where he met Anquetil who asked how things were going in the rear. He told him and Anquetil then rode back and was not seen again. Men were running up the hills, throwing their weapons away and control was completely lost. Captain Bellew rallied about forty horsemen to form some sort of advance guard. A few remaining horsemen galloped through the foot soldiers, trying to make their own way to Jalalabad, only to be fired on by the infuriated soldiers. Brydon, together with Bellew's men, slowly made their way ahead, with the watch fires of the predatory enemy in the hills. They were all dying of thirst and Brydon's shoeless foot in the only stirrup iron felt it was burning. Reaching the summit of the gorge, they were spared attacks for about an hour and could take stock of the devastation the enemy had caused. The ground was now more open which made it less easy for the enemy to snipe from and they reached the Sourkab River which they forded below the bridge at about 1 am. The pace had been reduced to about two miles an hour to enable the walking wounded to keep up. Fire was brought down on them as they forded the river from enemy on the bridge. Lieutenant Cadett of the 44th and several men were killed and wounded. At daybreak on the 13th, they found themselves at Gandamak.

At this stage they had lost all contact with those in the rear, including Brigadier Anquetil. The daylight showed up their predicament only too well. With enemy numbers increasing by the minute, the force now consisted of about twenty officers, with Major Griffiths the most senior, fifty men of the 44th, six of the horse artillery and four or five Indian sepoys. Among them, they could only rustle up some twenty muskets. 300 camp followers were still with them.

Brydon, who knew the countryside quite well having stayed there for three months earlier on, recommended an alternative route to Jalalabad over the hills, rather than through the Neemlah valley which contained a large village. There was no one really in command, so he left the main body with six officers, another doctor, a sergeant and five or six European soldiers.

Captain Souter gives an account of what happened in a letter, much later, to his wife. This is an extract;

'At Jugdulluck General Elphinstone and Shelton went over to Akbar Khan and other chiefs to offer terms, which they agreed to accede to.

While this was going on we were suddenly attacked, our men falling very fast and fighting bravely at the time during which, seeing the perilous situation of our Colours, I tore one from the staff and wrapped it about my person. Cumberland took the other, but was unable to button his great coat over it; he then handed it to Serjt. Carey, who secured it about him, but he fell during the night of our last march; the enemy pressing so close prevented our disengaging the Colour, and it was unavoidably lost.

Elphinstone and Shelton were not allowed to return to us, but were detained prisoners. In this state of affairs a night march was determined upon. The 44th, reduced to between 70 and 80 men capable of carrying arms, a few artillery men and the 5th Cavalry, and still an encumbrance of camp followers, etc, started at 8 o'clock at night. We soon came upon an encampment of the enemy who commenced following up our march, looting (stealing) and cutting up stragglers in the rear, until we came to a gorge between two ranges of low hills. Here the road was barricaded in two places with bushes, the progress of the column was stopped, and a hand to hand fight took place with the enemy, who had been in wait for us.

Here my horse fell with me, or rather, a trooper of the 5th Cavalry who, trying to pass me, pushed me down the side of the hill; the horse, from weakness (having been hit by two balls and having eaten scarcely anything for four days), was unable to rise, and I was unable to rise either, until two men raised the horse a little and I extricated myself. I lost the horse with my only remaining clothes that were on his back, and I felt the effects of the fall for a considerable time after.

At this time and place fell Brigadier Anquetil, Major Train, Dodgin, Dr. Harcourt and poor Halahan, Captain Nicholls, of the Artillery, and many other officers, including Captains Bott, Blair, and Bassett, of the 5th Cavalry.

On clearing the gorge, we mustered but half the force we started with. At 8 o'clock we continued our march, the enemy fearing to come near us, though we were reduced to a handful of men, but they kept up a fire upon us at a distance.

I took a trooper by force from his saddle and mounted his horse. We approached Gandamak as daylight appeared, which displayed to the enemy the smallness of our force.

The enemy increasing in numbers with the daylight, we were compelled to leave the road and take to a hill, before ascending which the trooper's horse was shot under me, staggered a few yards and fell. Some Affghan horsemen appeared, to whom we made a sign to come to us, which they did. Firing ceased, Major Griffiths and a Mr. Blewitt accompanied the party to negotiate with a neighbouring chief for a certain sum of money to let us proceed to Jalalabad. A great number of Affghans came up the hill, and appeared friendly with our people until they commenced snatching swords and pistols from the officers; this we could not stand, but drove them from the hill, and the fight commenced again.

After two hours, during which we drove the Affghans several times down the hill, our little band, (with the exception of about twenty men and a few officers of different regiments) being either killed or wounded, the enemy suddenly rushed upon us with their knives and an awful scene took place, and ended in the massacre of all except myself, Serjeant Fair (our Mess Serjt.) and seven men, that the more than usual humanity displayed by Affghans were induced to spare.

In the conflict my posteen flew open and exposed the Colour. Thinking I was some great man from looking so flash, I was seized by two fellows (after my sword dropped from my hand by a severe cut on the shoulder and my pistol missing fire), who hurried me from this spot to a distance, took my clothes from off me, except my trousers and cap, led me to a village, by command of some horsemen that were on the road, and I was made over to the head man of the village, who treated me well... my wound attended to.

Here I remained a month, seeing occasionally a couple of men of my regiment, who were detained in an adjoining village. At the end of the month I was handed over to Akbar Khan, and joined the ladies and other officers at Lughman'.

Eighteen officers and fifty men were killed at Gandamak bringing to an end one of the worst episodes in British military history.[15]

Brydon and his party, of course, were on another route, completely avoiding this and had no idea of the catastrophe. After the separation, they proceeded through the hills without seeing anyone for an hour or so, then rested and let their horses graze. Brydon's saddle was a high-pommelled wooden Punjabi version, carrying a heavy bag containing saddler's tools, bullets, a pistol, which none of the bullets would fit, a chain and spikes for picketing horses or spiking guns. He threw these all away but kept the pistol in his pocket. Shortly afterwards they came in sight of the village of Futtehabad on the plain, about fifteen miles from Jalalabad. It seemed quiet so Captain Bellew said he would go and see what the situation was. In a short time he was back saying all was well and that if they waited, he would go and collect some bread, promised by the headman of the village. In about a quarter of an hour he returned, regretting that he had been betrayed, as from the village, which was on a mound of high ground, he could see cavalry approaching from all sides. He guessed some signal had been given by the villagers to summon the cavalry. (They had actually seen a red flag waved, so that was probably it). He told the party to keep together and move slowly on. The

---

[15] A fragment of the Regimental Colour, rescued by Captain Souter, is today in the Regimental Chapel at Warley, Essex.

armed villagers approached, calling him to come back as they were friends. He did so and was immediately killed. At the same time the villagers opened fire and the cavalry charged amongst the group. An Afghan aimed a cut at Brydon, which he parried, then cut down Lieutenant Bird. It then became a complete rout with only Captains Hopkins and Collyer, Doctor Harper, Lieutenant Steer and himself escaping. The three former, being well mounted, left Brydon and Steer, saying they would send help. After riding a short distance, Steer said he could go no further, as both he and his horse were done. The horse was bleeding from the mouth and nostrils. Steer said he would hide in one of the many caves he knew in the hills about half a mile to his right. Brydon tried to persuade him to push on as the plain was sprinkled with people tending sheep and cattle, who would see him. He adamantly refused, so Brydon went on alone for a short distance unmolested. He then saw a group of about twenty men blocking his way. As he approached, they began picking up large stones, many of which were lying about. With difficulty, he set his pony at the gallop, and, taking the reins in his teeth, cut right and left with his sword as he went through them. They could not reach him with their knives and he was only hit with one or two stones. A little further on, he met a similar group, so he tried the same thing but had to prick his pony with the point of his sword to make it gallop. One of the enemy, on a mound, had a gun, which he fired close to him, breaking his sword, leaving a blade of about six inches. As he broke clear of them, he realised his poor pony had been shot in the loins and could hardly carry him.

As he moved on very slowly, he saw some five horsemen dressed in red. Supposing they were friendly irregular cavalry, he made towards them. To his horror, as he closed with them, he realised they were Afghans. They were leading Captain Collyer's horse. Brydon tried to escape but his pony could hardly move. The Afghans sent one man after him, who made a slash at him, defending himself with what remained of his sword, it was severed at the hilt. His assailant passed him and then turned round and charged again. Brydon then desperately threw the handle of his sword at the man's head and, swerving at the same time, managed to avoid the main thrust and only suffered a cut to his left hand. Feeling disabled, he reached down to his right to gather up the reins. His assailant clearly thought he was going for a pistol, and rapidly rode off. Brydon felt for the pistol in his pocket but it had gone. He was now totally unarmed.

He was now on a disabled horse, absolutely done in and with Jalalabad not in sight. Just as he was about to give up, he was spotted from the far off battlements of Jalalabad. 'About 2.0 pm on the 13th January some officers were assembled on the roof of the loftiest house in Jalalabad. One of them espied a single horseman riding towards our walls. As he got nearer it was distinctly seen that he wore European clothes and was mounted on a travel-hacked yaboo, which he was urging on with all the speed of which it yet remained master. A signal was made to him by someone on the walls which he answered by waving a private soldier's forage cap over his head.'[16]

Captain Sinclair, of the 13th, rushed out with his servant, who bound up Brydon's foot and he was taken into Jalalabad where his wounds were treated; he had a light

---

[16] Captain Henry Havelock, Adjutant of the 13th.

sword wound to his left knee, apart from his head and hand cuts and a graze where a ball had gone through his trousers. He had a good meal and then a sound sleep. A search party was despatched to scour the countryside for stragglers but only came across the bodies of Captains Hopkins and Collyer and Doctor Harper. A night later, a Mr Baness, a civilian employed by the Company was brought in but died of exhaustion the following day.[17]

Contrary to popular myth, Dr Brydon was not the only survivor of the retreat but one of a very few. Florentia and her group had left the main body as 'guests' of Akbar Khan on 9 January.

What had happened to them?

---

[17] The iconic painting of 1879 by Lady Butler 'Remnants of an Army' portrays Doctor Brydon arriving at the gates of Jalalabad.

CHAPTER 11

In the Hands of the Sirdar

Late in the evening of 13 January, Florentia and her party met up with the Sirdar's other hostages, General Elphinstone, Brigadier Shelton and Captain Johnson at Jagdalak. Little did they realise that, on that day, the remainder of the Army had been completely annihilated at Gandamak.

The next day they all started out at 9 o'clock, accompanied by Akbar Khan and about 600 of his cavalrymen, amongst whom were some deserters from the British army. The road was particularly rough with many ups and downs, which, on first sight, looked totally impracticable. In the 1000 foot ascent of the Adrak-Budrack pass, Florentia had to grip her horse's mane in case both she and the saddle should part company, but there was a superb view from the summit. In normal times, she thought, she'd have been very frightened, not being accompanied by a groom, but there was no time for that. Still, she enjoyed the wonderful scenery of the defiles they went through, but irritated by constant stopping and starting by those in front. Along the route, they passed 200 to 300 Indian soldiers who had escaped the massacre of the 12th up this unfrequented road. Most were naked and frostbitten, wounded and starving. They'd set fire to the surrounding shrubbery to try to keep warm. Florentia later learned that very few of them survived even after resorting to cannibalism. After an exhausting ten hour journey, the party had travelled some 24 miles and arrived at Fort Kutz, on the right bank of the River Punjsheer. It belonged to a Ghilzai warlord, Mohammad Ali Khan. They were forbidden entry so had to make do with a bivouac outside and, although they had descended into a milder climate, the wind was bitter. Enviously, Florentia saw the General, Shelton, Johnson and Melville invited into a cowshed filled with dense smoke from a blazing fire in the centre, but nice and warm. To make matters worse, these lucky officers were then asked to dine with Akbar Khan in the fort, where they had a sumptuous dinner. Florentia and the rest had some half-baked cakes of unleavened bread, lumps of tough mutton and some hot tea at midnight.

The next day, they started early and crossed two branches of the Kabul River, which was deep and rapid. To give them their due, the Afghans gave everyone a lot of help, Akbar Khan even carrying Mrs Waller behind him on his horse. Another rode alongside Florentia in the river, keeping her horse's head facing well upstream. In spite of their efforts, five horsemen lost their lives in the torrents. To their pleasure, a number of the camp followers' ferocious and mangy dogs, which had attached themselves to them, were left behind on the bank. At about 3 o'clock, having ridden a barren and waterless twenty miles to the north-east, they arrived at the fortified town of Tigree, in the rich valley of Lughmanee. The valley was studded with small forts and settlements, the inhabitants of which gave the group a good deal of invective, including to Eyre's gentlemanly surprise, to the ladies, whom they called immoral sluts and looking like scarecrows. The men they slanged as infidels and baseborn dogs who would face certain death before many hours had elapsed. The captives stonily ignored them. An important Afghan pilgrimage site, the tomb of Lamech, the father of Noah, was encountered on the way. They knew this was some twenty-five miles from Jalalabad. They spent a better night there with the General, Shelton and Johnson staying with the Sirdar and the rest farmed out to other houses in the town. Florentia and Alexandrina found themselves in an apartment of Gholab Moyenoodeen's fort. Somewhat to their surprise, they were very well looked after, their condition sympathised with and any request honoured where it could. They were given a lump of molasses filled with pistachio nuts; a popular delicacy. It was delicious. Vincent Eyre commented favourably on his Afghan gentry travelling companions, 'possessing a ready fund of easy conversation and pleasantry, with a certain rough polish and artless independence of manner, which, compared with the studied servility and smooth-tongued address of the Hindoostanee [Indian] nobles, seldom fails to impress our countrymen in their favour.' Not a bad accolade for men of a race that had just slaughtered his countrymen.

They stopped there for a day which must have been most welcome. Being a Sunday, out came a bible and a prayer-book that had been picked up at Boothak, and Florentia and her companions had a little Service. No sooner than it ended, when there was a sound of firing. It was nothing to do with them but a quarrel over some of the plunder that had been looted from the column or some blood feud with the neighbours. To their relief all went quiet after a good deal of shouting and noise.

On 17 January they were ordered to prepare to go higher up the valley. This was disappointing as it was *away* from the Jalalabad direction. The Sirdar had wanted to pause for a couple more days in Tigree but the population was becoming steadily more antagonistic. Hopes were dashed, and it was now very obvious that they were virtual prisoners, dependent on Jalalabad being evacuated and Dost Mohammad being replaced on the throne. They now had an additional escort of 200 Afghan infantrymen. This did not prevent the locals helping themselves to some of the remaining items of baggage the group still had. A number of their Indian servants also deserted, convinced the Sirdar had it in for them. They progressed along the valley, via a line of forts, for eight or nine miles, to Buddeeabad at the top of the valley in the hills towards Kaffiristan. They were accommodated in a large, new fort belonging to Mohammad Shah Khan, the Sirdar's father-in-law. It was built in a square of 80 by 80 yards, with 25 foot high walls, towers at each corner and a faussebraye[18] on the outside. The group were allocated six rooms, which formed two sides of an inner square. It was run by the Khan's secretary, the Meerza. Florentia speedily organised the allocation: Room 1; Lady Macnaghten, Captain and Mrs Anderson and two children, Captain and Mrs Boyd and two children, Mrs Mainwaring and one child, Lieutenant and Mrs Eyre and one child and Hester Macdonald. Room 2; their servants and baggage. Room 3; Captain Mackenzie and his Madras Christian servant, Jacob, Mr and Mrs Ryley and two children and Mr Fallon, a clerk from Captain Johnson's office. Room 4; Florentia and Alexandrina, Mrs Trevor and

---

[18] A faussebraye is a defensive wall located outside the main walls of a fortification. It is of a lower height than the main walls, and is protected by a ditch.

her seven children, her European servant, Mrs Smith, Lieutenant and Mrs Waller and child and Mr Mein. The remainder crammed themselves into the other two. For the seventeen European soldiers, two European women and one child (Mrs Wade, Mrs Burnes and young Stoker) there was a tykana.[19] Apparently, the rooms were intended for the chief and his favourite wife; those for his three other wives were in an outer court, not yet roofed in. It didn't take long for Florentia and Alexandrina to settle in with one mattress and a quilt between them and the clothes they were wearing when they left Kabul. Akbar Khan visited them, assured them they weren't prisoners and hoped they would be as comfortable as possible. He was happy for Florentia to write to Robert in Jalalabad and receive letters from him. She took advantage of this and wrote him a few guarded lines to say that they were safe. Little did they know they were to be there until 11 April.

The fort had no well but access to a small river nearby. (Surprisingly, it was unusual for forts to have wells inside the walls which, of course, made them very vulnerable to besiegers). Nevertheless, there was clean water to drink and plenty in which to have a proper wash, which they hadn't really had since leaving Kabul. It was a painful process as the sun and snow had taken toll of their complexions and skins had peeled. They had a good breakfast of dhal and large hot radishes which had gone to seed. The chapattis were made of coarse ground wheat which was not so good, and more than three of these could cause indigestion. Barley and rice was parched to make coffee. A couple of

---

[19] Cellar of a sort.

sheep were killed every day and the meat boiled in a pot with the rice, producing great greasy lumps of skin and bone. The chapatti was used as a plate and the food eaten with fingers. Rancid ghee, of the quality that Florentia would not even use in her lamps in India, was poured over the rice.

Mohammad Shah Khan had never acknowledged Shah Shuja, hated the British and had a malign influence over Akbar Khan. He was reputed to have been behind the seizure of the Envoy but not directly involved in his murder. Also present was Akbar Khan's cousin, Sultan Mohammad Khan, known as Sultan Jan, a handsome, vain and boastful man. Akbar Khan informed the group that the wounded Doctor Brydon, the sole survivor of the massacre he said, had reached Jalalabad. This fulfilled the prophecy, as they left Kabul, that the whole army would be annihilated with the exception of one man who would reach Jalalabad to tell the tale. Not a good omen for the rest of their trip. However, the Sirdar's plans had been completely thwarted by Sale's refusal to give up Jalalabad. The Sirdar still clung to the hope that an order from Major Pottinger (in theory the Envoy's replacement) to Captain Macgregor, the political authority there, to evacuate Jalalabad would be obeyed. He failed to understand that, with the prisoners he had, however powerful and senior he was, he was simply not free to act as he wanted. He was optimistic that Sale would have honoured the 'treaty', left Jalalabad for Peshawar, through the Khyber Pass, and be annihilated on his way by the Khyber clans.

The days in the fort were spent trying to improve their living standards and obtaining news, particularly, of course, their own fate. The Afghans were masters of spreading false rumour and obfuscation, what nowadays would be called 'fake news.' However, the captives, for that is what, realistically, they must be called, were no slouches at gaining their own intelligence. For instance, on 18 January, Akbar Khan and Sultan Jan departed with lots of noise about attempting the taking of Jalalabad but Florentia received a letter from Robert, dated the 19th, saying the force could hold out in Jalalabad for six months and she calculated that Colonel Wylde must have arrived there, with 5000 men on the 22nd. There was also the rumour that General Pollock was on his way across the Punjab with an army. Anyway, Akbar Khan and Sultan Jan called on Florentia on Sunday 23rd and were happy to take a letter from her to Robert. Abdul Guffoor Khan, an ally although on the Khan's staff, said that Robert was quite well. So what happened to the Sirdar's attack on Jalalabad? Nothing more said. Another absurd rumour was that Shah Shuja had demanded Conolly and the other three hostages be given up to him to have them executed. This was refused by Zeman Shah Khan, who had them in his custody. Another *canard* was that General had given permission for Anderson's cavalry to desert to the enemy. This was hardly likely, especially as he had suggested that Anderson should return from captivity to his men as their morale was suffering in his absence. So, lots of rumours and gossip floating around.

Clean clothes were becoming a problem for the party and, to their horror, the ladies discovered lice amongst their garments. To persons of a delicate constitution this was a nightmare but Eyre sardonically observed that, after time, even they could look these intruders in the face without screaming. Akbar Khan obtained a quantity of chintz which they divided amongst themselves to make new clothes;

many of them now adopting Afghan styles out of necessity and common sense. He also produced eight pieces of long cloth which looked suspiciously as though it had come from their own looted baggage. To manage their administration, a Mehmandar – a man of all work, a factotum – was appointed, one Moossa Khan. This individual spent most of his time feathering his own nest at the expense of the captives; a rogue even by Afghan standards. He hoodwinked Lady Macnaghten into paying him with expensive Cashmere shawls and, twice, induced her to pay him twenty rupees for recovering her favourite cat, which he had stolen himself. Anyway, as a trusted intriguer of the Sirdar's, he was removed for other nefarious tasks and replaced by Meerza Bawndeen Khan. This individual had originally styled himself Syud, a holy man, but changed his name to Khan as being more warlike and distinguished. On the outbreak of the rebellion, he had been imprisoned on the suspicion of favouring the British but, on the arrival of Akbar Khan, was released since he had befriended the Khan when a prisoner in Bokhara. Although he was boorish and took little trouble to be pleasant, he was better than his predecessor. An additional improvement to their lives was to have their meals cooked by their own Indian servants rather than the Afghans who would produce boiled mutton and rice, and unleavened bread at irregular intervals.

Akbar Khan and Sultan Jan, whose headquarters was now in Trighurree where they were preparing for the siege of Jalalabad, paid a visit on 23 January to ask Major Pottinger to write to Captain Macgregor, in Jalalabad outlining everything that had occurred since the Army left Kabul. Presumably to help this along, the Sirdar distributed 1000 rupees to everyone but still could not help interfering with the draft of the letter. Mrs Trevor's boys and some of the men were allowed to walk in the sugar-cane fields outside the fort, which they enjoyed.

What, of course, they didn't know was that Elphinstone had been relieved of his command. On 28 January, the Governor-General, Lord Auckland, wrote this to General Sir Jasper Nicolls, Commander-in-Chief:

'We do not doubt that Major-General Nott will have rejected the authority of any directions which may have been sent to him by Major-General Elphinstone, of a like nature to those sent to Jalalabad ; we would request your Excellency expressly to instruct him to act for himself, independently of such directions, upon his own distinct military responsibility. Your Excellency will communicate to Major-General Nott, that it is of the highest importance that he should maintain his position at Candahar, in concentrated strength, until he should receive further orders from the Government.

We have not received, since the commencement of the insurrection at Cabool, any dispatch, either in the political or military department, from the British authorities at that place; and, on our present information, we are disposed to view the conduct of Major-General Elphinstone in command of the force there, with the most severe displeasure and indignation. Your Excellency will of course cause a full military inquiry to be made into all the circumstances connected with the direction and conduct of our troops at Cabool, at the earliest period at which such an inquiry may be practicable. In the meantime, we think it right to direct that Major-General Elphinstone shall not retain the command of the troops to the west of the Indus, but that the command of the force at, and beyond, Peshawar shall remain with Major-General Pollock. It is our direction also, that the local command at Jalalabad should be vested in Major-General Sale, subject only to the direction of Major-General Pollock, and the authority of Major-General Elphinstone should at once wholly cease.'

The final nail in poor Elphinstone's coffin.

29 January was a memorable day; the prisoners received a batch of letters and newspapers from Jalalabad, together with a quantity of clothes and other comforts. It was a real morale raiser to have communication with the outside world and know that their plight was at the forefront of their brother officers' minds. There was some sort of basic code of dotting letters in the newspapers which would be indecipherable to the Afghans. Thus they were told the news of Wylde's failure in the Khyber Pass and withdrawal back to Peshawar, and General Pollock's march from India. There was also news of Doctor Brydon's epic escape and the deaths of those who had been with him, and other survivors of the massacre near Futtehabad.

Amazingly, Robert managed to send Florentia a chest of drawers containing her clothes. They came entirely untouched and unexamined. She wrote to him by hand of her new friend Abdul Guffoor Khan. She managed to keep up her correspondence with her husband, sometimes intermittently, but, given the circumstances, it was a major achievement. Robert also sent her some boxes of books and 'many useful things' which were a great treat. On the other hand there was gloom at the news that their horses and servants were to be removed. This may have been due to the Sirdar's anger at suspecting, with a certain amount of justification, that a secret correspondence had been going on between Pottinger and Macgregor. Furthermore, for the same reason, the officers were told to hand over their arms which, up to now, they had been allowed to keep. When challenged, Pottinger freely admitted to holding onto them on the basis that he had given the Sirdar no promise that he would not do so. The art of the double negative; he was not a 'political' for nothing. Akbar Khan warned him to desist and darkly reminded him of the Envoy's fate. The arms were then removed from the officers with the promise that they would be returned when they left. Florentia took her son-in-law's sword herself to Akbar Khan and begged the Sirdar to keep it personally that they might be sure of its safe-keeping as it was invaluable to his widow. However, the Afghan chief would not take it and insisted, with much feeling and emotion, that she should keep it. However, not content with taking the arms off the officers, the Afghans pretended that their servants were concealing more, so they were thoroughly searched and fleeced of the few remaining rupees they had. Florentia received a large batch of letters from her family in India and from friends in England but nothing from Robert.

On 15 February, the tedium of prison life was relieved by the arrival of Major Griffiths, 37th Native Infantry, and Mr Blewitt, a pay clerk who had all taken prisoner at Gandamak. Griffiths explained what had happened at Gandamak and how he and Blewitt, as interpreter, had tried to parley with the enemy. They had been made prisoner and taken to a village a couple of miles away where they were later joined by Captain Souter, who had been spared by wrapping the Colour round his waist. That night they were taken to the Sirdar's fort, four or five miles further into the hills, where they found three or four European soldiers who had escaped the massacre and been taken prisoner. Some days later, five more Europeans were brought in. Communication was established with Jalalabad and Griffiths had high hopes of obtaining their release by ransom. However, nothing could be arranged owing to the jealousy of Ghobam Jan Uzbezee, in whose power they were. After twenty days in captivity, Sergeant Major Lisson of the 37th was allowed to go to Jalalabad to explain the situation. Two prisoners died in the meantime. The man who accompanied the Sergeant Major to Jalalabad returned the third day and told them all was well. He had received 500 rupees ransom for the Sergeant Major who remained in Jalalabad. Hopes, though, of release were dashed when Akbar Khan heard about it and demanded they remain his prisoners. After some discussion, it was agreed and the prisoners were marched to Charbagh, and then on to join the others in Buddeeabad. Major Griffiths had been severely wounded in the arm earlier on and his wound was now in a bad state. A couple of days later, Captain Souter arrived, having been handed over to the Sirdar by the chief who had captured him.

Gunfire could be heard in the distance but it was thought to be some sort of salute being fired in Jalalabad. Quite what for, no one could guess. There was yet another rumour that Shah Shuja was still in Bala Hissar and raising a force to attack Jalalabad. Why and how, they asked themselves? This force was to be commanded by his son, Fatteh Jang. But no more was heard of it. Anyway, the captives discovered that their horses were now *not* to be taken away and everything was to be done to make them more comfortable. Florentia, sardonically, commented, 'Fair words butter no parsnips.'[20]

On 19 February, the air was extremely close and had been since a very heavy fall of rain a few days before. Then at 11 o'clock, there was a violent shuddering of the earth, which got so bad that it was difficult to stand. Large chunks of the main walls fell in with thunderous crashes. Subterranean rumbles were heard, seeming like a boiling sea of lava, lifting up the ground in waves, rocking the buildings. Florentia had gone upstairs in her house to see to her laundry, which was drying on the flat roof when the earthquake struck. She kept her balance as well as she could until she felt the roof giving way. She shifted her position just as the ceiling of their room fell in. As she descended the stairs, the ceiling there fell in around her but, by some miracle, she was unhurt. Of course, she was mainly worried about Alexandrina and could only see a pile of smoking rubbish. To her joy, there was cry that all were safe, and the others were delighted to see that she was all right. The earthquake originated in the hills in the upper part of the valley and rumbled downwards; in Florentia's self-admittedly soldiers' words, 'like the action of an exploding mine.' There were several more shocks during the day, then a number at night. They, sensibly, spent the night in the courtyard. The end wall in Lady Macnaghten's room had sunk by two feet and the beams damaged. General Elphinstone was ill in bed but rescued by his soldier servant, Moore, a private in the 44th, who carried him out in his arms. Whatever people might have thought of the General, he was

---

[20] *Fine* words butter no parsnips – 17th Century expression.

much respected by the soldiery and they were devoted to him.

The Afghans were terrified. Although seismic shocks were fairly common, this one was particularly violent and was the worst in living memory. The fort was relatively unscathed compared with the rest of the area but many of the others were badly damaged and scarcely a house remained standing in Tirghurree, with hundreds killed. When workmen arrived to clear the rubble, they said that this fort suffered least of about forty in the valley. In one, a tower collapsed, killing five women and a man, with not a wall remaining standing. Lady Macnaghten's cat was buried in the debris but dug out again unharmed; one of its lives gone.

The following day, Florentia wrote to Robert to tell him they were safe but they'd had a bad night. The officers gave up their largest room to Florentia's party as hers was now roofless. It had been very cold overnight and, by morning, their clothes and bedding were saturated with dew. Minor shocks continued throughout the day. Some people rigged up awnings over areas of the courtyard in which to sleep but Florentia and Alexandrina preferred to be indoors. A prop was erected to keep up the ceiling, but a shockwave seemed as though a heavy ball had been rolled over it. By now, happily, Florentia's wounds had completely healed. The Afghans, once they had recovered their poise, were very optimistic that the earthquake had levelled the walls of Jalalabad and they were just going to walk in. Clearly it was an auspicious sign from the Prophet to help them on their way. (In fact their prayers were answered; walls of the fortress, which had been painstakingly built up by Robert's men on arrival, were indeed demolished by the earthquake on 19 February. However, urged on by the encouragement and strong leadership of their officers and non-commissioned-officers, his men rebuilt the perimeter walls in a remarkably short time).

On 23 February, Captain Bygrave, who was a paymaster, so not someone one would expect to be in the forefront of the battle, arrived with a story of his adventures. He was not in good shape, having lost all the tips of his toes to frostbite. After starting from Jagdalak on the night of the 12th January, he was one of the first to get over the road-block of thorns choking the Pass. Collecting some soldiers who had done the same, he gave them a rousing talk about holding together and keeping discipline to save their lives. If they did so and if they wished it, he would lead them but they would have to obey his orders. The men cheered him and promised to obey such a leader. For three or four miles they kept their cohesion and held the pursuing enemy at bay. However, under repeated Afghan cavalry assaults, the little band started to disintegrate and simply could not push on down their route. The only thing for it was to leave the main road and head into the hills to find an alternative way to Jalalabad. He left the few remaining men and, with Mr Baness, a merchant supplying the Army, he struck off northwards to avoid the pursuing Ghilzais. Sensibly, by day, they took cover, sometimes in the tall bulrushes of the mountain streams, sometimes in the thick foliage of the mountainside evergreen shrubs. All they had to live on were a few grains of coffee and the wild liquorice root growing on the banks of the Sourkab River. Travelling only by night, they found navigation, without map or compass, extremely difficult. At one point they found themselves on a road, which looked promising, until they came across the mangled body of a European soldier. Fearing they were walking into more mayhem they retraced their steps for a number of miles. This continued for four long nights and days, with Bygrave becoming more and more incapacitated through frostbite and lameness. He suggested to Baness that they should find the nearest village and throw themselves on the mercy of the inhabitants. Baness thought this far too risky and, despite his reluctance to desert his companion, for the sake of his large family, he said, he must make his own way to Jalalabad. Even having left, he returned to Bygrave twice to try to persuade him to fresh exertion, without success.[21] After a long sleep, Bygrave managed to walk and crawl a few miles further. The second night after Baness's departure, he came upon a Ghilzai village (Kutch Sourkab, four miles north of Gandamak and twenty-eight from Jalalabad) where he lay up under some straw in a cave. He gave himself up the following morning to the first person who approached the cave. With a bribe of some gold, which he still had, he was taken to the hut of the village headman, Nizam Khan, who treated him with the utmost kindness and consideration for a number of days before handing him over to Akbar Khan. The Sirdar was then camped at Charbagh, preparing gun ammunition for the siege of Jalalabad. He had several of the British abandoned guns from which the Afghan smiths managed to remove the spikes.

Florentia would have loved to have known the contents of a letter written on 24 February by the Governor General to Major General Pollock but, sadly, even her intelligence sources were not up to the clandestine communication

---

[21] Baness made it, exhausted, to Jalalabad but died two days later.

between these luminaries. In essence, it suggested that there was no reason to make any great effort, at present, to contemplate the re-occupation of Afghanistan. Obviously, this was highly secret because, if known, it might encourage some of the opposition. It was left up to the judgement of Major General Pollock how to handle such incendiary information.

The letter went on to maintain Pollock's first priority was the rescue of the prisoners and bring them safely to Peshawar. How it was to be done was up to him. However, it was considered that this might best be achieved by 'reserve and delay' rather than by eagerness and ready expenditure which would only encourage others to take advantage of enriching themselves. Furthermore, Pollock was advised, rather than use his own official agency, to employ the private channels of Hindu merchants and bankers but nothing should be paid until the captives were safely in Peshawar or, at least, on the eastern side of the mountains. Pollock, and his subordinate officers, were urged to take particular care over the financial arrangements of such transactions. While the freedom of Lady Macnaghten was highly desirable, it must not jeopardise the general release of the other hostages. Although negotiation with Akbar Khan is generally discouraged, in this case it would be acceptable as long as no commitment was made in relation to the freeing of Dost Mohammad. This was a matter of state policy and must be decided by central Government. [A note dated 29 March from Captain Macgregor in Jalalabad to General Pollock made it quite clear that Akbar Khan would not negotiate unless the terms included freedom of his father, Dost Mohammad, and his family.]

In other words, over to you Pollock but spend as little as possible and don't commit yourself to anything. So no change there then.

Rumbling of the earthquake went on for several days, described by Florentia as a heavy ball rolling over their heads or a snake writhing in the sea. At times, she said, it was just like waves crashing into the side of a ship. More rumours abounded. One was that Sultan Jan had lured troops from Jalalabad to pursue him into an ambush and inflicted considerable casualties. Another was that General Pollock had arrived, with full political power, in Peshawar with an army of 5,000 to deal with Afghanistan. Dost Mohammad was said to have accompanied the army, others, that he had escaped from Ferozepore. A day or so later, a man arrived from Jalalabad confirming that there had been some action but nothing like the rumour; four of the 13th had been killed and four taken prisoner. Sultan Jan had a narrow escape, many of his men having been cut up.

On 3 March, Lady Macnaghten's and Captain Lawrence's possessions were searched on some hollow pretext. Lady Macnaghten's collection of Cashmere shawls were minutely examined, no doubt to establish their worth, but, to the disappointment of the searchers, no jewels were found. Nothing, though, was taken from her on this occasion. More happily, though, Florentia received two letters from Robert, dated 11 and 16 February. Disgracefully, every servant whose feet were frost-bitten, was stripped and evicted from the fort. Some of their limbs were withered and blackened and others had lost feet at the ankle. They were dragged over rough ground to the fields, without food or shelter. The author of this atrocity was the fort's owner, Mohammad Shah Khan, but it was the Meerza who had to carry out the order, quietly letting some back into the fort by night.

At night, a week later, there were shouts of, 'Murder, murder.' A servant girl of Florentia's was attacked by a disappointed suitor, one Mr Husnoo, and, when she put up a fight, he ran, and, jumping over a wall, hurt his back. Quickly apprehended, he was severely flogged and narrowly escaped hanging by the intervention of the officers who persuaded the Meerza merely to banish him from the fort.

On 11 March, Dost Mohammad (another Dost, not Akbar Khan's father) appeared from the Sirdar's camp and had a long conference with Major Pottinger. Of course, this riveted the captives. What could it mean for them? Not unnaturally, rumours flew with abandon. It was supposed that Akbar Khan had made some sort of overtures to the Indian government to have his father released. Khoda Bux Khan, a powerful Ghilzai chief, had left Akbar Khan's circle and there was clearly some power struggle going on. It was guessed, therefore, that Pottinger was being sounded out as to whether Macgregor, in Jalalabad, would sanction, politically, the British joining the Sirdar against Shah Shuja. Colonel Palmer, at Ghazni, sent Macgregor a draft of the terms for handing over the town. Macgregor refused to ratify it and forwarded the draft to General Pollock who passed it back to Pottinger via Akbar Khan. In the meantime, Ghazni was to be provisioned by the chiefs. Dost Mohammad said, although quite how Florentia knew, that Shah Shuja had written to Macgregor telling him to vacate Jalalabad, but, at the same time, the messenger was, verbally, to tell him to do no such thing. Wheels within wheels. None of this had any effect on Robert Sale at

Jalalabad, who led a strong sortie out of the fort to deal with some Afghans trying to mine the walls. The enemy were then lured into an ambush on their retreat and many of them killed.

The Meerza hedged his bets by cajoling the captives to sign a document to say how well they had been treated. This did not fool any of them, least of all Florentia who clearly saw through it, but probably told the others to sign. She also found out that the Sirdar had asked Lady Macnaghten that if she had no need of the three grooms over at another fort, he would send them to Peshawar. To Florentia, this was cynicism in the extreme, her ladyship had no need for grooms; she had no horses, they had been taken from her by Akbar Khan himself or Mohammad Shah Khan. Mrs Boyd gave birth to a child, adding, as Florentia unkindly put it, 'another to our list of female captives.' She was very quiet though, at this point, about the pregnancy of her own daughter. She was told that Jalalabad had fallen which was totally untrue and the Meerza took the trouble to come to tell her that the news was false and she shouldn't upset herself about it. More bet hedging? Anyway, he was replaced a short time later by the Nazir, the head of the household, so maybe the Sirdar worked out what he was up to. Florentia now referred to her husband, no doubt with pride, as 'Fighting Bob' Sale.

Assassins were now on the prowl. The Sirdar was shot in the left arm by one of his own followers who had been bribed by Shah Shuja with a lakh of rupees. He was caught and disembowelled in accordance, as Eyre laconically put it, 'with Afghan custom in such cases.' Florentia was told it was all an accident but before the wretched man could prove it, he was burnt alive. There was even a rumour that

Macgregor had instigated the same thing but bribed Akbar Khan's cousin to do the deed. The cousin was found out and his complete family were then put to death. Florentia observed that nothing was too savage or brutal for Akbar Khan who once had a man skinned alive, starting at his feet and working up his body until he died. However, even bigger news was the assassination of Shah Shuja. No rumour, he really was killed by Shuja Dowla, the eldest son of Nawab Zeman Khan, with a double-barrelled shotgun as they were travelling to the camp at Seeah Sung. The old king had been at his killer's birth and given him his name. He was, therefore, his god-father. This now threw a major factor into the Afghan melting pot of loyalties and treachery.

Florentia had not been idle; she organised a temporary shed for those turned out of their rooms by the earthquake, obtained stools to sit on, *charpoys* (sort of bed/hammocks) to sleep on instead of the ground and a *cujava* (block of wood) with boards nailed on it for a table. She had also fallen in with the new Nazir, who said that the Meerza cheated the captives out of their allowance, and that two sheep and twenty chickens were to be distributed daily, together with one *seer* (a little over a kilogram) of rice and one of ground wheat to each room, with a proportionate amount of ghee. Raisins, sugar and tea was to be issued monthly. It would not be long before he came under her control, just as she had had the Meerza doing much of her bidding. 'Little fingers' and 'wrapping around' were words which came easily to mind.

A little ominous on 21 March; the inhabitants of the valley were said to be moving their families and property into the hills for safety. The Afghans maintained that it was merely the nomadic Ghilzais moving their cattle, as normal in the spring, to higher pastures, having wintered them in the warmer Lughman valley. Nevertheless worrying for the captives; was there something that the Ghilzais knew that they didn't? A good sign of the arrival of spring was Lieutenant Melville presenting a bouquet of narcissus to the ladies but not so good was the shoeing of their horses by a blacksmith. Did this mean an imminent move? A report came in from Jalalabad that some troops had at last arrived there having lost a considerable number of men forcing the Khyber Pass. The nearby forts were filling with wounded Afghans and Akbar Khan had failed to have any success with his skirmishing at Jalalabad.

The Nazir tried to sound out the captives as to what ransom they thought they were worth. He thought one and a half to two lakhs of rupees might be about right? Part of the deal would be that the General, Major Pottinger and Captain Lawrence would remain in Afghan hands until the money was paid. The General held a conference with the officers to discuss it. Florentia was furious that she was excluded from a decision personally affecting her in which she had had no say. Anyway, it was referred to Macgregor and felt to be merely a feeler by the Afghans to see how much their prisoners were worth. What Florentia called, with a curl of the lip, Afghan 'wit.' Letters arrived from Jalalabad with the good news that all was well although one officer was wounded and another hit with a spent ball. Substantial reinforcements were expected by 1 April. News was that they were already approaching the Khyber Pass, whose tribes had been bought over by the British political agents, but Gholab Singh, a Sikh warlord, had claimed the honour of keeping the Pass open. Sultan Jan and

Mohammad Shah Khan were said to be taking 3000 (Eyre reckoned nearer 1000) men to oppose this force which could be a nuisance in the Cholah Khyber, between Lallpoorah and Hazar-i-now. Ghazni had surrendered to the Afghans, after the destruction of the 37th Native Infantry, but, contrary to earlier rumours that the prisoners were going to be taken to Bokhara to be sold as slaves, the officers were well, safe and taken care of. On Easter Sunday Florentia wrote to her husband, no doubt to include the news of four earthquakes before breakfast and more that night.

Further good news from Jalalabad; Macgregor had agreed the captives should be ransomed and Robert Sale made another successful sortie, obtaining a large number of cattle. Rumours of a possible move were getting stronger and the locals were becoming very civil and asking that their lives be spared. Florentia assured them they would be safe and well treated if they behaved properly. What Florentia called a 'famous hoax' was going the rounds that they were all going to be ransomed for three lakhs of rupees, they were to leave Buddeeabad the following Wednesday, Sultan Jan had been defeated in the Khyber and that Akbar Khan had fled to Kabul. Additionally, Akbar Khan had withdrawn all his patrols, hostilities had ceased, Dost Mohammad had arrived at the Attock and that, as soon as he entered the Country, all prisoners would be released and the British were to leave the Country, leaving the Dost to rule as best he might. Sanity and equilibrium was regained with a letter to Florentia from Robert proposing to have more shoes made and sent to her. There was nothing of the foregoing and she surmised they were not going to leave the Country soon. Pottinger, gloomily, reinforced this by reckoning they were going to remain there for another six months.

Meanwhile, in Jalalabad, Macgregor had seized a flock of 200 sheep, 20 head of cattle and 20 camels which were passing by the fort. Apparently, Akbar Khan, understandably infuriated by this, made a plan to snatch the garrison's ponies when taken out to water. However, an early morning patrol saw his troops moving to take up position and there was enough time for Sale to set up an ambush with a couple of rifle companies and kill 200 of them. He clearly had influence, as three local chiefs supplied grain to the garrison which they left outside the gate at night. Florentia was fascinated by the story of a brass 6-pounder gun. The Nazir told her that it had been brought in from the Khyber. It was now in the Sirdar's camp. The gun was the one possibly taken at Ali Masjid, the other end of the Pass, and, by bringing it into his camp, Akbar Khan wanted people to believe he had given up the idea of defending the Khyber Pass. The gun had been on the road for a month, exhausting six camels on its way. Actually, it was the one taken at Jumroad three months ago when the cantonment troops were out foraging and nothing to do with Ali Masjid and the Khyber Pass.

More gossip; the Nazir admitted that the two lakh ransom money was merely an opening gambit to test the resolve of the captives and their British commanders. For that, an emissary would go to Peshawar to negotiate and Pottinger held answerable for his safe return. More news came through; all the officers at Ghazni, less eight, had been killed. The garrison at Kandahar made frequent successful sallies. Shah Shuja got no further than the Bala Hissar gate when he was cut down by the son of Zeman Khan and sliced up into pieces. Three senior chiefs and 1000 Afghan cavalry went over to Macgregor and told him his enemy was ill prepared. Consequently there was a surprise attack on the Sirdar's camp at Charbagh with much slaughter and men running for their lives. Three guns were recaptured. Shah Khan escaped and Akbar Khan was dead.

No, he wasn't. He was eight miles away and heading their way.

Then Mohammad Shah Khan arrived at the fort to tell them that, apparently, there had been some earlier debate amongst the Afghans as to what to do about the prisoners. Some were for having them all killed straightaway but other, wiser heads, realising their ransom value and insurance in case things went against them, prevailed. Major Pottinger tried to negotiate their release but was, politely, told that they were to follow the fortunes of the Sirdar and to be prepared to head for the hills the following day.

Packing, unpacking, ready to move and then told they were staying. What was happening? Worrying for the captives and Florentia's morale raising abilities tested to the full.

What next?

CHAPTER 12

Death of the General

The next day, 10 April, they were indeed told to move early in the morning. However, no camels arrived until 3 pm. During a certain amount of disorder, Shah Khan seized the opportunity to plunder the captives' belongings, yet again. His first act was to select all their best horses for himself, although Vincent Eyre managed to hang onto his good one. He then went through Lady Macnaghten's baggage, helping himself to a number of valuable shawls and jewels. He also went through Captain Lawrence's kit. He demanded to see Florentia's boxes but did not go through them, knowing perfectly well that she had arrived with nothing. He had clearly forgotten that Robert had sent her bits and pieces from time to time. The Meerza returned and, together with the Nazir, promised Florentia that they would send a box of hers, which she could not carry, to Robert at Jalalabad, together with some servants, who were not allowed to travel with the rest of the party. She was highly suspicious when she saw them putting it into their own store and strongly expected them to keep it for themselves. However, to her glee, there was only rubbish and some small bottles in the drawers. She hoped the Afghans would drink the contents of the bottles, thinking they contained medicine, whereas one held nitric acid and another a strong solution of lunar caustic.[22]

After this circus, the group eventually set off. The European soldiers were left behind with the promise that they would be ransomed. The General's and Alexandrina's camels immediately collapsed and the General was stretched out on the ground until another could be brought. Lieutenant Melville gave his horse to Alexandrina. The Meerza, further ingratiating himself, took the fur-lined cloak and sword belonging to James Sturt, much treasured by Alexandrina, ostensibly for safe keeping. Unsurprisingly, he 'forgot' to return them later, such was the dishonesty of the man. It was, however, great to be leaving the harsh walls of the fort, their prison since the cold, dark days of January. Spring had now arrived and the valley was lush and green, with small trees in leaf. After about four miles towards Alishung, they were met by a party of horsemen who galloped up, joyfully waving their arms and shouting, 'Shabash' and 'Bravo.' The reason for their happiness was, they said, that the British had been cut up in the Khyber Pass and all their guns taken by Sultan Jan. Additionally, Jalalabad had fallen. Despite the improbability of this news, it cast understandable gloom on the captives who were told to turn round and return to the fort. On the way back, the horsemen related, with much satisfaction, how the British had bribed the Khyber Pass tribes with three lakhs of rupees for safe passage. No sooner than half the money was paid in advance than the bandits

---

[22] Lunar caustic is an effective oxidizing agent for removing warts, destroying damaged or diseased tissues, and for stopping superficial bleeding. Nasty to drink though.

colluded with Sultan Khan to ambush the leading and rear elements of the army in the narrowest part of the Pass.

However, the reality was that on 5 April, Robert, in Jalalabad, had heard through his spy network that General Pollock had met stiff resistance in the Khyber Pass. The following day a gun salute was fired by Akbar Khan's forces to celebrate this setback to their enemies. Robert therefore decided that his garrison could no longer wait for the relieving force to arrive. Surrounded by Akbar Khan's considerable army, he decided to take his chance. On 7 April, Robert left the town with his brigade and directly engaged Akbar Khan's besiegers. Attacking with three columns of infantry each with 500 men supported by guns of his field battery, they achieved considerable success against an enemy reckoned to amount to some six thousand men. By 7 am the following day, the enemy were in full retreat towards Lughman and the siege raised. Four guns, previously lost by the British were recovered. In just a few hours, Robert's force destroyed the Afghan enemy whilst suffering the comparatively low casualty rate of 14 killed and 66 wounded. Sadly, one of those killed was Colonel Dennie, commanding officer of the 13th. After the engagement, local chiefs accepted defeat and ensured that plentiful supplies came in to the market which was established outside the walls. Pollock's force finally managed to break through the Khyber Pass on 9 April and arrived near Jalalabad on the 15th. Robert arranged for the regimental band of the 13th to play them in with the old Jacobite air, *'Oh! but ye've been lang o'coming'*. Such was the achievement that the battle honour "Jalalabad" was awarded and a silver medal was later issued to those involved.

Depressingly, the party arrived back in the fort, though to the joy of those who had been left behind who, hearing shots, had thought them all killed. To Florentia's annoyance, a number of their comforts had been removed and mats etc. taken. However, the soldiers busied themselves to be useful, restrung Florentia's *charpoy* and brought a lamp and stools for her and Alexandrina. Some chickens were cooked and they had a good supper. These small kindnesses were very good for morale. The better news, however, was, as suspected, the horsemen's story was rubbish. The real cause of their about turn was a dispute among the chiefs, which might have led to an attack on the group, so the return was sensible, but they were told to be ready to leave again the following day. The inhabitants of the valley were fearful of an attack by the British and were sending their families into the hills for safety, as the captives had guessed earlier on.

After an early breakfast, they started off again. As before, the soldiers were left behind with the European women, Mrs Wade and Mrs Burnes, and the child, Seymour Stoker. Various maimed and disabled servants were also left. Florentia really thought the women should have come with them but was unable to persuade anyone in authority to allow it. After three miles on the Tirghurree road, they struck off to the hills to their right. The effects of the earthquake were very visible, no building was intact, very few habitable and most in ruins. They were now travelling in a westerly direction, skirting the base of the hills for four or five miles, then crossed a low bridge into the cultivated valley of Alishung. After crossing some rapids, they came across Akbar Khan in his palanquin. He looked ill and worn out but was very polite to them. Three tents had been pitched for them in a pleasant green spot. It was a beautiful area of cultivation with masses of flowers in bloom. They ate supper of some pretty tough mutton, their one meal of the day. That night it came down in torrents but they were reasonably dry in their tents.

During the night, Sultan Jan arrived with about thirty to fifty horsemen of the five hundred to a thousand he had taken to the Khyber. Florentia noticed how sunburnt he was. Tanned Englishmen, she thought, looked like Afghans but weathered Afghans looked like Indians. The Sultan was in a pretty bad way as a result of his defeat and, unlike the Sirdar, was sharp and uncommunicative with the captives. Akbar Khan, in Vincent's eyes a proper gentleman, was truly brave and attributed his setbacks to the fortunes of war while extolling the courage of the troops led by Robert Sale. The Khan was, clearly, a man of many parts; on the one hand a bloodthirsty killer and, on the other, a man of some sensitivity and empathy. Today's psychologists would be intrigued. Florentia was not so easily persuaded, though, as Vincent. He may well have had some of the qualities that Vincent applauded but, nevertheless, he was, unquestioningly, an out-and-out murderer.

Interestingly, the guards on their camp were entirely made up of Sikhs. They were under command of a Muslim Rajah who, having been banished many years ago by Ranjit Singh, had attached himself to Dost Mohammad when in power at Kabul, and remained loyal ever since. A fine looking man, he was well disposed towards the group and expressed his disgust with some of the Afghans who, when he left the Charbagh camp to do battle on their behalf, took the opportunity to plunder his men's possessions.

Setting off the next morning, the single men were separated from the rest of the group and started off on different routes. This was totally unacceptable and Captain Lawrence sought the Sirdar's permission to stay together. He also took the Sirdar to task for dragging the women and children around in such harsh conditions. They were simply, he said, not up to being treated like this. It was a disgrace. At this, Mohammad Shah Khan, who was present, flew into a rage. He said that the captives were to follow wherever he went, if their horses flagged they would have to trudge on foot. If they lagged behind, they would be dragged along by force. This was exceedingly unpleasant and Lawrence realised the power this man had over the Sirdar. However, Akbar Khan rebuked him for his rudeness and allowed the party to reunite and travel together. Surprisingly, Florentia made no comment on this; perhaps she did not know what had happened. On they pushed among low hills and gentle ups and downs, with one very steep ascent leaving the Adanek Beeduck Pass to their left. The country was arid, with no habitation or cultivation. The little water they came across was so shallow and sandy the horses refused to drink it. At one point, Akbar Khan passed them; bowed, smiling as he did so. Florentia was not fooled and remembered her Shakespeare, 'He can smile, and smile, and be a villain.'[23] They crossed a small stream about half way and then, after twelve miles or so, they arrived at the camp pitched in a narrow ravine, through which a small rivulet flowed. The ground was covered with tall reeds, to which the Afghans set fire at night. Quite why, Florentia

---

[23] 'That one may smile and smile and be a villain,' Hamlet Act 1 Scene 1

puzzled? Maybe to keep warm? Supper was two old goats which were completely inedible, so were sent back. They were replaced by some particularly tough old sheep. Moyenoodeen turned up from the Khyber, looking rather down in the mouth, according to Florentia, who shook his hand. Clearly, he was shy of making his acquaintance with her too public but asked, confidentially, how her wound was. He had been a friend of Robert Sale's in Kohistan and still professed to be a friend of the British but not openly, for obvious reasons.

Another twelve mile trek followed and, during one particularly difficult ascent, the ladies had to get out of their camel panniers and walk. Florentia always rode a horse and had her own saddle. Other women rode in what Florentia called 'gentleman fashion', presumably astride, sitting on their bedding instead of saddles. On the way, they gathered quantities of a curious herbaceous plant, the under surface of whose leaves were covered with a beautiful crimson dewy-looking substance, which the Afghan ladies used as rouge. Eventually they came to a partially cultivated valley with two small forts, badly damaged by the earthquake. The inhabitants had the reputation of being the greatest thieves in the Country, which rated them very bad indeed, said Vincent. There they pitched camp. The tents, really strips of ordinary soldiers' canvas, were small and hot. They lay in rows, crammed together on their bedding, nestling against each other.

The next day they covered about twelve to fourteen miles over rocky ground but easier than the day before. The exception was a 1600 foot ascent through the Bad-push, or Windy Back, Pass. With her soldier's eye, Florentia reckoned, with 100 Sappers, it could be made feasible for guns in a few days. There was much vegetation; hollyoak, wild almond, myrrh, ilex and a tree called Khinjuck which had a fragrant sort of gum which the Afghans use to treat flesh wounds. There was lots of mistletoe in its branches and a profusion of an evergreen shrub with a jasmine-like flower. At the far side of the Pass they were met by Mohammad Shah's sons with bouquets of tulips. They then marched on a tolerably good road, crossing the same stream at least twenty times. Following this stream for about six miles, they arrived on the left bank of the Kabul River which thundered down between some precipitous hills in a fast moving torrent, twenty feet deep in places. About a hundred yards from the bank, stood a small fort. From there they managed to cross the river on rafts, supported by inflated bullock hides. The horses had to make a four mile detour by crossing at a ford higher up although some more courageous swam the river. The river was not navigable from there to Jalalabad because of rapids and whirlpools. Their baggage and tentage was brought up at dusk but some of it had to wait until the following day. Akbar Khan was already there in his palanquin, so they paid their respects. It is interesting how the relationship between prisoners and their gaoler had developed into a relatively mutual acceptance of their different roles.

They didn't start until midday the following day but only covered a short journey of four or five miles. The scent of amaryllis and Persian iris filled the air. It was very hot and the ladies were irritated at not having camel panniers, so had to ride horses. The poor General was in a pretty bad way. He had left Buddeeabad very ill and the travelling had done him no good whatsoever. He was sinking fast. They had kept to the bank of the river for about a mile, and then suddenly turned up a ravine to the right. Two miles more brought them to a valley connecting with the Tezeen valley, about a mile up which they camped, not far from the fort, at Surroobee where they had last been on 12 January. One of the captured mountain-train guns was still there as were a number of their Indian servants who had been well treated by Abdoolah Khan, at least, those who had survived frostbite. There was a nasty rumour that the hostages left at Kabul had been murdered.

They spent the next three days where they were, which, in some ways, was a relief. However, they were warned to expect a long march into the Tezeen hills where they were to be hidden by the Sirdar. If pursued by a small force, the Sirdar would take them on into the Khoord Kabul, if large, he would immediately capitulate, so he said. News from Kabul was that there was considerable inter-faction rivalry between the Duranis and the Barakzais. The rumour was that the officers left behind in Kabul would be sent to join the captives at Tezeen, then everyone was to march to Herat which would take two months, after which they would go to Balkh. Akbar Khan was trying to rustle up support from amongst the local chief as his adherents were deserting him in droves. The Ghilzais, true to form, were stirring up the locals against the English with lurid tales of their barbarism and cruelty. Florentia went down with a fever.

The 19th was a really miserable day. It had rained solidly all night and now the prisoners had to walk sixteen miles through a continuous downpour to Tezeen. Florentia was still feeling very ill to the extent she could not ride her horse. Akbar Khan could only get hold of two camels with panniers but gave up his palanquin to Lady Macnaghten and Florentia. Even so, it was extremely uncomfortable; she had to sit backwards with nothing to lean against, with very little room, and maintain a balance with Lady Macnaghten and Mrs Boyd's baby. So there was little to say for it except the grandeur of the equipment. She shivered in her turban and clothes which were soaked through by the rain. The road was up a narrow valley the whole way, crossing a stream twice before reaching Seh Baba. There they were confronted by a putrid smell from the decomposed bodies lining the route. In some places, the bodies were piled high, not just with those killed by the Afghans but a number who had simply died of starvation and exposure. With some self-satisfaction, their Afghan gaolers told them that some had had to resort to cannibalism. From Seh Baba to Tezeen the road went steadily upwards, through a half a mile wide valley, hemmed in on both side by lofty crags. They passed several Ghilzai nomadic encampments but were left unmolested. Everyone was soaked to the skin, despite their sheepskin coats, so it was with relief that they arrived at Mohammad Khan's fort where they were to stay. The fort had been badly damaged by the earthquake and therefore their accommodation was scanty, nevertheless, they were greeted with kindness and three large log fires. The courtyard of the fort was a sea of thick mud and that evening the Afghans carried Florentia and the other ladies on their backs across it to a room where they were to spend the night. The ground was covered with coarse felt carpets, although their bedding was saturated. A meal was cooked for them of rice, sour curds, with ghee poured all over it. Florentia could not stomach this but, luckily, had some tea and sugar in a container strapped to her saddle. She was given some milk and this did her well. They then stretched out for the night still in their wet clothes. Having a shivering fit in the night, Florentia was covered with a cloak kindly given to her by Captain Anderson. Thirty-four of them slept in a room 15 feet by 12 beside the fire. Others were in a dark hovel or, like Vincent, bedded down with their horses in a stable. This journey effectively decided Elphinstone's fate. He was now clearly dying.

They stayed where they were the following day, still in wet clothes, having nothing dry to put on. Mrs Waller gave birth to a baby girl. It was astonishing how there had been three other births among the captive women with no suffering or ill effects. The power of Mother Nature. Captain Mackenzie was warned for a secret mission to Jalalabad to liaise with General Pollock on behalf of the Sirdar. He would not be permitted, to Florentia's annoyance, to take any private letters. However, she did secrete one, in pencil, to Robert, with a trooper who was to accompany the Captain. Akbar Khan had convinced himself that if caught by the British, he'll be blown from a gun or hanged. Having said that, he regarded himself as the only man who could safely escort the prisoners through the country. He was probably right on both counts. Alternatively, he reckoned he could raise 5000 men to attack the British. His anxieties were surfacing. It rained solidly all day, with a few earthquakes.

The next day started with sunshine, and tents were pitched away from the fort. Everyone, less the General, the Eyres, the Wallers, Major Pottinger, Captain Mackenzie and Doctor Magrath, moved over to them. There they were told that they were going to remain there for a day then move to Zenganah, where the snow was four feet deep, and remain there for four months. The owner of the fort, Atta Mohammad Khan was annoyed by the conduct of his kinsman, Mohammad Shah Khan in fomenting rebellion and hinted at his own wish to side with the British government. It seemed he was promised remuneration by Captain Macgregor for the damage done to his property by General Sale in October 1841, so that may have had something to do with it.

At a meeting, at which Major Pottinger was present, the Sirdar lost his temper. He shouted how he had been betrayed and deserted by his countrymen. All along he had acted entirely at the instigation of the chiefs in Kabul, especially, in the murder of the Envoy and the destruction of the British army. Now these very men refused to support him. If he ever got the power, he would make a severe example of them. Pottinger, sensing a kink in the Sirdar's armour, took him to task. It was barbarous, he said, to treat women and children like this; driving them about the country as he was doing. When the Dost and the ladies of his family, including Akbar Khan's wife, daughter of Mohammad Shah Khan, travelled to India, they went with every conceivable comfort and probably more than they would have experienced in their own country. The Sirdar accepted what he said and replied that he would do whatever they wished but Mohammad Shah Khan had gone to Kabul and he, Akbar Khan, who was totally reliant on him, could do nothing until he returned. He said he'd had a letter from India saying that the Dost was closely guarded by twenty sentries night and day and offered to show it to Captain Lawrence. It was irrelevant because, quite clearly, it was a fake. The Dost had a guard but far from being unpleasantly confined, he was allowed considerable freedom to go hawking and everywhere he went, he was escorted by a troop of cavalry as befitted his station, reflecting the status of the royal families in Delhi. Any restraint his ladies were under was entirely his affair.

That night, the ladies of Mohammad Shah Khan and other chiefs travelling with the captives, asked Mrs Eyre to dinner. She found them exceedingly kind and attractive. They were well dressed and good looking. They asked the old question as to the gender of the Company Sahib and were awestruck to learn that Great Britain was governed by a woman. They expressed their dread of Captain Macgregor whom they regarded as some sort of ogre out of a child's fairy tale.

Very early the following morning they were all woken and ordered to get going as soon as possible. A messenger had arrived from the Sirdar for Dost Mohammad Khan. With no warning, and the belief they were going to be there for a few days, confusion reigned for a time. Florentia was still too weak to ride her horse, so Mrs Boyd kindly gave up her place in a camel pannier to her, but she had to carry Mrs Boyd's baby. It was the first time Florentia had ridden like this and, being tall, and because the pannier was one of the smaller kind, she found great difficulty in tucking her legs under her in the approved fashion. According to Florentia, the reason for the sudden move was that a letter had arrived from Fatteh Jang, son of Shah Shuja, in the Bala Hissar in Kabul, saying that he was coming with 400 cavalry to carry off the prisoners to be used as a bargaining chip. Zeman Shah Khan, acting king in Kabul, also wanted the prisoners but Akbar Khan was determined to keep them. However both he and they were in the hands of their implacable enemy, Mohammad Shah Khan. Those in the camp, as opposed to those in the fort, left separately for the Zanduh valley, near the Aman Koh, about eight miles south of

Tezeen, while those in the fort were hurried off at 9 o'clock for a small fort higher up the valley. This virtually finished the General, who was so weak he could not stand, but was made to ride a horse the whole way. Florentia's group marched about twelve miles, crossing and re-crossing a stream many times. At one point they passed a mountainside fall, caused by the earthquake, near a cave where there were a large number of bodies. There was much blood around, indicating that cannibalism had probably taken place. Three wretches were seen, crawling on hands and knees just within the cave. They called out to the party but there was nothing the captives could do except give them their pity and the hope that their suffering would soon be overtaken by death. Ill and horrified that she was, Florentia still managed to make the military assessment of the ground and going: no guns, except the mountain train, could cope and infantry would be badly exposed to enemy on the heights, she reckoned. Taking a right hand valley, they did not go directly towards Tezeen, but headed in the Jubhar Khail direction, considered the strongest of the Ghilzai mountain fastnesses. They passed a small camp of mud huts inhabited by charcoal burners, who paid them scant attention. Ice was now six inches thick at the side of the road and deep snow further in.

Not fully recovered from her fever, and thorough soaking, Florentia was pleased to be told that they were going to stay in the next place for eight days. Akbar Khan sent their horses back to Tezeen, saying he could not feed them here. He did, however, receive 6000 rupees from Kabul, probably from his uncle, Nawab Jubbar Khan. Apparently, people were leaving Kabul in droves, terrified of being caught by General Pollock's army and no one was prepared to oppose his advance. This convinced the Sirdar to resurrect his plan to send Captain Mackenzie to Jalalabad to negotiate with General Pollock. Mackenzie was therefore put on short notice to move. In the meantime, someone had told Akbar Khan that Vincent Eyre was a bit of an artist, so he sent for him. What he really wanted was to quiz Vincent, an artillery officer, on fuses, port-fires, how shells were fired from mortars and howitzers, and how to measure the length of a fuse for different distances. Vincent gave away just enough to allow the Sirdar a little knowledge but not enough to be useful. Before he left, he asked Vincent to draw one of his followers and a favourite horse. Vincent did so, not terribly well he thought but the Sirdar seemed pleased. A sextant was then produced and Vincent explained how it worked but it was too damaged to be any use, so the Sirdar had the lenses removed to be made into glasses to protect his eyes from the glare. Sunglasses?

At 7 pm on 23 April, the General died. It was a happy release from all the physical and mental hardships he had so stoically borne. He had been totally unfit for the job and was the victim less of his own faults than the errors of others. He was respected for his humanity, patience and Christian benevolence by all, whether Afghan, Indian or British. The Sirdar had not realised how far gone the General had been and, had he known, he said, he would have released him earlier on but his supporters had deliberately kept him in the dark in order to use Elphinstone to their own ends. At 8 am the following day, Captain Mackenzie was sent on his mission. At midday, there was an alarm. Everyone was put on horseback and taken to a nearby fort. In the confusion, Mrs Waller and her two children were left behind. Mr Waller approached someone who could speak Persian to remonstrate with the Sirdar as to how shocking it was to leave a lady and two children to have their throats cut. With that, a small group went back and fetched them. An old camel pannier was found, strung together and some Afghans carried it on a pole, with the children perched on it. Their mother followed on foot. Three wives of one of the chiefs were also left behind in a great state of terror but they also managed, somehow, to catch up. Florentia, as usual, gripped the situation. Mohammad Shah Khan said he was not going to give the captives anything except *ottah* (ground wheat). Florentia suspected he was keeping everything else for the chiefs' wives. Not good enough in Florentia's view and she made Mohammad Rufeek, their current administrator; buy twelve sheep for them and Akbar Khan to send twelve camels to Kabul to collect rice and ghee. She organised small thick mats to sit on and their quilts and blankets to be hung up for walls and a roof, making it not uncomfortable to sit in by day.

On the 25th, the General's body was sent to Jalalabad for burial. A rough wooden framework was constructed by an Afghan carpenter and, having been well wrapped up in felt blankets, his corpse was packed into it. Spaces were filled with highly scented wormwood. At 2 pm it was slung onto the back of a camel and set off with a small guard of Ghilzais and his British orderly, Miller, disguised as a local. There was a report that Macgregor had negotiated a swap of Florentia's ladies and children for an equal number of Afghan wives and children in Ludhiana, with a release date in a few days. While in conversation with the Sirdar, letters arrived for him from Ludhiana, saying his family had been starved for a whole week. Everyone immediately condemned this as utter nonsense at which the Sirdar, bombastically, announced that true or false, it would not deflect him from his purpose. He then resumed the conversation with Vincent as though nothing had happened, telling him that, way back in Kabul, the daily loss of life from guns fired from the cantonments, when under siege, accounted for about thirty or forty casualties but the shells fired from the Bala Hissar did little or no damage to life or property in the city.

News came that the poor General's cortege was intercepted on its journey near Jagdalak. The group ran into the camp of a band of Ghilzai nomads and were challenged. They thought the best way was to assume an air of confidence and nonchalance and halt for the night. Miller was covered up in a thick blanket and warned to keep quiet until dawn. At about 10 pm, there were loud shouts of, 'Feringhee' and 'Kafir.' A rush was made to where he was lying and the covering over his head snatched off. Slashed in the arm with a sword, the thick felt of the blanket saved him from other cuts. He was rescued by a chief who hurried him off to his tent. The bandits then stripped the General's body and pelted it with stones. They would have burned it had not the Sirdar's men threatened them with untold vengeance from the Sirdar if they did so. When he heard this, Akbar Khan was apoplectic and sent as many men as could be spared to re-pack the General's body and rescue the European orderly.

In the course of conversation with Major Pottinger, the Sirdar asked him whether he would swear that he had written nothing to Jalalabad apart from that which the Sirdar knew about? There was a long silence, and then the Major said that, had the treaty been honoured, not a British soldier would now be in Afghanistan. Like a good politician, he did not directly answer the question. 'Swear this is true', the Sirdar insisted. Pottinger acceded, to which the Sirdar seemed now, for the first time, to believe what he had so vehemently doubted before. He looked around to his followers with an expression on his face which said, 'What a miserable fool I have been.'

It is possible that Akbar Khan suspected that Pottinger had sources of intelligence and some clandestine communication both with Robert Sale and General Pollock although he could not prove it. Eldred Pottinger was a past master in this sort of art and may well have had his own spy network with access to secret contact between Central Government and Pollock. He might well have been aware of the gist, if not the detail, of a communiqué of 26 April between Maddock, private secretary to the Governor General and General Pollock which read, 'It is naturally a subject of anxious consideration in what manner it may be most expedient to endeavour to effect the restoration to their country, of the prisoners now in the hand of the Affghans. The only safe and honourable course for a Government to pursue under such circumstances, is to effect the release of prisoners by a general exchange. The redemption of prisoners by the payment of a ransom, is a measure unknown to the modern practice of civilized nations, and which the Government of India cannot consent to revive. If the Affghans had any regular Government with which it was possible to treat for the general exchange of prisoners, such a measure would be the most consonant to policy, and there would, on our part, be no reservation whatever of any prisoners in our hands. But it is apprehended that the British prisoners are rather to be considered as being in the power of individual chiefs, and so held for the personal benefit of such chiefs in the matter of exchange or ransom, than as being the prisoners of any one chief, or the State; and it may be impracticable to make their release the subject of a general arrangement. If such should be the case, you are authorized to make such partial arrangements for the exchange of prisoners as you may deem most advisable, with this reservation, that the person of Dost Mohammad is not to be surrendered, in pursuance of any such partial arrangement, without the express authority of the Governor General; nor is any expectation to be held out, that it will be so surrendered. Your attention will naturally be, in the first instance, directed to the release of the female prisoners; the sympathies of all are engaged in their fate; nevertheless, the Governor General feels it to be right to remind you, that all British subjects have an equal claim upon the consideration and protection of the Government, and it is as much the duty of yourself, and of all the British authorities, to endeavour to effect the release of the last Sepoy, as that of the first European, by all means not tending to establish an injurious precedent, and consistent with the honour of the British Government.'

Still separated from Florentia's group in the Zanduh valley, Pottinger and Akbar Khan paid them a visit. The Sirdar asked Florentia not to be angry; things were very difficult to get hold of here but he had sent camels to Kabul for supplies. In the meantime, he produced some locally made shoes and cloth for them. Florentia organised some floor mats into arbours, woven with juniper but these failed to provide sufficient cover against the rain and hail that descended before nightfall. Back at their base, Vincent and Lieutenant Waller amused themselves by watching the

Afghans (Juzailchees – soldiers armed with the Juzail musket) at target practice. They were very accurate at 100 yards but so slow to reload that a British soldier would have got off four or five shots to their one. However, Florentia's earlier observation as to the accuracy of the Afghan marksmen against the wild firing of the British held true. To everyone's relief, the General's orderly, Miller, was returned unharmed. The bandits who had attacked him were now abject in their apologies for having offended the Sirdar, as well they might. The General's body had been repacked and sent on its way to Jalalabad.

A runner, carrying a message from Captain Conolly in Kabul to General Pollock, was intercepted by Akbar Khan's men, severely beaten and detained. If the contents were true, it was dynamite. It covered an agreement with Amenoollah Khan to be paid three lakhs and said that Kuhandil Khan (the Dost's brother), with 8,000 Persians was approaching Kandahar. Did this signify a rapprochement with Persia or what? Who was against whom? The Sirdar, returning to his base camp, was having his own problems paying his men, a number deserting for lack of back pay. On top of this, Amenoollah Khan and some other chiefs demanded that Pottinger, or twelve lakhs of rupees instead, should be handed over to them. Unsurprisingly, Pottinger's bills of credit for fourteen and a half lakhs, guaranteed by the Government, dependant on the safe arrival of the Kabul force at Jalalabad, had been dishonoured. The chiefs, furious, were now trying to extract the money from the Indian accountants, blaming Pottinger and Lawrence. The culprit, of course, was Akbar Khan.

On 1 May, the Sirdar sent the captives a large bundle of English newspapers and letters from Jalalabad. Some letters were eight months old, although Florentia had had her private ways and means of communicating with her husband. Captain Mackenzie had arrived there safely, they were told. Akbar Khan summoned Vincent to examine a cavalry saddle with him. He wanted to know whether it was made of pigskin? It was a difficult question, Vincent said, as it was hard to distinguish between cow and pigskin. With a knowing wink, the Sirdar was, clearly, not going to give up a good saddle on account of religious scruples but he had to be careful as his priest was in the room. Vincent collared Waller and they both agreed to say that the saddle was undoubtedly made of cow hide. They knew perfectly well that Akbar Khan was not going to allow some minor religious qualm stand in his way. It demonstrated, again, the sometimes curious relationship between the Sirdar and his prisoners. Here was the bloodthirsty architect of the destruction of the British army, guarding a number of prisoners purely as bargaining chips, yet looking after them with kindness and compassion. The Sirdar set much store by the advice and cooperation of people like Florentia and Vincent Eyre. It was doubtful whether he could ever bring himself to sacrifice them. Further underlining this relationship, Vincent was summoned by the Sirdar late that night. He tried to persuade Vincent to fight for him in Kabul against Amenoollah Khan and Fatteh Jang. He appreciated, he said, that no Englishman would fight against his own countrymen, but these were enemies equally hostile to the British, so that, by fighting for him, he would be serving his own country. A bit of neat logic, he thought. Vincent replied that he was already badly wounded and tired of fighting. Furthermore, he was entirely ignorant of Afghan politics and could not possibly decide the rights and wrongs of the case. Anyway, no English officer or soldier was allowed to take up arms under a sovereign power without having obtained the consent from his own Monarch. Understandably, Akbar Khan was bitterly disappointed and Vincent argued with him long into the night before he was allowed to return to his bed.

The Dost was also involved. Florentia knew that he had written to Akbar Khan saying that if there was any chance of regaining the throne, he was to fight for it. If not, he was not to drive his women and children prisoners around the country as it was not in their interests that they should be ill-treated. To be fair, he probably pitied the wives of the Afghan chiefs who were accompanying the captives. While they had the best and largest camel panniers, many of them were very unfit to ride a horse, with or without side or ordinary saddles. As far as Florentia went, she had rather walk or ride a horse than be packed into a pannier again. She was, of course, an accomplished horsewoman.

There was considerable turmoil in Kabul. Amenoollah and Fatteh Jang held the Bala Hissar while Zeman Shah Khan and the Barakzais, who had sixteen guns, were in the city. The latter wanted those in the citadel to join them but they refused saying that they were the assassins of Shah Shuja. Neither group had anything to do with Akbar Khan who, they said, played a double game and massacred the British army. They tried to inveigle him to Kabul but, sensibly, he was not for it, well knowing what the outcome would be. Conferring with Pottinger and other British officers, and the Afghan chiefs, the Sirdar became very overexcited. He maintained that he had acted purely as a result of the *jihad*, holy war, being raised. He had killed the Envoy and slaughtered the British as a consequence. Now, the vengeance of the British was being poured down upon him and he was being deserted by his men. So far, he had kept his feelings pent up but no longer. Betrayed, were he in power now he said, he would exterminate every Moslem who had abandoned him and left him so humiliated. At that point, a runner from Kabul arrived to say that Zeman Shah Khan had been victorious, one of Amenoollah's sons had been killed, Hamza Khan had been wounded but Amenoollah and Fatteh Jang still held the Bala Hissar. In revenge, Akbar Khan sent his cousin, Shamshudeen, with a body of troops, to lay waste to the Loghur country, destroy the forts and capture the women, all for the promise of 30,000 rupees. From whom? The Sirdar? Very unlikely; he hadn't any money.

On 3 May the Eyres and the Wallers rejoined Florentia's party in the Zanduh valley. Mackenzie had returned from his mission to Jalalabad just before they left, bringing with him a letter for Florentia from Robert. There was no immediate prospect of the captives release but negotiations were constructive and friendly. He then hurried off to report to the Sirdar. Allegedly, Nawab Zeman Khan had offered the crown to Akbar Khan. With that, he excitedly summoned Pottinger and Troup to accompany him to Kabul and Mackenzie was sent back to Jalalabad to resume negotiations. He tried, again, to persuade Eyre to come with him to sort out the gunnery, but to no avail. The hostages in Kabul were now said to be under the protection of a holy man, son of the Chief Priest. Amenoollah tried to abduct them but had been driven back into the Bala Hissar by Nawab Zeman Khan, whose house was burned to the ground. There was a pretty baseless rumour that, in three or four days' time, the prisoners would be taken to Ghazni.

With her ear to the ground as ever, Florentia had discovered the substance of Mackenzie's negotiations at Jalalabad. Firstly, what was the sum proposed for release of the captives? Two lakhs of rupees and the sooner they were handed over, the better relationships would be with the Government. As a consequence of the protection given to the captives by Dost Mohammad and Mohammad Shah Khan, their families and possessions would not be attacked. Peace or war, though, and the settlement of the country, was a decision for the Governor General. The Sirdar's response, by hand of Mackenzie, was that he did not want money but the friendship of the British nation. He was prepared to release the women and children but not the officers and men yet. General Pollock issued a proclamation that those remaining calm and quiet would not be molested. Pollock had also been told on 15 May, 'The Governor General is at a loss to imagine what propositions, relating to himself, Mahomed Akbar can have laid before you. That person is not only the acknowledged murderer of the late Sir W. Macnaghten, but he deceived and betrayed a British army into a position in which it was destroyed. It is not consistent with the honour of the British Government to enter into terms for the making of a provision for so great a criminal. We might engage to spare his life, if he were to fall into our hands, because it would be difficult so to bring him to trial as to protect the Government from a colourable charge of violently prosecuting an unworthy revenge; but no more than this can be done, and this only, if he should promptly do all he can to repair the crimes he has committed.'

The threat to the captives was that if British troops moved any further west than Gandamak, they would be taken 20 miles deeper into the hills. There were two problems with this. The first was that they were well above the Tezeen valley in the Jubhar Khail country. The people there would not allow them any further and, if they came, they would be handed over to the British for fear of vengeance being brought down on them. Secondly, they had no transport. The riding horses and baggage ponies had been removed. While Mohammad Shah Khan would have no compunction about them having to leave their clothes and possessions behind, they could not possibly be expected to walk. Incidentally, Florentia had lent her horse to Mackenzie. It arrived lame at Jalalabad but was looked after by Robert. News came of further treachery at Ghazni. By whom?

Snow still covered the tops of the hills and there was hard frost where they were camped. It had become bitterly cold and Florentia kept a good fire going in the bower. One of her servants took the water bag down to the stream to fill it and, by the time he got back, it had frozen solid. Their administrator was now one Mohammad Rufeek, with whom Vincent struck up a good relationship, going for a long walk with him into the hills south of the camp. He was kind, thoughtful and became a great favourite with the prisoners. An Afghan arrived with a whole lot of Vincent's sketches for sale, which, being rather flattered, he immediately purchased. Sergeant Deane's wife, a Persian, had been taken by force and married to a younger brother of Mohammad Shah Khan. It was said that whenever he enters her presence, she salutes him with her slipper. (Ribaldry amongst the European women). She had only recently been told of Deane's death and had been very attached to him.

She was a very pretty young woman. To their intense joy and surprise, Captain and Mrs Anderson's 4 year-old eldest daughter arrived. She had been abducted in the Khoord Kabul Pass on 8 January and since been looked after by Nawab Zeman Khan's family. She had been treated with every possible kindness and taught to say, 'My father and mother are infidels, but I am a Moslem.' Captain Troup, who had negotiated her release, wrote that he and Major Pottinger had been staying in Nawab Jubbar Khan's house in Kabul. The city was in turmoil, with faction against faction and the inhabitants siding with whoever paid them most. A later note from Pottinger stated that he had just witnessed an engagement between the Barakzais and the Duranis which he described as more comical than effective, a 'battle of spurs' he called it. Florentia's view was that the city was steadily being ruined by a stagnant trade situation and, with a show of force, the inhabitants would undoubtedly side with the British. She criticised the Government for weakness and what she called 'dilly-dallying' just because a handful of captives were in the hands of Akbar Khan. What was the honour of the Country compared to a few having their throats cut? Not that she wanted her throat cut, she emphasised, but it was certainly worth it to see the British flag once more flying over Kabul. She was quite happy to see the Dost returned to power but first let the Afghans know who the victors were and the treacherous chiefs ground into the dust.

One of the men taking the General's body to Jalalabad returned, very pleased to be given 200 rupees for his work. He reported there was good turn-out for the General's funeral with salvoes being fired and the troops looking magnificent. In the prisoners' camp, it was said that the

Ghilzai ladies with the captives were surreptitiously packing their kit and were going to give the group the slip on hearing that four British Divisions were on their way. The leading elements had already arrived in Tezeen at four in the morning and had looted the town. The consequent threat was that the prisoners therefore were going to be sent a further forty miles up into the hills. A reconnaissance party set out and returned to say the snow was two feet deep and the going thoroughly impracticable. All this was highly unlikely as the Sirdar had sent a message saying that whenever the captives were to be moved, he would provide camels, horses and ponies for all their needs. There were none to be seen. Brushing aside any British threat therefore, Akbar Khan laughed at the offer of two lakhs ransom for all the captives, presumably from MacGregor's sources, and professed to be not interested in money, however, quietly suggesting that eight lakhs might do the trick. An offer of five? The opinion was that everyone would remain prisoners until everything was settled. This was firmly endorsed by Pottinger. In the meantime, Fatteh Jang had written to his brother, Timur, (another son of Shah Shuja) at Kandahar to come and help him. Timur sent him 3,000 infantry and told him he was coming up with the British army. In Kabul, Fatteh Jang appeared to be king, Akbar Khan, vizier, and Zeman Khan, the chief Sirdar, but when some of Mohammad Rufeek's people arrived from Kabul, they said that Akbar was king, waiting for his father to take over. Where were the Persians? All a bit of a muddle, but Florentia and Alexandrina were sent some tea and sugar by a well-wisher so their morale was not that bad.

Vincent took the opportunity, with his friends Boyd and Waller and a couple of Afghans to go for a trek into the hills to the west. They had wonderful views of the Hindu Kush to the north and Sufeed Koh to the south. At 2,000 feet the farmers were only just beginning to plough, whereas in the Zanduh valley, the crops were already green. Descending to a stream bed, they noticed an abundance of wild onion growing on the banks. In Eyre's own inimitable words, 'A beautiful fritillia was also common; and an asphodelous plant bearing a gigantic spadix of yellow flowers, which I took for an ornithogalum.' They were overtaken by some tough Ghilzais of the Jubbar Khail who offered to escort them to Jalalabad. The Afghans, with the officers, took fright and hurried them back to the camp. On return, Mohammad Rufeek was given a rocket by Dost Mohammad Khan for allowing the officers to go so far. Vincent thought him a thorough boor whose ideas and manners, always exhibiting some silly, mean suspicion, were very low grade. If the Khan had had his way, they would all have been locked up in dark cells or narrow cages long ago, he thought.

May 16th was Florentia's 33rd wedding anniversary. To celebrate, she dined with the ladies of Mohammad Shah Khan's family. It turned out to be an extremely uncomfortable party. They had two female servants to interpret. There were three of Shah Khan's wives, some of Dost's, with the mother of the two chief's wives and two of their unmarried sisters. Florentia was pretty scathing about their appearance. They were, she said, generally speaking, inclined to *embonpoint*, 'largely formed, and coarsely featured,' their dress inelegant, and of the coarsest materials. The favourite wife, and the best dressed, was attired in common Kabul silk, with a coarse piece of chintz inserted at the back, evidently for economy's sake. The dress, which covered her whole body, looked like a common night-dress. They wore their hair in innumerable small hanging plaits; these were arranged once a week after taking a bath and the tresses were then stiffened with gum. The Kabul women were addicted to white and red paint. They coloured not only their nails, like the Indians, but their hands right up to the wrist which made it look as though they had been plunged into blood. After a bit, an extremely dirty cloth was spread over the mats, and dishes of pillau, and sweet and sour curd were spread in front of them. Those without spoons ate with their fingers, a habit Florentia had not got used to, and water was drunk out of a tea-pot. The gentlemen were given dinner by Abdoollah Khan in his tents about two miles away, nearer the snow. That evening, Mackenzie returned from Jalalabad, bringing with him a letter from Robert to Florentia. It is hoped he remembered what the day was.

At this stage General Pollock was well established in Jalalabad, and had been reinforced by Brigadier England, and General Nott was about to set out for Kabul from Kandahar. Florentia's assessment was that they would wait for the right time, and orders from Lord Ellenborough, who had relieved Lord Auckland as Governor General, before conducting a joint attack on Kabul. Akbar Khan was boasting that he had 12,000 men to take on the enemy but Florentia reckoned there were now at least that number of British soldiers in Jalalabad, with 18-pounders, and could comfortably take Kabul. Had they attacked even earlier, when there was so much dissension and division among the tribes in Kabul, it would have been even easier she thought. Mackenzie returned from his second trip to Jalalabad without any news about the captives' release. Akbar

Khan's terms to General Pollock were that he should be made governor of Lughman province, and be exempted from attendance at court and control by British political officers. Pollock took no notice whatsoever of these demands. No doubt he had in mind a note from the Governor General's office which reminded him, 'It cannot but be a subject of much regret, that you should have considered it necessary, under any circumstances, to have any communication whatever of a diplomatic nature, with Mahomed Akbar Khan, in whom it must be impossible for anyone to place any trust.'

Near Jalalabad, a European and some natives were murdered and, since nothing happened, the criminals became over confident and a lance-corporal in Tait's Horse was assassinated. When the killer took refuge in a village, Tait's men surrounded it and demanded the hand-over of the perpetrator. Nothing happened, so Tait, after consultation with General Pollock and MacGregor, told the villagers that if the man wasn't delivered to him within a certain time, the village would be burnt and everyone in it killed. Florentia was unsure of the outcome but was convinced that, while cruel, this was the way to prevent further bloodshed in the future. The Sirdar was nursing three broken ribs and some inflammation after a fall from his horse. Was there a very small note of sympathy in Florentia's tone? Much to her satisfaction, she heard that part of her letters about the siege of the cantonments had been put in front of the Court of Directors of the East India Company.

Lady Macnaghten and a few of the ladies, but not Florentia, had breakfast with the Dost's ladies and were told that if the Sirdar took the Bala Hissar, the captives would go there, if not, they'll go to Jalalabad. The Dost was much taken with Mohammad Rufeek's rendering of the 'Sermon on the Mount' in Persian. He was also an admirer of the Lord's Prayer and the Christians' stock went up when it was explained to him how prayer in private worked rather than the more outward expressions of the Muslim faith. Corporal Lewis of the 44th was brought into the camp. He had been held prisoner in Tezeen. He had been starved and ill-treated by his captors until he renounced his faith and adopted Mohammadanism with the given name of Deen Mohammad and daily attendance at prayers. It was unrecorded how quickly he reverted to his original Faith. Maybe he didn't?

Florentia received two notes from Robert dated 15 May. He wrote that he had had a highly gratifying letter from Lord Ellenborough and another from Sir Jasper Nicholls, regarding the defence of Jalalabad and the surprise attack on Akbar Khan's camp. The 35th were to be given the honour of being called Light Infantry and the Company's troops were to be decorated with a medal bearing the inscription 'Jalalabad' and have a crown woven onto their Colours. Lord Ellenborough was asking for the 13th to be similarly honoured. Chintz, sugar, tea and cheese were also sent from Jalalabad, and some Turkish red cotton cloth and boots and shoes for the men. Florentia, understandably, in good spirits recounted the story of the Sirdar's departure from Tezeen for Kabul. His followers had asked him what tentage they should take for him. In equally good humour, as he really thought he was going to ascend the throne, replied, 'The ladies and people above have got all our tents here; but you may send my salaam to General Sale, and ask him to lend me one of those he took from me.' No doubt sycophantic laughter from his entourage.

On 22 May, thirty-three ponies arrived from Kabul. These were not nearly enough to carry the whole group, so the officers told Dost Mohammad that camels would be required. He agreed and the potential departure that day was delayed until the following day.

The final objective was Kabul. Tomorrow they were to reach Khoord Kabul, a seventeen mile march.

Was this to be the first of the final legs of their long, hard journey?

CHAPTER 13

The Final Months

Mules arrived but no camels, even so they started out, on 23 May, at about 9 or 10 o'clock in the morning for what they hoped, would be the final stage of their imprisonment. But how was it going to end? Three of the officers walked and the ladies were installed on panniers on the mules. Florentia was mounted on a pretty second rate horse. They retraced their path down the bed of the stream to the fort where General Elphinstone had died. They crossed a branch of the Tezeen valley and then took a short cut over the hills to the foot of the Huft Kotul. Here they encountered putrefying bodies, strewn along the road as far as Khoord Kabul. The body of Major Ewart was still recognisable but they couldn't do anything about it. Further on, just past Kubbur-i-jubbar, they passed two caves either side of the road, full to the brim with rotting carcasses. As they progressed to Tungee Tureekee the sight became worse and the stench indescribable. Mohammad Rufeek nervously asked if this wouldn't infuriate General Pollock's army? Yes, Vincent Eyre coldly told him, he wouldn't be surprised if every house in Kabul was levelled to the ground. Turning off the main road, they passed a large ruined village, then arrived at the fort of Khoord Kabul where they had last been on 9 January. It had been an exhausting twenty-two mile trek.

Setting off the following day there was no question of traversing the Khoord Kabul Pass; it was completely impassable due to the piles of dead bodies and the overpowering stink. They therefore took the direct route to Kabul, with Alexander the Great's column in view almost the whole way. The first three or four miles were over a barren plain, then the road entered a gap in some hills and came out overlooking a wide valley. They paused in the middle of the valley by a deliciously clear spring, filling a small tank of fish. Pushing on they had a difficult ascent before reaching Alexander's pillar, one of the most famous antiquities of the time. Seventy feet tall, it crowned the crest of the mountain range which bordered the plain of Kabul to the south-east. Below them was an outstanding view of the Kabul valley two thousand feet below. A hundred miles away, the snow-capped mountain ranges of the Hindu Kush and Kohistan fringed the horizon. In the distance, the Bala Hissar could just be seen and the occasional roar of a cannon heard. The descent was difficult. Florentia would have been happy with a horse she was familiar with but she was on a hired pony which hated the scramble. Shaking with fear, it clambered down from rock to rock. Nevertheless, thought Florentia, it was better than walking and they came through safely. After passing a succession of small forts in well cultivated countryside, they came, unexpectedly, to Noor Mohammad, the Meer Akor's fort. The Sirdar had, in fact, given instructions for them to be taken to Mohammad Shah Khan's fort about two miles away, but the latter wanted to keep it solely for his family, so re-directed the prisoners to this one at Spewakee, not far from Kabul itself. Nothing had been prepared, so they were shown to two open cow sheds down a narrow alleyway in the outer square.

This was totally unacceptable to Florentia and, since no one was doing anything, she bearded Dost Mohammad Khan and Mohammad Rufeek herself, accompanied by Lieutenant Melville. As a consequence, she secured a pleasant room over the gateway of the inner fort for the ladies, with the promise of better accommodation the next day. Florentia passed a sleepless night from the pain in her wounded arm and incessant firing from the Kabul direction. Her stress level was not helped by the gossip that their speedy departure from the Zanduh valley was as a result of a plan by a couple of chiefs, Azaid Khan and Aziz Khan, to carry out a surprise attack, with 2000 men, on their guards and rescue the prisoners for a reward from MacGregor.

However, the next day, things looked up. A sally was apparently made from the Bala Hissar, nearly catching Akbar Khan, who had just time to escape to a fort near the Shah's camp behind the Seeh Sung hills. The Afghan female occupants of Florentia's fort had been transferred elsewhere thus freeing some excellent accommodation for the prisoners. As well as having sleeping quarters, they were allowed to sit by day in an octagonal room in a tower with open lattice windows. It was cool and had wonderful views; worth all the trouble of getting there, Florentia thought.

Akbar Khan was in a real muddle, as well he might. On the one hand, he contemplated retiring to the Kohistan, allow Pollock to take Kabul, then he would offer to go to India and replace his father if the latter was allowed to rule Afghanistan again. On the other, he couldn't resist the thought of the treasure lying in the Bala Hissar. He knew, though, that Fatteh Jang was holding out there in the hope of being relieved by the British. He earnestly desired, he told everybody, to be on good terms with the British and regretted that, in early life, he had not been better acquainted, then his recent prejudices against them would have been unfounded. Florentia would have seen through that little charade without much difficulty. General Pollock had offered to exchange Akbar's family of four wives and their children in Ludhiana for Florentia and her party. However, due to Akbar's instability there was nothing doing.

On 26 May, Captain Troup, who was liaising with Akbar Khan's closest colleagues, arrived and told them that the Sirdar was now living on the outskirts of the city about two miles away. He was to have a friendly meeting with Fatteh Jang, but the whiff of treachery was never far away. Morale was very low in Kabul, he said, with much begging on the streets, the merchants and shopkeepers losing trade and those in the army dying to get back to their fields and crops. Additionally there were a lot of people appalled and disgusted at the assassination of Shah Shuja. The European hostages and prisoners were being very well treated. The Sirdar, Troup said, wanted Florentia's group to send him a note listing anything they wanted and he would do his best to comply.

Captain Troup left the following day, with a note for the Sirdar and a letter to Robert from Florentia although, he said, he couldn't guarantee to send it immediately. Everyone was allowed to walk in an adjacent garden and, untold luxury, the gentlemen were permitted to bathe in the canal near the fort now the weather had become much warmer. The conference between Fatteh Jang and Akbar Khan was arranged. The Sirdar's terms were that Jang would leave the Bala Hissar, keep his guns and establish himself in one of the stronger forts in the neighbourhood. He would have to give up his army to the Sirdar who would use it against the British. Florentia thought that this was hardly likely to be agreed and hoped that Fatteh Jang would hold out until the arrival of the British.

Florentia reminded herself that in the General Election of July 1841, Sir Robert Peel's Tories had replaced Lord Melbourne's Whigs. Peel wanted to be rid of Afghanistan and replaced the instigator of the disastrous foray of the Army of the Indus, Auckland, with Lord Ellenborough as Governor General of India. Ellenborough had been given strict instructions to extract Britain from Afghanistan. Even before the disaster of the retreat from Kabul, he realised that Britain was failing badly and decided that British prestige required a final demonstration of military and political might before departure. The last thing he wanted was an aggressive Afghan state to the north-west of India which might invade Peshawar or other North West Frontier provinces. Additionally, there were still a number of British hostages in Afghanistan and he wanted to negotiate their release from a position of strength. The Army of Retribution was born with General Pollock put in command of the troops in Peshawar.

By the end of 1841, General Nott had been based in Kandahar with a small garrison and given the task of keeping the west of Afghanistan and the southern passes open as communication routes for the British. As peace seemed established, he was ordered to reduce his force levels and return troops to India. However when a detachment of his, on a routine mission from Kandahar to Kabul, was annihilated by the Afghans, he realised the danger he was in and withdrew all his outlying patrols and garrison troops into Kandahar. He sent another force towards Kabul but it could get no further than Ghazni. The situation worsened when one of Shah Shuja's sons defected from Kandahar and fell in with the surrounding Afghan tribes. Nott immediately despatched a force to disperse the enemy outside the city. Hearing of the murder of Macnaghten in Kabul he realised that there was a full scale insurrection against the British taking place. He then received the astonishing order from Elphinstone to withdraw to India with all his force. He decided to ignore it calculating that the order had been written under pressure. He hedged his bets by maintaining that he would await confirmation from Calcutta before proceeding with the evacuation.

The appalling news of the slaughter of those on the retreat from Kabul reached them and the massacre encouraged the Afghans to take on other objectives. The first to fall was Ghazni which had been commanded by Colonel Palmer. He had accepted terms of safe passage out of the citadel to return to Peshawar. On leaving the relative safety of the citadel, they were set upon by hostile Afghans. All the soldiers were killed and some of the British officers were taken hostage. Colonel Palmer was tortured into revealing the whereabouts of British money and gold which the attackers assumed had been buried and hidden by the British. Eventually the remaining nine British officers were taken to Kabul.

Meanwhile, a force of 12,000 Afghans surrounded Kandahar. Nott expelled all the Afghans from the city in order not to use up essential supplies and reduce the chances of betrayal. Ultimately he managed to disperse the besieging Afghans and the city was saved on 11 March

1842. He had been hoping to be reinforced from Quetta by General England. However, England was repulsed in the mountains and had had to return to Quetta. Nott was now running out of food, supplies and money to pay his troops. He ordered General England once more to attempt to break through to Kandahar but this time through the Khojak Pass. Nott sent a force of his own to his end of the pass to help England's force to push through to Kandahar. Nott became aware of yet another enemy army massing on the River Arghandab. He moved out with a part of his force, leaving General England, who had now arrived, with a smaller element to protect Kandahar itself. On 29 May Nott attacked and defeated the Afghans at Kelat-i-Giljye, and drove them in confusion and with great loss across the river. He had cleared Western Afghanistan.

With the British generals now firm in Jalalabad and Kandahar, the Afghans began to lose confidence and slide back into their usual chaotic state. Ellenborough arrived in post and considered abandoning his plans for an army of retribution but the two generals implored him to allow them to seek vengeance on behalf of their fallen comrades and release the hostages before evacuating the country. Ellenborough conceded to their request with rather vague instructions to withdraw via Kabul. Nott had an easier distance to go against Pollock's more difficult route through passes and defiles but both were hampered by a lack of transport animals which had to be brought through the Khyber and Bolan Passes. As Pollock's force went through Gandamak, they soon saw for themselves the results of the retreat disaster; mutilated men and women, and infants frozen to death. Retribution was not going to be difficult.

But back to the captives. On 31 May, they had an interesting visit from Shuja Dowlah, Shah Shuja's assassin. He was a handsome, quiet-looking man, whom few would have guessed had been the perpetrator of such a crime. He tried hard to persuade them that the Shah had deceived and betrayed them and what he had done was fully justified. The murder was instigated, he said, by Dost Mohammad Khan, the Ghilzai, in revenge for the attempt on the life of Akbar Khan by the Shah's agents at Charbagh. Few believed this and the Nawab Zuman Khan banished him from his house forever. His visit was followed by one from Shah Dowlah, another son of the Nawab. He enquired particularly how well the group had been looked after by the Sirdar. What was behind this? Clearly, the Sirdar's prospects were not prospering as the Kuzzilbash, a tribe within the city, had, as a body, risen against him. They were reported to be holding their part of the city, and strengthening the Bala Hissar, until the arrival of the British.

The officers were now stopped from leaving the fort to bathe and the ladies were closely guarded when walking in the gardens. This, though, was later rescinded. Every night they were locked in the square and servants were not allowed out of the fort for any reason. Mohammad Rufeek was sent away under suspicion as his family, allegedly, had helped General Nott. News of Nott's success at Kandahar reached them and Pollock was expected to be with them by 15 June. Clearly, tensions were rising.

Fatteh Jang apparently had offered a large reward to anyone seizing and escorting the prisoners to the Bala Hissar. This was hardly through altruistic motives or the welfare of the hostages but, no doubt, to give him extra bargaining counters with the British. That night he beat off a determined assault on the Bala Hissar by Akbar Khan. Captain Troup then arrived, bringing two parcels from Robert for Florentia. There were some bits and pieces for the ladies, which Florentia distributed but what really excited her were copies of letters to Robert from Lord Ellenborough and Sir Jasper Nicholls (now Commander-in-Chief). These were so complimentary that Florentia shook off her fever and, with great happiness, regained her health. General Pollock had written to Akbar Khan expressing his dismay that he had attacked women and children, contrary to the rules of war. It was hoped this would shame the Sirdar into releasing his women and children hostages. This had absolutely no effect but he did send the ladies some coarse cloth, soap, tallow candles and an Afghan wash-hand basin. Troup thought that the Sirdar might well take the Bala Hissar. He had mined one of the bastions but was loath to demolish it as he wanted to preserve the integrity of the defence when he succeeded in capturing the citadel. Anyway, he said, he did not want to make it easier for the British to enter. Florentia suspected it was merely a ruse to frighten the defenders as she reckoned that the Sirdar's sappers and miners had made a number of attempts but met solid rock. If he had been able to take the fort, she thought, he would have done so by now.

On 6 June, the prisoners heard considerable noise of gunfire from Kabul. Fatteh Jang was said to have sallied out from the Bala Hissar and carried off a quantity of Akbar Khan's stores and camels. The Sirdar had seized Amenoolah Khan, whom he had, with good reason, suspected of colluding with Fatteh Jang. The Khan was said to be worth eighteen lakhs of rupees on which the Sirdar was eager to get his hands. Amenoolah was the son of a camel driver, but with cunning, bravery and hard work had pulled himself up to be one of the most powerful chiefs in the Country. He owned the whole of the Loghur valley and could draft 10,000 men into the field. He was the chief instigator of the rebellion and the murder of Sir Alexander Burnes. He played either side against the middle and was an extremely dangerous man; definitely a target for the British to keep in their sights. The Sirdar really needed to have him on his side, so taking him prisoner was an unwise step and likely to provoke his family and followers. Maybe he thought he could 'sell' him to Pollock? Contradictory reports had circulated. One, quoted by Florentia, was that the Sirdar was in possession of the Bala Hissar. This was extremely unlikely though his former henchmen, Mohammad Shah Khan and Sultan Jan, had been inside the citadel for three days, conferring with all sorts of people. They asked the Sirdar to meet them at one of the gateways, attended by only five followers. Akbar Khan, sensibly suspecting treachery, would go no further than John Hicks's tomb[24] just outside the gate. He had warned them not to trust Fatteh Jang but perhaps they were now in his camp? A bad move by the Sirdar; although Mohammad Shah was junior to him, he had the troops available and could lay his hands on ready cash. Sultan Jan was the fighting leader of the trio. So, while Akbar Khan laughed and joked, and squeezed those whom he thought had money, the other two

---

[24] A tomb in the Muslim burial ground. 'Here lyeth the body of John Hicks, son of Thomas and Edith Hicks, who departed this life, the eleventh of October 1666.' He was probably in the service of the Emperor of Delhi, either in trade or a mercenary and may, being buried where he was, have embraced Islam.

were plotting. Craftily, though, the Sirdar kept all the records of what the prisoners had asked for, and what he had provided, plus any notes of thanks he had received from them – just in case. Even so, with just one lakh of rupees to hand, the Sirdar could still do a lot of mischief by organising a fighting force for a few weeks. Florentia was always astonished how quickly effective these men could be. She was so used to seeing Indian recruits being drilled and trained long before they became proper soldiers. Of course, she realised that the Afghans were born warriors; every boy carried several knives and became an expert shot from a young age. In his hands, the accuracy and range of the juzail musket was superior to the British matchlock. He was used to hard living and going without food and water for long periods. He was a natural horseman and indoctrinated by the mullahs to attain everlasting glory in heaven with scantily-dressed Houris if he fell in battle. However, he was ill disciplined, easily discouraged, treacherous and only fought for his family/tribe or the last person who paid him.

Captain Troup returned to the Sirdar the following morning, presumably on some sort of liaison visit. The man who went with him came back later to say that Akbar Khan had blown up the Bala Hissar bastion nearest to the bazaar. Unlikely, said Florentia, as he also reported that the Sirdar's men were parading around on top the very bastion they were meant to have destroyed, throwing dead bodies over the wall. She thought it was a pity that Pollock's men hadn't arrived yet as Fatteh Jang was paying Indians a rupee a day just to guard the gates as he didn't trust Afghans. She was also told that there would be lots of opposition to the removal of the captives from where they were as various competing groups wanted to keep them in their clutches.

Further reports came in that afternoon. There had been a considerable battle outside the Bala Hissar; the attackers were commanded by Sultan Jan and when he tired, his place was taken by Mohammad Shah Khan and when he became exhausted, the Sirdar took over. When he brought a gun to bear on the mine below the tower, Fatteh Jang fired from one of his own and destroyed the Sirdar's. There was then a nonsense; the mine was blown, failed to destroy the bastion and killed 300 of the Sirdar's own men. However, Fatteh Jang, it was said, capitulated and Akbar Khan became master of the Bala Hissar. Florentia was very aware, however, that the news the captives received was highly coloured by the Khan and his guard. While a number of the prisoners spoke Persian, they don't understand Pushtu, which was the language spoken by their captors, so eavesdropping on their conversations did not work too well.

Two tin boxes and two baskets arrived from Tezeen, supposedly originating from Jalalabad. They were quickly locked away until the Sirdar gave permission for the contents to be distributed. Mostly, they contained medicine for Doctor Magrath and some letters and newspapers which were handed over to Akbar Khan. As they were going into the garden to take some exercise, they heard that the Sirdar had sent his greetings and he was now in command of the Bala Hissar. This was, though, not actually the case. He had taken the main tower which dominated the citadel but not the whole garrison. He had no guns up there but, as Florentia knew well as she had seen it in operation, mountain train guns could be pulled up on mules. Another rumour was that Gool Mohammad was going to capture them in a surprise attack in four days' time. Florentia had become fairly immune now to these persistent rumours which, usually, quickly evaporated but, nevertheless, always raised little anxiety. There was, reported their servants, more gunfire that night but neither Florentia nor the officers heard it. Fatteh Jang was alleged to have taken two of the Sirdar's tents, some ammunition and killed forty of his men. It was said that the Sirdar had sent Zeman Shah Khan to negotiate with Fatteh Jang to propose that the latter should remain king but that he should hand over all his guns and troops to the Sirdar with which to fight the British. Fatteh Jang held onto Zeman Shah Khan until he had a response from the Sirdar to his agreeing to the terms but that all the captives were to be placed in his hands.

Captain Mackenzie appeared on 9 June with the letters that had been snatched by the Sirdar and to report that the Sirdar *had* sprung the mine under one of the towers of the Bala Hissar near to the bazaar on the 6th. Much damage was done to the buildings in the city nearest to the explosion and some sixty men of the storming party were killed by the defenders. It was then that Fatteh Jang, realising his support was waning, decided to make terms with the Sirdar. In Florentia's experienced view, there was no need for surrender; a traverse wall could have been thrown up to repair the breach and secure the place against the Afghans. However, she reckoned that the occupants of the citadel had been intimidated by the explosion, something which they dreaded, and Fatteh Jang, having held out for a month without relief from Pollock, had become disheartened. The towers were handed over to the chiefs while he retained the royal residence. With all the different factions and loyalties, this was a guarantee of some sort of mayhem. All of them had an eye on the treasure supposedly hidden by Fatteh Jang, who was now in a life-threatening position with his enemies in charge of the city. It turned out that Akbar Khan *hadn't* seized Amenoolah Khan after all. However, the two old Nawabs, Zeman Khan and Jubbar Khan openly quarrelled. The former seized the latter's beard, exclaiming, 'You are the fellow who first brought the Feringhees (foreigners) into the country, and to whom, therefore, all our troubles may be attributed.' Upon which Jubbar Khan's son drew a pistol and threatened to shoot Zeman Khan for insulting his father. Akbar Khan, laughing heartily, enjoyed the whole scene.

The captives, dying to hear news of Pollock's progress, were disappointed to learn of sickness debilitating his men in Jalalabad due to the heat and bad water. Additionally, there had been difficulty over the resupply of camels and oxen from Peshawar, which struggled to get to Jalalabad. Once there, they would be ready to start out. Nott was still based north of Kelat-i-Giljye. Ominously, the Sirdar somehow had his hands on 18 lakhs of rupees; with this amount, if true, he could be a lot of trouble. However, what power did he really wield, Florentia wondered? The Kuzzilbashees held one of the gates which guarded their sector of the city, Mohammad Shah Khan occupied another, Fatteh Jang still lived in the interior of the Bala Hissar and Akbar Khan inhabited a house in the bazaar. The Afghans were increasingly nervous of their captives receiving news and doubled the guard to 30 men. One brave individual, bringing articles for Captain Johnson, was caught, fined 6000 rupees, tortured and had all his nails torn out. Two other luckless individuals, suspected of bringing news, were severely beaten. The prisoners were allowed, though, fruit from the garden on payment of a few rupees but the grapes needed another six weeks to ripen and the sour plums were only good for making jam. Worrying information, perhaps orchestrated by their captors, was that, while some troops were at Gandamak, others at Jalalabad and Kandahar were withdrawing to what Florentia called the 'provinces' ie India. Very unlikely but that and more earthquakes added to their unease. They were told that they wouldn't leave the fort even if Akbar Khan negotiated it as the other factions would try to keep them in their hands as bargaining counters with the British. There was a view that the Sirdar had overplayed his hand by transferring the prisoners towards Kabul, their ultimate destination, as others were waiting to pounce. Better, though, was the production of some wonderful mulberries from the garden. They had been cooled by the stream and covered with rose petals. The prisoners sat under the vines and ate them, being promised by the gardener some delicious sherbet the following day.

The gossip of the day, what Florentia called the *'on-dit,'* was that 4000 Sikhs would hold Jalalabad while Pollock advanced on Kabul. The Afghans reported that eight British regiments were now at Gandamak and on arrival of the British, the Sirdar and Mohammad Shah, they said, would flee but not many of their followers would accompany them. The prisoners would be taken with them and transported to Mecca or Room. By 'Room' they meant Constantinople. Further, that Fatteh Jang was a prisoner and that Kamran, who they heard had been earlier put to death, was coming from Herat to form a coalition with Fatteh Jang, Akbar Khan, the Ghilzais and other chiefs to fight the British. If successful, the prisoners would remain where they were, if not, they would be sent to Turkistan via Charikar, north of Kabul. Such was the flight of febrile imagination; not by Florentia, but the Afghans.

Probably more reliable information was that Pollock had left Jalalabad and was on his way. If so, the prisoners could expect an imminent move. Fatteh Jang was, indeed, in captivity and the chiefs were bent on having him put to death but there were wiser heads against this, not for any love of Jang, but better policy in view of potential outcomes. The Ghazees, though, were determined to sink the chiefs into a sea of blood to prevent any possibility of making any deals over the prisoners. If the latter, they say, are moved out from Kabul, they will kill the Sirdar and any of the chiefs involved. Zeman Khan, one of the more level-headed chiefs, implored Akbar Khan to allow him to go to Jalalabad, with the captives, to negotiate terms. The Sirdar would have none of it and there was a blazing argument which developed into a fight.

18 June – Waterloo Day. The latest was that the prisoners were to be transferred to Bokhara via Kohistan and Mackenzie sent a letter warning them of a move, but certainly not to Bokhara. Ali Mohammad, their current gaoler, told them that the Sirdar was going to Jalalabad, with Fatteh Jang and a number of other chiefs, to pay his respects to General Pollock. There was a pitched battle in the city between the Sirdar and Zeman Khan. Although the former lost some sixty to eighty men, he captured Zeman Khan and two of his sons but released them after stealing their guns, ammunition and treasure. Captains Mackenzie and Troup arrived at the captives' fort with the news that, after his success, the Sirdar now ruled Kabul. The Kuzzilbashees reluctantly submitted to him and gave up Mohun Loll who was immediately tortured. The two captains had been allowed to visit the hostages in the city who were under the protection of Meer Wyze, the chief

mullah, and to whom they had been handed over for safe keeping by Zeman Khan. When they were in the latter's house, they were in constant danger from the Ghazee assassins. At one point these brigands had got into the house, fully intending to slaughter the hostages and were only prevented by Zeman Khan falling on his knees, ripping off his turban and entreating them not to dishonour his roof by committing violence against those under his protection. When he transferred the hostages to Meer Wyze's house at night, he lined the streets with his own men with instructions to shoot anyone who so much as looked out of a window. He not only accompanied them himself but sent his family ahead as a vanguard. Captain Conolly, one of the hostages, had solid proof that Shah Shuja had instigated the rebellion as a way of getting rid of Burnes, whom he detested, and several of his rival chiefs who, he hoped, would fall victim to British vengeance. Little did he realise what disasters were to be generated by so doing. Burnes had made few friends amongst the chiefs. He was arrogant, aloof, and certainly far too close to some of their women. They saw him as an opportunist sent to spy out their land with a view to betraying them to his masters. They weren't far wrong. They dreaded him taking over as Envoy from Macnaghten. In their own camp, they were not much better with Akbar Khan in the treachery stakes. On 6 January, the day the retreat from Kabul began, he and Sultan Jan, armed to the teeth, appeared before the assembly of chiefs. On being asked by Zeman Shah what his intentions were, he replied, 'I am going to slay all the Feringhee dogs, to be sure.' Again, when the stragglers were passing through the Khoord Kabul Pass and he was bringing up the rear, he called on the Ghilzais, in Persian, which the British understood, to stop firing, while, in the same breath ordered them, in Pushtu, to slay everyone. If there was ever any mystery about the responsibility for the massacre, it was now solved; Akbar Khan was indeed the chief traitor.

On 21 June, Florentia noted that it was Henry's birthday. He was their youngest child, born in 1829, so now thirteen but she didn't say where he was. One assumed in Calcutta with her uncles but she didn't seem particularly maternal. To the captives' surprise, the soldiers who had been left behind in Buddeeabad fort arrived. They had been starved and ill-treated. They put this down to the malign influence of Mrs Wade. She was the wife of a sergeant who, after Florentia's group had left the fort, turned Muslim, left her husband and consorted with an Afghan in Akbar Khan's service. She took every opportunity to insult and threaten her former comrades; taking what little they had and relaying to her new friends any plans the prisoners had to escape. This nearly resulted in them having their throats cut. Knowing her husband had a couple of gold coins sewn up in his boot, she had them cut open and removed. Mrs Wade herself made her way to Kabul, no doubt with the assistance of her lover, taking with her the 3 year-old orphan, Seymour Stoker. Florentia tried to get Captain Troup to intercede with the Sirdar to have the child, a son of a man in Robert's Regiment, brought to them, sadly, without success. The enraged Sergeant Wade swore that when General Pollock reached Kabul, he would ask him to hang his treacherous wife.

The weather was abominably hot and only relieved by bleeding with the help of a penknife. One man, with a broken arm, died of lockjaw. The Indians left behind were stripped and searched, even to the extent of having their bandages taken off their wounds, to see if they were concealing anything. They were then expelled from the fort. A few made it to Jalalabad, but most perished. Not a pretty story. However, better news was that Sergeant Fare brought with him the Colour of the 44th, which Captain Souter had tied around him, saving his life. At Buddeeabad, Brigadier Shelton asked that it be given to his soldier servant, Moore of the 44th, to sew it up in a piece of cloth to preserve it. Thus it was saved for posterity; an important item in Regimental history now in their chapel in Warley.

It was said that Colonel Stoddart and Captain Arthur Conolly (different to the John Connolly, a hostage in Kabul) were prisoners in Bokhara. Conolly had been actively trying to have slaves in Kokan released but when the ruler of Bokhara subdued Kokan, he imprisoned Conolly in an underground dungeon. He and the Colonel were kept there for 126 days in the dark, with food being let down to them every four or five days. They couldn't wash or change their clothes. Conolly was later beheaded. Ominously, there was a rumour that Florentia and her fellow captives were to be sent to the same place; a fate which they were extremely keen to avoid. However, since this emanated from the disgraced Mrs Wade, it was treated with contempt. Fruit was ripening in the garden and Florentia and the captives ate the first really ripe apricots and cherries which were brought in from the City. Green plums and peaches had ripened but were inferior to the ones Florentia was used to. Nevertheless, it made a change to their monotonous diet.

Yet another fairly severe earthquake on 29 June. Captain Troup called in before setting off for Jalalabad on a mission for the Sirdar. He took part of Florentia's journal and her letters for Robert. He said that Fatteh Jang was back as king in Kabul and that Akbar Khan was content, for the time being, to be the Vizier but a number of his supporters, who were known to be friendly to the British, had left for the hills. Some of the prisoners were going down with fever, including Mackenzie, Waller and Melville but Florentia was well. Pollock's troops were reported to be in the Lughman valley but, it was suspected, were merely foraging parties. There had been hopes of a prisoner exchange of Florentia's group for those Afghans in Pollock's custody but talks failed as Pollock was ordered to march on Kabul. An infuriated Akbar Khan swore that as Pollock advanced, he would take his prisoners to Turkistan and make presents of them to the various chiefs. In the last resort, perhaps the most likely destination would be, in fact, Herat, well beyond the reach of the British.

The Sirdar took up residence in the Bala Hissar and intimated that all the hostages in Kabul, except Conolly, were to be sent to Florentia's fort. Troup, who had returned from whatever mission the Sirdar had sent him on, which was not clear, and Pottinger were to follow him to the Bala Hissar. Florentia had done some calculations as to how soon Nott's men from Kandahar would reach Kabul. A messenger arrived from there on 6 July, having taken 8 to 10 days to travel, with the news that the force had already started out three days before he left. Florentia reckoned it was a 22 day march from Kandahar to Kabul and, with possible fighting on the way, they could not be expected before the 25th, but more likely around 1 August. Sadly, Mrs Burnes's child died and was buried in the lee of the hill, with Vincent Eyre performing the ceremony.

News filtered through to the captives from Troup and Conolly in Kabul that the Sirdar had ordered the ditch round the Bala Hissar to be cleaned out and was to send Mohammad Shah Khan with 6,000 men to occupy the passes between Kabul and Jalalabad. His concept of operations, if he had one, was to fight on the plain in front of the Bala Hissar. Florentia, clearly, thought little of that and her derision increased when she learned that anyone not calling Akbar Khan, 'Vizier', would be fined. Other information came to light that when the British began the retreat from the cantonments in January, Zeman Shah Khan wrote a note to Conolly, which reached Pottinger at Boothak, warning him of the Sirdar's treasonous intentions. Pottinger, therefore, must have known this when he was negotiating with Akbar Khan at Boothak but still went ahead, ostensibly trusting the Sirdar. In reality, he probably realised he had few other options and hostages were made over to the Afghans. A letter from Macgregor in Jalalabad, had also been found on Shah Shuja's dead body telling him to hold out for another fifteen days when he would be rescued. Zeman Shah Khan, though, was a steadfast friend of the British, spending some two lakhs raising 1000 men to fight Akbar Khan. He also fed hundreds of wretched Indians, starving in Kabul, some of whom had been sold for one or two rupees each and transported to Turkistan. Zeman had tried to prevent it but was now very short of money. When little Tootsey, the Andersons' child, had been abducted in the Khoord Kabul Pass, she was taken to Kabul where Sultan Khan rode up and down the streets, offering her for sale for 4000 rupees. After negotiations over the price, Conolly bought her and put her under the protection of Zeman Shah Khan. She was later returned to her parents. Amenoolah Khan, in whose hands the child had been, then, out of revenge, hatched a plot to kill Conolly. Conolly was to be lured to the Bala Hissar on the pretext of thanking the king for his kindness over the child and when he reached a gate, assassinated. However, he was warned in time and stayed away.

On 11 July, Pottinger returned to the prisoners, Troup having left for Jalalabad a couple of days earlier. Typhus and dysentery was rife amongst the captives but Florentia was not affected. Mrs Trevor gave birth to another girl – she already had seven children, all accompanying her in captivity (it will be remembered her husband had been killed with Macnaghten on 23 December). Doctor Campbell, medical officer of the 54th, arrived from Kabul where he had volunteered to look after the hostages when Elphinstone's force left the cantonments in January. Worried about Mackenzie's and some of the others' state of health, he decided to stay with them. Reports were coming in that the British were building a fort at Jagdalak, 70,000 men were assembling at Ferozepore, 15,000 were now at Kandahar, 20,000 at Jalalabad and 10,000 on their way from England. Would they be in time to rescue the prisoners? The Sirdar planned to move them in a few days but the Kabul citizens would not allow it. Conolly arrived with a letter from Pollock containing an offer to exchange all the Afghan prisoners in India for those in this country. If it helped by Conolly going to Jalalabad with Afghan chiefs, sympathetic to the British, for discussions, then he should do so. The letter also outlined the British forces now available, including an army under Sir Jasper Nicholls, and that if they were driven to the extreme by the Afghans, then punishment and retribution would be fearful. If Akbar Khan was sincere in his wish to be friends with the British, he had better, for a start, hand over all the guns he had captured.

Akbar Khan then came to the fort to hold a conference with a number of his cronies, including Sultan Jan, who now called himself Sirdar-i-Sirdaran, a sort of Commander-in-Chief. As far as Florentia was concerned nothing came out of it except that, to her infuriation, they stripped the garden of its fruit. They did, however, receive letters and papers from Jalalabad although she suspected Akbar Khan of holding onto them for over a month. Lady Macnaghten recovered some of her jewellery, albeit damaged. The prisoners were put on half rations, ostensibly, Florentia sarcastically commented, to make up for the lavish expense their gaoler, Ali Mohammad, had had to spend on Akbar Khan's party. She suspected Ali Mohammad of being on the take and playing both sides against the middle. However, to Florentia's great joy, on 24 July, Alexandrina safely gave birth to a daughter, Julia Florentina. Her grandmother merely said, 'another female captive.'

Troup appeared back from Jalalabad with no news as to their release but did bring some bits and pieces for them: arrow root, cotton gloves, reels of cotton, tape, soap, jalap (a cathartic drug) and cream of tartar. He arrived with three ponies, one of which carried a box of money. The Afghans realised this and the ponies promptly disappeared. Florentia was not so upset by the loss of money but, particularly, medicine. They had virtually none and were now plagued by malaria from mosquitoes breeding in the stagnant rice paddies. She had hoped that once the Afghans had stolen the money, the ponies and the baggage, including medicine would be returned. Sadly, not. Later, Troup left to see the

Sirdar in Kabul but expected to return to Jalalabad so Florentia gave him some more of her journal for Robert.

There were reports of severe Afghan losses at the hands of Nott's men moving up from Kandahar, infuriating Akbar Khan who, again, threatened to take the prisoners to Bamiyan and sell them there to the chiefs. Florentia's frustrations bubbled over: what was Nott doing? He was only meant to go to Ghazni to release the prisoners, not to fight except to defend himself, then join Pollock. Kabul was not to be attacked but everyone was to come together and evacuate the country 'hand in hand' as she, sarcastically, put it. Thus giving the Afghans, after waiting for their ally, *the snow*, an opportunity to destroy yet another even larger British army as it wound its way through the mountain passes back to India. She bitterly regretted the loss of the courageous Skinner who would know what was going on and have enormous influence and authority with the Afghans. He had been deliberately singled out and killed at Jagdalak on the Sirdar's orders. The latter was worried that Skinner, and, indeed, Trevor, a close confidant of Macnaghten, knew far too much and had to be eliminated. Skinner had played a clever and dangerous game of pretending to be a dupe of the Sirdar's but, in reality, becoming very close to him to gain intelligence. Clearly, Akbar Khan realised this and, not only feared his power but was jealous of him. However, Florentia still believed that the Sirdar would not cut their throats; through no love for them but they were simply too valuable, in the eyes of the other chiefs, as bargaining chips and ransom money.

Apparently, the whole of the Lughman valley was in Pollock's hands, with every fort from Tighree to

Buddeeabad destroyed. Akbar Khan had sent a force to oppose him but it halted at Boothak, the commander nervous, with some justification, that he was too weak to take Pollock on. More of the prisoners went down with malaria and Conolly was very ill indeed. Zeman Shah Khan's party seemed to be in the ascendancy again which was good news for the captives as the owner of the fort they occupied was a crony of the Khan's and, if approached by the British, would side with them, to the extent of arming the prisoners to resist their abduction. Letters had been sent to Pollock from several influential chiefs in Kabul, promising that if he did not sack the city and respected their possessions, the captives would not be transferred elsewhere. One or two of them hoped, that by doing so, they would regain their old positions; one family, for instance, being the hereditary Viziers of Kabul. The Governor General's directive of 3 August to Pollock, though, was quite clear, 'In the event of Mahomed Akbar Khan's coming into your hands, without any previous conditions for the preservation of his life, I request that you will inform him, that he will be tried for the murder of Sir William Macnaghten, and confine him accordingly, as you would any other person accused of a similar crime, and try him as you would any other person, and deal with him, if he should be convicted, as you would any other person found guilty of murder under similar circumstances. You will not hurry his trial, so as to commence it with insufficient proof of his undoubted and admitted guilt. The only other circumstance which should induce you to delay his trial is, the consideration that British subjects still remaining, at the capture of Mahomed Akbar, in the hands of the Affghans, might possibly be made to suffer in the event of his execution. Upon this point you will act according to your discretion.'

On 7 August John Conolly died. A coffin was sent for and a request to convey his body to Jalalabad was made. However, the Sirdar refused to allow it until Troup returned from there. If, he said, all was not well, he would not allow him to go, alive or dead. Curious; did he mean Troup or Conolly, who was dead anyway? Some camels turned up but none were strong enough to carry the coffin so Conolly was buried at sunset in the fort's garden.

Pollock made it abundantly clear that if any attempt was made to transfer the captives beyond reach, he would lay waste to Kabul. In the meantime, Nott had returned three regiments to Quetta, taking the advantage to get rid of his sick, non-combatants and extraneous baggage, before moving north towards Kabul. From Pollock's force, Sappers and Miners, normally in the vanguard of an advance to clear the way, cross obstacles and mine opposing forts, had been delayed at Charbagh for some time and, later, reached Gandamak. This was a good sign but, ominously for Florentia, there were eight camels, with their drivers, lurking at the captives' fort, looking as though there was a move afoot. Nevertheless, Troup and Lawrence turned up from Jalalabad bring Florentia letters from Robert. There was no hope of an early release, he wrote, and all that was happening, to Florentia's frustration was *talk*, though Pollock had threatened that if the captives were not sent to him within eight days, he would destroy Kabul. This was a hollow threat as Akbar Khan knew that he did not have the transport available. 1st Brigade had arrived at Jalalabad, together with the 3rd Dragoons and troop of horse artillery. However, in Florentia's military view, they would not manage the passes to Kabul without extra troops to protect the flanks and dominate the heights. There was weird story emanating from an Arab soldier of fortune who had offered his services to Pollock and been rejected on the basis he was probably a spy. He said that two European officers, disguised as natives, coming from Kandahar with thirty followers, had been arrested in Kabul trying to buy up all the gunpowder. They were either mercenaries or among the Ghazni prisoners escaping incognito. Anyway, they were now imprisoned with the other hostages. Interesting; Florentia wondered who they really were?

13 August was Florentia's 52nd birthday; hardly one to be celebrated, as she wryly put it, under the present circumstances. (For that time and place, and in those conditions, she was a remarkable woman for her age). The hostages from Kabul had now joined them and there was talk of them all being transferred to Sourkab, four day's march away, in the Loghur country, or to the Kohistan, or Bamiyan. Robert's Brigade, the 3rd Dragoons and the troop of horse artillery were due to leave Jalalabad on the 6th for Futtehabad which would bring them fifteen miles nearer the captives. They packed up what little they had, purchased two ponies, and awaited the order to move. There was an opinion, but maybe only a figment of a prisoner's wild imagination, as Florentia put it, that the Sirdar was fed up with carting the women and children around with him. If he had to flee, he would run with just four hostages; Pottinger, Lawrence, Troup and either Shelton or Johnson. The rest were to be abandoned or, perhaps, killed?

By 15 August, Nott had left Kandahar, accompanied by Timur Shah, a son of the late Shah Shuja. Florentia worked out a probable route, hitting Gulnarye, about 90 miles from

Kandahar, then striking north to Ghazni. This would be better than crossing the mountains via the Gholary Pass which would be more difficult for their guns. Akbar Khan said he had sent 5000 men to oppose them and that if the Jalalabad troops moved up, he'd send the prisoners off at half an hour's notice to a 'fine climate, with plenty of ice.' Florentia thought all this unlikely but, if true, was probably Bamiyan. He also said he'd sent 5000 men to face the Jalalabad advance. Florentia reckoned nearer 400. Mrs Smith, Mrs Trevor's servant, died of fever and 'water on the chest,' probably pneumonia.

The Sirdar's troops who headed for Kandahar were soundly beaten by Nott. Fatteh Jang had escaped from Kabul by cutting a hole in the roof of his prison and letting himself down by rope. It was likely he had made for Jalalabad. Akbar Khan wrote to Lord Ellenborough to say that he would only treat with him and would have nothing to do with Pollock who was 'a fool.' Charming, Florentia thought, Pollock may have been a number of things but 'fool' he wasn't. The situation was warming up; there was a good deal of firing heard from the city and several Afghans had been killed by the British at Gandamak. Revenge must have been sweet. Akbar Khan said he would despatch a further 5000 men there. The Kandahar force was now within two day's march of Ghazni. Three horses, at the fort, were kept saddled ready for messengers and the word was that the captives would not be there three days hence.

With the arrival of a number of English newspapers, Florentia was tickled by their, usually, uninformed comments, particularly about her. In one, there was an on-going controversy between a correspondent who claimed that Lady Sale, in her letters, evinced a strongly favourable view of Akbar Khan. Another wrote that she only did so because she was a prisoner. The response was that it was unlikely that Lady Sale would write anything that was false. Florentia agreed that she would not have written on the subject at all unless she wrote as she thought. If people misunderstood, that was their fault, not hers. Another said that she should not have written anything. This was possibly so, thought Florentia, but the editors lacked detailed knowledge. Her letters to Robert covered information sufficiently important enough to be relayed to the Governor General and Commander-in-Chief. They were then forwarded to the powers that be in England. As for her favourable view of Akbar Khan, all she wanted was Nott to release all the prisoners in Ghazni and then simultaneously join Pollock in Kabul. Once in power there, she hoped they would place Akbar Khan, Mohammad Shah and Sultan Jan *hors de combat*. They should befriend those Afghans who had maintained loyalty to the Crown, and helped them, and allow Dost Mohammad back on the throne. He and his family were only an expense to the British in India and he could be made a friend again. However, the Afghans should be shown that the British were capable of conquering them and would not allow the massacre of so many troops go unavenged. The British should not, then, sneak out of the Country like whipped Pariah dogs. Waxing further to her theme, Florentia maintained that had they followed Sturt's advice and left Kabul without baggage (she was, probably, including the camp-followers as baggage), at speed, and with the protection of men standing by them (although unlikely as they were so worn out and dispirited) then their escape would have undoubtedly featured alongside Xenophon's retreat of the 10,000.[25]

She was not drawn, however, into the debate as to whether it had been right to replace Dost Mohammad with Shah Shuja or maintain ascendancy over an uncivilised people far from a base from which supplies of everything had to come. Let the Governor Generals and the Commanders-in-Chief deal with that, while she knitted socks for her grandchildren. However, as a soldier's wife, she had no intention of sitting calmly by while honour was tarnished by savages. To be fair, Akbar Khan, was described by Florentia as a William Tell,[26] who had delivered his Country from the hateful yoke of an oppressor. However, he was a man riddled with deception and hypocrisy; the slayer of the Envoy, not by proxy, but by his own hand. Florentia gave him the benefit of the doubt that he had intended to keep the Envoy prisoner in the hope of ransom money but, as a man of ungovernable passion, he had completely lost his temper. He was a jovial and smooth-tongued man who fooled many of the British into thinking he was a friend. However, the warning letter that Conolly had received at Boothak should have alerted the British to his real intentions. He followed the retreat with his bloodthirsty Ghilzais, taking every opportunity to slay those on the convoy, while pretending he could do nothing about it as he only had 300 men. He

---

[25] The expedition of the Greeks, generally known as the 'Retreat of the Ten Thousand,' was led by Xenophon in BC 401. Florentia knew her Classics.

[26] William Tell the Swiss folk hero, whose defiance encouraged the population to open rebellion, marking the foundation of the Swiss Confederacy.

was under the evil influence of Mohammad Shah Khan, the most inveterate enemy of the British. The reality was that they were in it together and anyone caught befriending the British would be tortured and threatened to hand over money on pain of death, then probably beheaded.

Florentia stated that a woman's vengeance was fearful and hers was no exception. The objects of her revenge were Akbar Khan, Sultan Jan and Mohammad Shah Khan. She had to admit, though, that ever since they had been in Akbar Khan's hands, they had been well treated and honour was respected. It was true they had few comforts but no less than the Afghan women who always slept and sat on the floor. They had bought *charpoys*, beds made with ropes criss-crossing a framework of poles, which gave them some comfort. She shared a room with Lady Macnaghten, Mrs Mainwaring, Mrs Boyd and, of course, Alexandrina. There were no men with them – Captain Boyd had a bed space on the landing – except for the Boyds' two little boys and Mrs Mainwaring's baby son who had been born on 13 October just before the insurrection broke out in Kabul. His father was with Robert's Brigade in Jalalabad. The child was called Jung-i-Bahadur (literally, the boasting warrior). Florentia declared it was a relief not to have the permanent presence of the gentlemen, day and night. They were given rations of meat, rice, flour, ghee and oil and, more recently, fruit. Afghan cooking was greasy and disgusting, so they took it on themselves, trying to cater for all tastes. For instance, to them a strong cup of coffee was a luxury but bitter and detestable to an Afghan. It was true they were carted about the country, exposed to heat, cold and rain but so were the Afghan women. It was, in Florentia's view, very disagreeable but they were, *de facto*, prisoners and, as such, were reasonably treated by the Sirdar who called them 'his honoured guests.' They were provided with coarse chintz and cloth to make their clothes and so doing gave them an occupation to take their minds off their predicament. They suffered most from a lack of cleanliness. It was, it will be remembered, ten days after leaving Kabul before they could change their clothes, even to take them off, wash, and put them on again. It was not until they reached their present location they finally got rid of lice, which Florentia called the 'infantry' while fleas were termed 'the light cavalry.' She accepted the difference between the European and Afghan standards of cleanliness. Where the former enjoyed bathing twice a day, the latter were content with once a week and only then unplaited their hair which was normally kept in place with gum. She did say they washed their hands before and after meals but that was because they ate with their fingers but, at the same time, wore the same clothes for a month. Being able to walk in the garden of the fort was a great bonus. While heavily guarded, the sentries did not, on the whole, annoy them and left them in peace, apart from the odd thoughtlessness. It was understandable that, when on their travels, the Afghan wives had the pick of the camel panniers and horses; Mohammad Shah Khan had taken Alexandrina's horse in preference to his own but Florentia's had carried Mackenzie to Jalalabad and stayed there so, to her satisfaction, Robert had got it. She was still amused at the reporting in the English newspapers as to how she had 'led the troops.' She maintained that while she had been in the vanguard, it was merely that the chiefs had told her to accompany them for safety's sake rather than valour. She quoted Goldsmith's verse on Mrs Blaze, 'The king himself has followed her, when she has gone before.'[27] The public relations people of the time were already warming to this intrepid lady despite her protestations. The Grenadier in Petticoats' was their description of her. Secretly, she was flattered but what she really appreciated, however, was a subscription set up by the Indian newspapers to have a sword made to present to Robert in recognition of his leadership.

By 22 August, Fatteh Jang had made it to Jalalabad and declared he would take on Akbar Khan in a fair fight. As a result, showing off, the Sirdar paraded some 25,000 infantry and 5,000 cavalry on the Seeah Sung plain. He was mad, thought, Florentia. He could not possibly hope to defeat a disciplined British army in a conventional battle; much better to hold the defiles and passes of the mountains with his marksmen. Then, totally unexpectedly, the seven officer hostages from Ghazni arrived at the fort. The Sirdar said that everyone would be sent to Bamiyan, Zoormut or Sourkab in three or four days' time. There was a report that the Afghans had been severely defeated in a pitched battle by Nott's men but, more likely, by the Hazaras who had happily changed sides after bribes of British gold.

On 25 August, a sudden order came to move. The day was spent frantically packing and the group left that night. Mrs Anderson, being too ill to travel, remained behind with Doctor Campbell, together with Mrs Trevor and eight children. Was this to be the final phase of their captivity or just another move in the long series of journeys they had undergone?

---

[27] Oliver Goldsmith (1728-74), 'An Elegy on the glory of her sex, Mrs Mary Blaize.' (1759)

CHAPTER 14

Rescue

They left by the light of the moon. Camels, with panniers, were provided for the ladies and children, and Captains Mackenzie and Eyre, who were ill. Florentia was the only lady who rode a horse. They were escorted by 400 Afghans, many of whom were deserters from Shah Shuja's army. The rumour was that they were to be taken to Kulum in Usbeg Tatary (today Turkmenistan/ Uzbekistan) via Bamiyan. It was alleged that Akbar Khan was in league with the Ruler of Kulum who had dispatched 2,000 men to his frontier to escort the captives to the slave market in Bokhara. It was difficult to see their way in the dark but Florentia could just make out the line of jagged mountains and a succession of forts on either side of the tracks. They crossed the Loghur River and reached a fort called Killa Kazee which was about seven miles from Kabul, although their route was much longer having taken a detour to avoid the city. As dawn broke they were still travelling and found themselves only about two miles, as the crow flies, from Kabul itself. The city walls were quite distinct. Florentia reckoned they had travelled about eighteen miles. They reached their camp site beside a fort called Kundah but were refused entry. Apparently it was occupied by Sultan Jan and his reinforcements for Ghazni. This scotched the rumour that he was being held hostage in Kabul against the safety of the prisoners. He had about thirty men with him and some good horses, including the Envoy's grey which Florentia recognised. The prisoners were joined by thirty-seven European soldiers who had been left behind, sick, in Kabul when the retreat started. A letter arrived from Kandahar saying that Nott had left in three columns, totalling 6,000 men, and was within ten miles of Ghazni. He was expected in Kabul on 1 September. Florentia was highly critical of the Pultans assigned to guard them. They imitated British troops, marching up and down between sentry posts, but merely carrying a ramrod, having stuck the butt end of their musket into the ground. Easily overpowered, she considered.

On 27 August they left after midnight with a strong escort of Afghan cavalry. Lady Macnaghten's finely decorated camel was stationed in the vanguard, so easily identified if there was an escape attempt. They were eight or nine hours in the saddle along pretty rough roads in barren land. There was a long, but not difficult, ascent to Bala Maidan and, from the summit, a wonderful view, at dawn, of a cultivated narrow valley, studded with numerous forts. Willow trees and poplars lined the water courses. Again, they were refused admittance to a fort but had tents pitched for them. Florentia shared one with her daughter and granddaughter, Lady Macnaghten, Mrs Boyd and three children and Mrs Mainwaring and her child. There was news that Nott had arrived at Ghazni, blown up the new tower and put to death nearly every man, woman and child: not, perhaps, entirely true but unsurprising given the thirst for vengeance on the part of the soldiery. There was a plan hatched which, to her infuriation, Florentia only heard about by chance after it had been dismissed. This was to get Ahmed Khan, their gaoler, to make short marches and a number of halts to reveal the prisoners' location to Nott, who could then rescue them. Once successful, Ahmed Khan would receive two and a half lakhs. The ransom scale was Lady Macnaghten 10,000 rupees, Florentia 5,000, Alexandrina 5,000, Captain and Mrs Boyd and family 5,000 and so on. All were graded by rank and means, which Florentia regarded as preposterous. No one was that wealthy and she wondered where the money was coming from. Presumably India, although she reckoned the Government would have paid more. Florentia was, rightly, scornful of this private venture which she described as *zubberrdust*, literally strong-armed or overblown. Anyway, it came to nothing as Florentia would have easily predicted had she known about it at the beginning. It was a hopeless scheme.

They left the next day and Florentia remarked that she would have enjoyed the ride on a good horse instead of being hustled as a captive on a soggy baggage pony. They went through some beautiful scenery with clumps of trees and a crystal-clear river flowing to their left. They bivouacked that night near the town of Julraiz, surrounded by forts. It was a good spot, sheltered by poplars and beside a clear stream. Here they acquired some apricots, grapes, pears and apples. Setting off at daybreak they passed Sir-i-chushm after about three miles. This was a fortified town with a dominating fort called the 'head of the spring' containing tanks full of sacred fish. Later they passed a fine fort called Mustapha Khan Ke Killa, after the man who built it. His son, a gentle soul, wearing glasses, still lived there. He gave them *naan* bread and apricot paste. Infuriatingly, some of their guards again looted a couple of camels. They camped at Killa Nazari about eight miles from their previous camp.

Leaving at 2 am, they marched sixteen miles to Gurdundewar on the Helmand River. Passing through a narrow defile, the route then opened out onto a good road, wide enough for wagons and carriages. There was very little cultivation and few forts. They met a man on the way who said he was a messenger from Ghazni and that the town was in Nott's hands and Nott was on his way to release them. Shortly before arriving at their next halt, a dozen aggressive Hazaras were seen off by the captives' guards who fired about fifty shots, killing one, wounding two and taking two prisoner together with some loot. On 30 August, they left the Hah-i-Baba, about 18,000 feet above sea level, on their left and pushed on eight miles to the foot of the Hadje Gurk pass. The route went through a narrow, stony defile with a tributary of the Helmand running through it. Some of the enormous rocks either side looked almost as though they had been carved by human hand. Florentia thought it possible that they had been done by Buddhists or Brahmins in the distant past. Nearing their destination, the valley opened up and they arrived at a very dilapidated fort but still inhabited. Every breach in the walls was filled with armed men. The captives' guards marched up and down, to the sound of their two drums, one fife and a bugle, usually out of step and looking ridiculous to Florentia's practised eye but no doubt impressed the garrison. The Hazaras appeared to be manning the heights and the odd ineffective pot shots were exchanged. Florentia sardonically observed that, during a skirmish, the enemy took up a position behind a *sangar* (a clump of rocks thrown up as a defence) on an overlooking hill but fled the moment they were attacked. She was not impressed. The following day they had a hard march on very rough going to the forts of Kaloo through the

Hajigak Pass at over 12,000 feet. They crossed a river twice, alongside of which hay had been harvested into sheaves, reminding Florentia of fields in England. There was a report that Akbar Khan was fighting his fellow chiefs in Kabul and Pollock's men must have reached Boothak. The next day they climbed the four miles to the top of the Kalu Pass, 13,400 feet. It was a precipitous and narrow route, but little more than a steep path. However, from the summit there was an outstanding view of what looked like waves of a very rough sea, composed of hills of every colour and shape. From there they could see Bamiyan; a magnificent scene but not a happy one for people who expected to remain in captivity in that desolate region. After a seven mile trek they ended up at Killa Topchee in a narrow but highly cultivated valley. Moving again at daylight they covered the seven miles to Bamiyan. On the way they passed through a valley no more than a mile wide, but highly cultivated with grain, beans and peas. Tamarisk and barberry were abundant. Stopping by a fort where there were a number of cows grazing, they were given refreshing curds. At Bamiyan they were refused entry so pitched their tents under the walls of this ancient city which had been sacked by Genghis Khan and the 300,000 inhabitants slaughtered. Owing to some argument, they had to up sticks and go about a mile to another scruffy fort, much to their annoyance. Florentia issued a demand to be allowed to stay in their tents which was, unsurprisingly, granted - their captors had got the measure of Her Ladyship. The Khan promised to do better on the morrow.

Salch Mohammad Khan's wife came to visit Lady Macnaghten. She was young and fair, with a fat round face and came from Ludhiana where, it was said, she had been a dancing girl. She said that Fatteh Jang was either a prisoner or had been put to death and his family was expected in a day or two. The following days, the prisoners made small excursions to the local caves to make sketches. Vincent Eyre was a particularly good draughtsman but Florentia also copied the frescoes on the walls and ceilings. She was dying to get into the ancient city but was refused point blank on the basis that their guards had quite enough to do looking after the main body of the group. To make it easier for the guards, the prisoners were to be moved into what Florentia described as 'one of the horrid little forts.' However, all was not lost. Some time ago, to prevent any squabbling over distribution of food, drink and clothing, a committee of three had been elected by vote. These were Major Pottinger, Captain Webb and Captain Lawrence. The latter was designated the supplier and shared out the rations and food for the soldiers, with his own hands. So, on entering the fort, the committee having examined the miserable sheds built round the high walls with corner towers and a gateway, decided that the five least unpleasant rooms should be occupied by the ladies who were to draw lots for them and decide amongst themselves. This was then changed to choice by seniority with Lady Macnaghten first, followed, of course, by Florentia. The latter opted for a long, dark cow byre with the only light coming from the door and a hole in the roof. She occupied this with Alexandrina, the nurse and the child. They then set to, knocking two holes in the walls to obtain more light. In doing so they blistered their hands but achieved great satisfaction. During the night, an enormous bug flew in. It didn't alarm Florentia but the others spent the night trying to swat it and, the following day, requested tents to be put up for them near the gateway.

Clearly, at this point there were a number of Afghans who could see which way the wind was blowing and did not want to be on the wrong side when Pollock and Nott arrived with their Army of Retribution. The group also became aware there were a number of Indians in their guard who would be prepared to come over to their side. More importantly, Saleh Mohammad Khan, who was responsible for them, was open to bribery. (He was actually a Hazara, who had certainly been bribed by Akbar Khan, so was known as a man who could be bought). Johnson and Lawrence sounded him out but he laughed them off, pretending that he thought they were joking. However, early on 11 September, a conference was held in Florentia's room, being the most private in the fort. Major Pottinger chaired it with Saleh Mohammad Khan, the Syud (priest) Morteza Khan, Lawrence, Johnson, Mackenzie and Webb in attendance. It was decided to promise Saleh Mohammad Khan 20,000 rupees and 1,000 a month for life and that if it was not the Government which rescued the prisoners, they themselves would be responsible for the payment. The document was formally signed by the five officers in the name of Christ thus making it legally binding and certainly impressing the Afghans. Saleh Mohammad told them he had orders to take them further that night, to Kulum, but he also had a letter from Akbar Khan stipulating that anyone unable to march was to be put to death. He was extremely anxious that the prisoners should not receive any news from outside and, to emphasise this, two drummers were severely flogged for passing on information. This did not seem to inhibit Florentia's own ways and means for obtaining intelligence.

For instance, she found out that the Andersons, Trevors and Bygrave, who had been left behind, were now safely with the British forces but she queried it as the current information was that Pollock was still east of the Khoord Kabul Pass and Nott a day's march the other side of Ghazni. Saleh Mohammad hoisted a flag of defiance – white with a crimson edge and green fringe – on the walls. No one was quite sure whom he was defying? Nevertheless, two Hazara chiefs came over and swore their allegiance to Pottinger. The Nawab of the province had fled and his replacement handed Saleh Mohammad 1,000 rupees for the privilege of assuming the position. There was an exciting rumour that the prisoners were to be armed, though very unlikely, but Captain Johnson was appointed quartermaster to store up enough food to be able to withstand a possible siege by Akbar Khan until relieved by Pollock's men. Two more chiefs came over to their side with much ceremony and swearing on the Koran. One of them owned a fort which had been burnt by Doctor Lord some time ago but he was now prepared to hand over the remains to the captives. Its name sounded, in English, like 'fool-hardy;' not perhaps wildly inappropriate, thought Florentia, for their present predicament. Those against the offer were Shelton and Palmer, neither of whom seemed to take part in what was going on. The latter had been tortured in Ghazni so, understandably, was anxious to keep his head down. Shelton was nervous about antagonising Akbar Khan but both of them signed the document drawn up by the five other officers. Florentia wrote to Robert telling him of their resolve to hold out, even if it meant eating rats and mice.

More local chiefs came over to the prisoners' side and Florentia was full of praise for Pottinger who was, effectively, now the governor of the valley, with Saleh Mohammad in his grasp. His knowledge of Persian and the manners and customs of the people made him adept at dealing with the Afghans and able to take advantage of any opening for the betterment of the captives. He dealt with the chiefs, handing them promissory notes empowering them to receive Government rents on neighbouring land. All this was handled with great solemnity and formality, well knowing that these were mere scraps of worthless paper. Yet they had a magic all of their own and were highly valued; just what the prisoners needed. It is likely that Pottinger had wind of the Governor General's memo of 13 September to Pollock which strengthened his hand, 'The GovernorGeneral directs me to inform you that, in the event of the prisoners not being in your hands when you receive this letter, his Lordship deems it expedient that you cause it to be intimated to Mahomed Akbar Khan that, in the event of any further delay taking place in their delivery to you, upon the proposed condition of the release of all Affghan prisoners in our hands, it is his Lordship's intention to remove Mahomed Akbar Khan's family from Loodiana; and that it is under his Lordship's consideration, whether Mahomed Akbar Khan's wife and children should not be immediately sent to Calcutta, and eventually to England. Mahomed Akbar Khan must be aware that the Government in England cannot afford to any one education in the Mahomedan faith, and there are no means of obtaining it there.'

After hearing of turmoil in Kabul and that Pollock had reached Boothak and Nott, Maidan, the captives moved, on 16 September, to Killa Topchee, with only what they could carry in the way of supplies. While they had fine weather for the journey, nevertheless, they were still in immense danger. It was thought that one of the chiefs who had been with them had deserted over to Akbar Khan and revealed their plans. So everyone they met was treated with suspicion. Florentia, riding a horse, outstripped those being carried in the panniers and, together with the other horsemen, pulled over to a large group of rocks to seek shade from the sun while they waited to be caught up. Saleh Mohammad approached them and, speaking Persian to Lawrence, told him he had obtained some muskets and ammunition which he had with him on a camel. He suggested some of the captives should be armed and pretend to be the advance guard of a main body thus deterring any would be attackers. When Lawrence called for volunteers, to Florentia's shame, no one stepped forward. Exasperated by this, she said, 'You had better give me one, and I'll lead the party.' If he had done so, it is probable they would have followed out of shame and loyalty. But nothing happened.

They then had news of Pollock who had fought his way through the Khoord Kabul Pass, pursuing the enemy as far as the hills north of Kabul, while Nott had chased the enemy to the Seeah Sung Heights. The Kuzzilbashees had seized the city and were looting it. Pollock reached it on 16 September. Akbar Khan and Mohammad Shah Khan were nowhere to be seen. Nott was, by then, at Urghundee, close to the prisoners. Pollock, rightly, worried for their safety, asked Nott to send a brigade to rescue them. Nott refused, to the disgust of his officers, on the grounds that his men were worn out. At this, Pollock immediately dispatched Sale's brigade for the task. Making a forced march, Sale left Seeah Sung, two miles east of Kabul on 19 September (his 60th birthday) for Urghundee where he halted for the night. The following morning he left his camp standing and secured the Kote Ashruffee Pass with his infantry while he went ahead with the 3rd Dragoons. A group of Sultan Jan's men were around but were frightened off by the Juzailchees.

As Florentia and her fellow captives shaded their eyes against the sun, they could nervously see a strong body of cavalry coming at them at the gallop through the dust of the desert. With great joy it turned out to be not Akbar Khan, intent on final murderous revenge, but Sir Richmond Shakespear[28] and 600 Kuzzilbashees, closely followed by Robert and his men. Florentia and Alexandrina were at last reunited with husband and father. After nine months captivity, immense danger and physical hardship, they had survived. Florentia could hardly express her emotions. As they reached the infantry, they received rousing cheers and the men of the 13th pressed forward to shake their hands or touch the hems of their skirts. For the *memsahib* of the stiff upper lip, this was too much and the tears ran down her cheeks. On arrival at the camp, Captain Backhouse fired a

---

[28] In 1839, Richmond Shakespear had been appointed Political Assistant to Major d'Arcy Todd's Mission to Herat. Shakespear was sent by Todd to negotiate with the Khan of Khiva for the release of a number of Russian hostages, whose captivity provided an excuse for an unwelcome Russian advance into Central Asia. Shakespear was successful in his negotiations, and marched with 416 Russian men, women and children, to Orenburg, where the arrival of his weary group was received with both astonishment and gratitude. From there, Shakespear was posted to Moscow and thence to St Petersburg, where he was received by the Tsar. He eventually returned to London and was knighted by Queen Victoria on 31 August 1841, at the age of twenty-nine. By 1842 he was on the Staff of General Pollock.

royal salute from his mountain guns and all the officers came out cheering to welcome their return. Even the hard-bitten warrior, Robert, was so overcome with emotion that, riding for a bit with Mackenzie, one of the released prisoners, could barely bring himself to congratulate him before digging his spurs into his horse and galloping off to be by himself.

On 21 September, they resumed their way to Kabul via Killa Kazee to be personally greeted in the City that afternoon by General Pollock. What a change in circumstances compared to the last time they had been there. The cantonments were in smoking ruins. The shops in the great bazaar were closed and the city was silent and desolate. The occupants sullen and cast down, awaiting the vengeance which was surely coming their way. The exhausted, but happy, former captives made their way to the camp at Seeah Sung where they were greeted with a 21-gun salute.

Their ordeal was finally over.

CHAPTER 15

Aftermath

In Kabul, Pollock considered, before withdrawing from the country, how to wreak vengeance on the people who had butchered so many? Blowing up Bala Hissar was an attractive demonstration of the power and might of the British Army but he was persuaded not to do so by those who, later, might find themselves defenceless against any further uprising. Instead Pollock destroyed the Great Bazaar where Macnaghten's body had been left hanging, rotting in shreds, and the Feringhee Mosque built by Akbar Khan. It took two days to destroy the massive structure with explosives. Discipline broke down and there was considerable plundering of the city, together with some revenge killing.

There were Afghan rebels still active in Istalif, a beautiful village belonging to the implacably hostile Kohistanees. A force was despatched to attack and burn it. Utter destruction was also the fate of Charikar, the capital of the Kohistan, where Codrington's Gurkha regiment had been destroyed. Zeman Khan, who had been a firm friend of the British throughout, and the family of the ill-fated Shah Shuja, were content to return to the exile in India which gave them safety and peace.

On 12 October, Robert, accompanied by Florentia, led the advance guard of Pollock's army on the return march to India, which was reached without mishap on 12 November, having burnt Jalalabad to the ground on the way. A large number of the mutilated and crippled camp followers of Elphinstone's army who had escaped with their lives were allowed to accompany them. As the Army of Retribution wound its way back through the Khyber Pass, its men saw, still, the mangled bodies and filth of war on the route of the retreat. There was nothing to be cheerful about, despite having won in the end, if one could call an Army of Retribution victorious. Lord Ellenborough was determined that the returning soldiers should be greeted as heroes but the realists were only too aware of the extent and depth of the disaster that had befallen the British in their unnecessary venture into Afghanistan. They were not to be seen in the land for another forty years.

On 17 December, at the head of the Jalalabad garrison, Robert crossed the Sutlej by the bridge of boats at Ferozepore and was received with great honour and an embarrassingly bungled ceremony by the Governor General. On 24 February 1843 the thanks of Parliament were unanimously voted to Robert, moved in the Lords by Wellington and in the Commons by Peel. On the death of General Edward Morrison, Colonel of the 13th, Sale received, on 15 December 1843, as a special promotion for distinguished service, the Colonelcy of his Regiment. For their distinguished service at Jalalabad, the Regiment was awarded the official patronage of Prince Albert and permitted to use his name, becoming the 13th (1st Somersetshire) (Prince Albert's Light Infantry) Regiment of Foot.

The British released Dost Mohammad unconditionally from captivity and he returned to Afghanistan to assume his position as leader. He deposed, without difficulty, Shah

Shuja's son, Fatteh Jang, who had claimed the throne on the death of his father. It was rumoured that Dost Mohammed had his own son, Akbar Khan, murdered in 1847. Maybe he feared the volatile and ruthless streak he knew his son had?

Ironically, Dost Mohammad went on to prove that he could be trusted by the British. He maintained reasonable order in his ravaged country; he kept the Russians at arm's length and played a subtle game with the Great Powers. Cleverly, he did not take advantage of the Indian Mutiny when it occurred in 1857. In practice, the North West Frontier was so stable that the British were able to reduce their forces on the frontier to fight the mutineers. They must have rued the day they made the wrong choice of whom to support on the throne.

The Sales returned to England in 1843 where they were treated as heroes by a public desperate for something to celebrate after the disaster the year before. They were fêted in Londonderry, Liverpool and Southampton. Florentia had not been idle and in 1843 John Murray published her book, *'A Journal of the Disasters in Affghanistan, 1841-2,'* to great acclaim, reaching a 7th edition by May. On 29 August 1844, the Lord Mayor of London gave the Sales a banquet in the Mansion House at which their health was drunk many times over.

On 30 October 1844, they dined with Queen Victoria at Windsor, who wrote in her Journal: 'Sir Robert & Lady Sale dined. Lord Ellenborough sat next to me. I was very pleased with Lady Sale, who is so simple, retiring & quiet, & so sensible. When asked she was quite ready to tell all about her misfortunes and adventures. When one thinks what the poor woman had had to endure in 9 months of captivity under Akbar Khan, & sees the thin & delicate looking person she is, one is filled with wonder that she should ever have come through such trials. She showed us her arm, which had been shot through & still bears the scars. Her poor daughter, Mrs Sturt was confined in prison, after her husband, Lieutenant Sturt had been killed on the retreat, but luckily the little girl is a very strong child. Akbar Khan was a remarkably fine man, Lady Sale said & like what one would imagine a Captain of Freebooters to be. Her horse was taken away from her & she was given a wretched beast, with a deformed foot, which stumbled at every step. They were kept on horseback from morning till night, & given horrid food without any forks or knives. Toward the end of the time they had 3 suits of clothes, which was a great thing; she used to wear a dressing gown & a pair of trousers. Akbar Khan was all the time encouraging the people to murder them. She was allowed to write to Sir Robert Sale, but her letters had to be sent open & sometimes word would come that Akbar Khan had received letters, but was in a bad humour & would not send them. She said the whole thing appeared to her now "like a very horrible dream", but that sometimes in the night, "she started up thinking all was being acted over again". She has not been in England for 22 years & Sir Robert Sale has been 45 years in India & only 3 in England. They are going back again in December, as he has been appointed Master General. Both were born in India. He is a frank, fine, good nature soldier, & appears to be a very strong man. After dinner I talked to Sir Robert Peel of the Sales, whom we praised, – of Lord Ellenborough, whose head Sir Robert thinks has been turned, which he regrets for so clever & so honourable a man. Lord Ellenborough had refused to be Privy Seal "as he was accustomed to great results", & Sir Robert laughed at his vanity.'[29]

They returned to India at the end of 1844 with Robert now Quartermaster-General of the Queen's troops in the East Indies. On the outbreak of the First Anglo-Sikh War in 1845 he served as Quartermaster-General of the army under Sir Hugh (afterwards Lord) Gough. This was the campaign in which Sir Harry Smith so distinguished himself.[30] Robert's left thigh was shattered by grapeshot at the battle of Moodki on 18 December, and he died from the effects three days later. Florentia was in Ludhiana at the time.

He was buried in the field after the battle of Ferozeshah on 22 December 1845. At Moodki he had been present as Quartermaster-General (responsible for the overall administration of the army) and not as field commander. An officer of his rank and responsibilities had no business to be in the forefront of the battle but, in Robert's case, it was unthinkable that he could have been anywhere else. His nickname, 'Fighting Bob' was, as ever, highly appropriate.

Florentia retired to a small estate near the comfortable hill station of Simla on an annual pension from Queen Victoria of £500 (£47,530 in today's money)[31] in recognition of her husband's great service. Her Will of 1850 showed her intention to build a small cottage on the estate; a codicil of 1852 added, 'the cottage called Springfield having been rebuilt.' Her Will also showed the loss she felt of the death

---

[29] Queen Victoria's Journal Volume 18, pages 135-137.

[30] See the author's book, 'In Love and War: The Lives of Sir Harry and Lady Smith.' Pen & Sword, 2008.

[31] Obtained by multiplying by the percentage increase in the RPI from 1845 to the present day.

of her son-in-law, John Sturt, on the retreat from Kabul. She shared an interest in antiquarian books with him and she was worried that no member of her family would appreciate the value of the ones she still possessed. So, in the end, they all went to Alexandrina, Sturt's wife, of course, and her collection of coins went to another son-in-law.

Alexandrina remarried. She and her husband, Major Holmes were assassinated, in the Indian Mutiny, on 24 July 1857 by men of the 12th Irregular Native Cavalry riding up behind their carriage and beheading them.[32] After doing so, the killers went on to Assistant-Surgeon H. S. Garner's bungalow where they murdered the doctor, his wife and a child, then set fire to it. One child, a little girl, escaped notice and was taken care of by the Tehsildar (a tax official).

Her daughter, Julia, by John Sturt, born in captivity, married Major Thomas Mulock in 1861. Whilst in command of the 70th Regiment of Foot during the New Zealand War of 1863-65 he was mentioned in despatches and received the campaign medal. In 1865 he was created a Companion of the Order of the Bath. Julia died in April 1910 and is buried in the graveyard of the church in North Cheriton, Somerset. His grandson, Evelyn, was awarded the Military Cross in World War 1. Evelyn's granddaughter, Susan Clark, is alive today; Florentia's great-great-great-great-granddaughter.

From 1846 to 1848, Florentia had been granted a Grace and Favour apartment in Hampton Court[33] and, in failing

---

[32] London Gazette 25 December 1857.

[33] Apartment 2 Suite XXI. Her granddaughter, Lady Sale-Hill later had Apartment 42 in 1924.

health, she decided to return to England and retire there or, perhaps, live in the benign climate of South Africa. Boarding the ship *Kent* on 23 March 1853, she arrived in Cape Town on 3 July, after an unaccountably long voyage. Sadly, three days later she died, aged 65. She was buried, with considerable ceremony, attended by the Lieutenant Governor, the Naval Commodore and heads of Government Departments, in Plot 117 in the English section of the Somerset Road cemetery.[34] The cemetery was closed to further burials in 1908 and a new cemetery established in Maitland. Her grave is now marked with a small granite obelisk, engraved, 'Underneath this stone reposes all that could die of Lady Sale. Her heroism, her fortitude and her patience under arduous circumstances are part of her country's story. Her piety, total abnegation of self, and the true tenderness of her woman's heart are best known to the sorrowing children, who raise this monument above her ashes.'

Thus ended the life of Florentia Sale, a supreme example of how to behave in adversity, her womanhood being no bar to dealing with fear and privation. A feminist's dream, she was of the stamp of those women who not only supported their husbands in remote and inhospitable parts of the Empire but, properly, carved their own names in history.

The real Lady of Kabul.

---

[34] Author's liaison with Selwyn Adams, Foreman, City Parks, Northern District, Cape Town.

ANNEX A

CIVIL AND MILITARY OFFICERS KILLED AT OR NEAR KABUL AND DURING THE RETREAT

12 October 1841 – 6 January 1842

Political

Sir William Macnaghten Bt	23 December
Murdered at a conference	
Sir Alexander Burnes	2 November
Murdered in his house	
Capt Broadfoot 1st Engr Regt	2 November
Murdered with Burnes	
Lt Rattray Bombay Inf	2 November
Murdered at a conference at Lughmanee in Kohistan	

Her Majesty's 44th of Foot

Lt Col Mackrell	10 November
Killed in action Kabul	
Capt Swayne	4 November
Killed in action Kabul	
Capt M Crea	10 November
Killed in action Kabul	
Capt Robinson	4 November
Killed in action Kabul	

Lt Raban 6 November
    Killed in action Kabul
5th Native Infantry
Lt Col Oliver 23 November
    Killed in action Kabul
Capt Mackintosh 23 November
    Killed in action Kabul
37th Native Infantry
Capt Westmacott 10 November
    Killed in action Kabul
Ensign Gordon 4 November
    Killed in action Kabul
35th Native Infantry
Lt Jenkins 12 October
    Killed in action Khoord-Kabul
Capt Wyndham 12 October
    Killed in action Jagdalak
Her Majesty's 13th Light Infantry
Lt King 12 October
    Killed in action Tezeen
Local Horse
Capt Walker 1st Native Infantry 23 November
    Killed in action Kabul
27th Native Infantry
Lt Laing 23 November
    Killed in action Kabul
Shah's Service
Capt Woodburn 44th Native Infantry 23 November
    Killed in action Kabul
Capt Codrington 49th Native Infantry 23 November
    Killed in action Charikar

Ensign Salisbury 1st Volunteer Regt 23 November
    Killed in action Charikar
Ensign Rose 54th Native Infantry 23 November
    Killed in action Charikar
Dr Grant Bombay Establishment 23 November
    Killed in action Charikar
Lt Maule Artillery 3 November
    Killed in camp at Kahdarrah
Capt Trevor 3rd Light Cavalry 23 December
    Killed in conference
Local Lt Wheeler 3 November
    Killed in camp at Kahdarrah

6 – 12 January 1842

Dr Duff, Superintending Surgeon 10 January
    Killed between Tezeen and Seh Baba
Capt Skinner 61st Native Infantry 12 January
    Killed in action Jagdalak
Capt Paton[35] 58th Native Infantry 8 January
    Killed in action Khoord-Kabul Pass
Lt Sturt[36] Engineers 8 January
    Killed in action Khoord-Kabul Pass

Horse Artillery

Dr Bryce 10 January
    Killed in action on march to Tezeen

5th Light Cavalry

Lt Hardyman 6 January
    Killed in action Kabul cantonments

---

[35] Previously wounded at Kabul. His left arm had been amputated.
[36] Previously wounded at Kabul

Her Majesty's 44th of Foot

Maj Scott — 10 January
    Killed in action on march to Tezeen
Capt Leighton — 10 January
    Killed in action on march to Tezeen
Lt White — 10 January
    Killed in action Junga Fareekee
Lt Fortye[37] — 10 January
    Killed in action Jagdalak

5th Native Infantry

Maj Swayne[38] — 10 January
    Killed in action Junga Fareekee
Capt Miles — 10 January
    Killed in action Junga Fareekee
Lt Deas[39] — 10 January
    Killed in action Junga Fareekee
Lt Alexander — 10 January
    Killed in action Junga Fareekee
Lt Warren — 10 January
    Killed in action Junga Fareekee

54th Native Infantry

Maj Ewert — 10 January
    Killed in action on march to Tezeen
Capt Shaw[40] — 10 January
    Killed in action on march to Tezeen

---

[37] Previously wounded in Kabul

[38] Previously wounded in Kabul

[39] Previously wounded in Kabul

[40] Previously wounded in Kabul

Lt Kirby   10 January
    Killed in action on march to Tezeen
37th Native Infantry
Lt St George   8 January
    Killed in action Khoord-Kabul Pass
Lt Wade   12 January
    Killed in action Jagdalak
27th Native Infantry
Dr Cardew[41]   10 January
    Killed in action Tezeen

After leaving Jagdalak on 12 January to the final massacre

Staff
Maj Thain[42] Her Majesty's 21st of Foot 12 January
    Killed in action Jagdalak Pass
Capt Bellew 56th Native Infantry   13 January
    Killed in action Futtehabad
Capt Grant 27th Native Infantry   3 January
    Killed in action Gandamak
Capt Mackay Assistant Provost Marshal Unknown
    Killed in action Unknown
Horse Artillery
Capt Nicholl   12 January
    Killed in action Jagdalak Pass
Lt Stewart   13 January
    Killed in action Gandamak
5th Light Cavalry

---

[41] Previously wounded in Kabul

[42] Previously wounded in Kabul

Lt Col Chambers	12 January
Killed in action Jagdalak Pass	
Capt Blair	12 January
Killed in action Jagdalak Pass	
Capt Bott	12 January
Killed in action Jagdalak Pass	
Capt Hamilton	13 January
Killed in action Gandamak	
Capt Collyer	14 January
Killed in action near Jalalabad	
Lt Bazett	12 January
Killed in action Jagdalak Pass	
Dr Harpur	14 January
Killed in action near Jalalabad	
Veterinary Surgeon Willis	Unknown
Killed in action Unknown	

Her Majesty's 44th of Foot

Capt Dodgin	12 January
Killed in action Jagdalak Pass	
Capt Collins	13 January
Killed in action Gandamak	
Lt Hogg	13 January
Killed in action Gandamak	
Lt Cumberland	13 January
Killed in action Gandamak	
Lt Cadett	12 January
Killed in action Soorkab	
Lt Swinton	13 January
Killed in action Gandamak	
Ensign Gray	Unknown
Killed in action Unknown	

Paymaster Bourke   12 January
    Killed in action Jagdalak Pass
Quartermaster Halaban[43]   12 January
    Killed in action Jagdalak Pass
Surgeon Harcourt   12 January
    Killed in action Jagdalak Pass
Assistant Surgeon Balfour   Unknown
    Killed in action Unknown
Assistant Surgeon Primrose   13 January
    Killed in action Gandamak

5th Native Infantry

Capt Haig   Unknown
    Killed in action Unknown
Lt Horsbrough   13 January
    Killed in action Gandamak
Lt Tombs   Unknown
    Killed in action Unknown
Ensign Potenger   Unknown
    Killed in action Unknown
Lt Burkinyoung   Unknown
    Killed in action Unknown
Dr Metcalfe   13 January
    Killed in action Gandamak

37th Native Infantry

Capt Rind   13 January
    Killed in action Gandamak
Lt Steer   12 January
    Killed in action Jagdalak Pass
Lt Vanrenen   12 January
    Killed in action Soorkab

---

[43] Previously wounded in Kabul

Lt Hawtrey 13 January
    Killed in action Gandamak
Lt Carlyon Unknown
    Killed in action Unknown

54th Native Infantry

Capt Anstruther Unknown
    Killed in action Unknown
Capt Corrie Unknown
    Killed in action Unknown
Capt Palmer Unknown
    Killed in action Unknown
Lt Weaver 13 January
    Killed in action Gandamak
Lt Cunningham 13 January
    Killed in action Gandamak
Lt Pottinger 13 January
    Killed in action Neemla
Lt Morrison 13 January
    Killed in action Gandamak

Her Majesty's 13th Light Infantry

Maj Kershaw Unknown
    Killed in action Unknown
Lt Hobhouse 13 January
    Killed in action Gandamak

Shah's Service

Brig Anquetil 12 January
    Killed in action Jagdalak Pass
Capt Hay 35th Native Infantry 13 January
    Killed in action Gandamak
Capt Hopkins 27th Native Infantry 13 January
    Killed in action near Jalalabad

Capt Marshall 61st Native Infantry 12 January
  Killed in action Jagdalak Pass
Lt Le Geyt Bombay Cavalry 13 January
  Killed in action Neemla
Lt Green Artillery 13 January
  Killed in action Gandamak
Lt Bird Madras Establishment 13 January
  Killed in action Futtehabad
Lt Macartney Madras Establishment 13 January
  Killed in action Gandamak

ANNEX B

SURVIVING OFFICERS OF THE KABUL FORCE

Political
Maj Pottinger CB　　　　　　　　6 November
　Wounded at Charikar
Capt Lawrence
Capt Mackenzie Madras Establishment 23 November
　Wounded at Kabul
Staff
Maj Gen Elphinstone　　　　　　12 January
　Wounded at Jagdalak
　　　　　　　　　　　　　　　23 April
　Died at Tezeen
Brig Shelton
Capt Boyd
Lt Eyre Bengal Artillery　　　　　22 November
　Wounded at Kabul
Horse Artillery
Lt Waller　　　　　　　　　　　4 November
　Wounded at Kabul
Her Majesty's 44th of Foot
Capt Souter　　　　　　　　　　13 January
　Wounded at Gandamak

Her Majesty's 13th of Foot
Lt Mein   October
    Wounded at Khoord-Kabul Pass
37th Native Infantry
Maj Griffiths   8 January
    Wounded at Khoord-Kabul Pass
Dr Magrath
54th Native Infantry
Lt Melville   10 January
    Loss of toes to frostbite Huft Kotul
Shah's Service
Capt Troup   8 January
    Wounded at Khoord-Kabul Pass
Capt Johnson
Capt Anderson
Dr Brydon[44]
    Escaped to Jalalabad
Paymaster
Capt Bygrave
    Loss of toes to frostbite
Mr Ryley Conductor of Ordnance

---

[44] Dr Brydon later survived the siege of Lucknow in Indian Mutiny and died peacefully in his bed on 20 March 1873. He is buried in the Black Isle, near Inverness.

ANNEX C

PRISONERS RELEASED ON GENERAL POLLOCK'S ARRIVAL AT KABUL TOGETHER WITH SURVIVING OFFICERS OF THE KABUL FORCE

OFFICERS

Lt Col Palmer, 27th NI	Ghazni garrison
Capt Burnett, 54th NI	
Capt Alston, 27th NI	Ghazni garrison
Capt Poett, 27th NI	Ghazni garrison
Capt Walsh, 52nd Madras NI	
Capt Drummond, 3rd Bengal Light Cavalry	
Lt Airey, 3rd BUFFS	
Lt Warburton, Bengal Artillery	
Lt Webb, 38th Madras NI	
Lt Crawford, 3rd Bengal NI	
Lt Harris, 27th Bengal NI	Ghazni garrison
Lt Evans, 44th Foot	
Ensign Haughton, 31st Bengal NI	
Ensign Williams 37th Bengal NI	
Ensign Nicholson, 37th Bengal NI	
Dr Campbell	
Assistant Surgeon Berwick	

Assistant Surgeon Thomson
Mr Fallon, Clerk
Mr Blewitt, Clerk

LADIES

Lady Macnaghten
Lady Sale
Mrs Trevor with 8 children
Mrs Anderson with 3 children
Mrs Sturt with 1 child
Mrs Mainwaring with 1 child
Mrs Eyre with 1 child
Mrs Waller with 2 children
Conductor Ryley's wife with 3 children
Private Bourne's wife (13th Light Infantry)
Sgt Wade's wife (Bengal Horse Artillery)

SOLDIERS

44th of Foot

Sgt Wedlock
Sgt Weir
Sgt Fair
Cpl Sumpter
Cpl Bevan
Drummer Higgins
Drummer Lovell
Private Matthews
McDade
Marron
McCarthy
McCabe
Nowlan

Drummer Branagan
Private Burns
Cresham
Cronin
Driscoll
Deroney
Duffy
Arch
Stott
Moore
Miller
Murphy
Marshall

Robson
Seyburne
    Shean
    Tongue
    Wilson
    Durant

Cox
Robinson
    Brady
    McGlyn
    Boy Grier
    Boy Milwood

13th Light Infantry

Private Binding
    Murray
    Magary
    Monks

Private Maccullar
Mc Connell
Cuff

Bengal Horse Artillery

Sgt McNee
Gunner Dalton
Sgt Cleland
Sgt Wade, Baggage sergeant to the Kabul Mission
Gunner A Hearn
Gunner Keane

ANNEX D

SIMPLIFIED FAMILY TREE

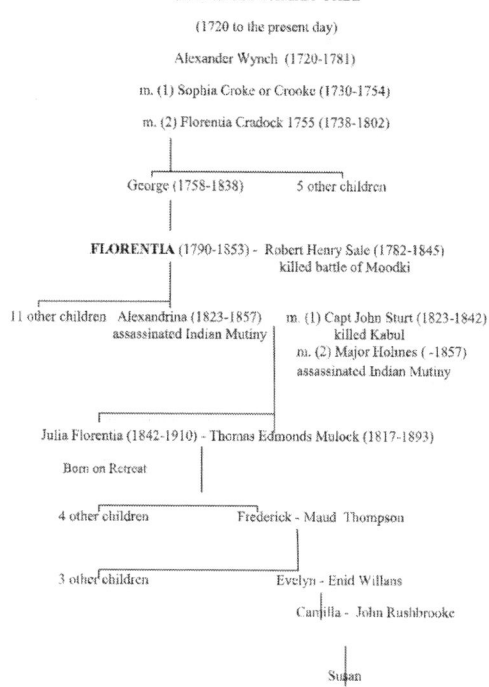

(1720 to the present day)

Alexander Wynch (1720-1781)

m. (1) Sophia Croke or Crooke (1730-1754)

m. (2) Florentia Cradock 1755 (1738-1802)

George (1758-1838)   5 other children

FLORENTIA (1790-1853) - Robert Henry Sale (1782-1845)
killed battle of Moodki

11 other children   Alexandrina (1823-1857)   m. (1) Capt John Sturt (1823-1842)
assassinated Indian Mutiny   killed Kabul
                                                    m. (2) Major Holmes (-1857)
                                                    assassinated Indian Mutiny

Julia Florentia (1842-1910) - Thomas Edmonds Mulock (1817-1893)

Born on Retreat

4 other children   Frederick - Maud Thompson

3 other children   Evelyn - Enid Willans

Camilla - John Rushbrooke

Susan

Printed in Poland
by Amazon Fulfillment
Poland Sp. z o.o., Wrocław